A Fresh Look at
WRITING

A Fresh Look at
WRITING

DONALD H. GRAVES

Heinemann
Portsmouth, New Hampshire

Irwin Publishing
Toronto, Canada

Heinemann
A division of Reed Elsevier Inc.
361 Hanover Street   Portsmouth, NH 03801-3912
Offices and agents throughout the world

Published simultaneously in Canada by
Irwin Publishing
1800 Steeles Avenue West   Concord, Ontario, Canada L4K 2P3

Every effort has been made to contact the copyright holders and students for permission to reprint borrowed material. We regret any oversights that may have occurred
and would be happy to rectify them in future printings of this work.

Acknowledgements for borrowed material begin on page 389.

Library of Congress Cataloging-in-Publication Data

Graves, Donald H.
    A fresh look at writing / Donald H. Graves
      p. cm.
    Includes bibliographical references and index.
    ISBN 0-435-08824-6
    1. English language—Composition and exercises—Study and teaching
(Elementary)   2. Creative writing (Elementary education)   I. Title
LB1576.G7264   1994   94-22478
372.6'23044—dc20   CIP

Canadian Cataloguing-in-Publication Data

Graves, Donald H.
    A fresh look at writing
ISBN 0-7725-2140-9
1.   Creative writing (Elementary education).
I.   Title.
LB1576.G73   372.6'23044   C94-931929-5

Acquisitions Editor: Toby Gordon
Production Editor: Renée M. Pinard
Interior Designer: Joni Doherty
Cover Designer: Jenny Jensen Greenleaf
Front cover photo and interior photos by Jim Whitney.

Printed in the United States of America on acid-free paper.
99 98 97 96   EB   4 5 6

To

DONALD M. MURRAY

A Writer's Writer

CONTENTS

ACTIONS

1.1: *Recall the teachers in your past who particularly affected your learning.*

1.2: *Post names of any teachers associated with the teaching of writing.*

1.3: *Identify important attributes of teachers in your past to plan the kind of teacher you wish to be in the years ahead.*

ACTIONS

2.1: *Practice listening to children.*

2.2: *Follow one child and record data about what that child does during a forty-five minute block of time.*

2.3: *Ask a child to tell you how his classroom works.*

2.4: *Find a child for whom words are probably not the easiest means of communicating what she knows.*

2.5: *Learn about the child beyond the walls of the school.*

2.6: *Get to know your children through a three-column exercise.*

III TEACH THE FUNDAMENTALS OF WRITING

IV BROADEN THE CHILDREN'S REPERTOIRE FOR WRITING

ACTIONS

18.1: Examine how your children use and understand characters in fiction.

18.2: Read the world for characters.

18.3: Sketch in a character.

18.4: Choose a situation that will reveal your character and write a short, ten-minute piece of fiction.

18.5: Conduct a short mini-lesson with children to help them see what questions best develop a character.

18.6: Ask your children to take out the fiction they are reading and make a list of anything they know about their characters.

18.7: Create a piece of fiction in which the children decide the elements that go into the story.

ACTIONS

19.1: Explore sources of nonfiction by reading the world.

19.2: Write a short ten-minute piece of nonfiction.

19.3: Take one school day and observe the opportunities for using nonfiction.

19.4: Consider the meaning of knowing something well.

19.5: Help your children begin to understand what it means to know an area well.

19.6: Help children work with nonfiction through the informal report.

19.7: Help children to use trade books as part of the process of writing the informal report.

19.8: Help children to get their voice into the text.

19.9: Line up several nonfiction books to read aloud to the children.

ACTIONS

20.1: Help children read the world for sources of poems to write.

20.2: Choose an episode from your exercise and experiment with a list poem.

20.3: Choose another episode from yesterday and write a five-minute poem after a three-minute list poem.

20.4: Help children get started with poetry.

20.5: Respond to children's poetry.

20.6: Read other poets aloud to the children.

V CONTINUE TO LEARN WITH OTHERS

ACTIONS

21.1: Choose a child and review her progress in preparation for a meeting with her parents.

21.2: Schedule a meeting with an administrator in which you share data about the learning progress and potential of specific children in your class.

ACTIONS

22.1: Schedule a meeting with two teachers, one who teaches as you do and one who teaches differently.

22.2: Continue to grow as a writer.

22.3: Contact a national, professional group dedicated to the improvement of literacy.

22.4: Investigate books written by teachers at your grade level.

22.5: Investigate courses in the teaching of writing or in writing itself.

PREFACE

It was my first year of teaching—thirty-nine seventh-grade students in a rural elementary school. Six of the students had repeated grades along the way and were several years overage. Those early fall days seemed to drag on forever. I looked forward to recess and lunch, even to the interruptions of physical education, music, and special programs. I knew too little about my subjects or my students to be able to fill up the time. I was advised "to be tough," to expect much of my students, and I assigned large amounts of reading and writing for homework, but the students wouldn't do it. Time stalled. I wondered if I would make it to Thanksgiving.

Yet those first difficult months of teaching were the last occasion when I felt I had unlimited time to teach. Although my students had many problems, my world and theirs was a simple one compared to the very complex reality faced by teachers today. Now we struggle for quality time with our students in the midst of inflated curricula, constant second-guessing by administrators and parents, and days punctuated by frequent interruptions. And strangely, the less time we have, the more we seem to waste it. We race through the day trying to stuff learning into tiny pockets of time. We feel the pressure of assessment and try to teach the skills that standardized tests cover. What is worse, we have so little time to learn about our children that our teaching bypasses their passions and abilities—but we can list by name the children for whom school is a waste of time, those who will leave it without becoming lifelong readers and writers.

With so little time to teach we have to decide what endures. In one sense, *A Fresh Look at Writing* is about how to use time well as a teacher of writing. My book *Writing: Teachers and Children at Work* discussed some of the basic elements that contribute to lasting learning, and these still hold true today. I stressed the importance of listening to children and learning from them, allowing them to choose their own topics, and the process of writing. For this reason I gave much attention to writing conferences, the place of revision, and publishing children's work. In fact, most of the teaching occurred through the conference.

Conferences are important, but now we've learned to place them in a different context. More important, we've learned much more about the essentials of teaching writing and how to use our time more effectively. Readers of my earlier book will find *A Fresh Look at Writing* to be more assertive: although listening to children is still the heart of the book, I think we now know better when to step in, when to teach, and when to expect more of our students.

As every study we've conducted over the last ten years has shown, we've underestimated what children can do. Teachers have led the way: it is teachers—who work at their own writing and thinking and then expect more of their students—who show us what children can do. We've learned that, right from the start, teachers need to teach *more*. For example, when first-grade children learn to spell, they need much more teaching than I've demonstrated in the past. Indeed, because spelling is the first stage in acquiring the conventions of language, it establishes important attitudes about learning and communication. The teaching continues through mini-lessons, which introduce other conventions and additional tools that writers use to rework their texts.

High on our new list is teaching children how to read their own work. We teach them how to read books but not how to read their own writing. I see too many folders and portfolios filled with papers that reveal little significant change. Unless we show children how to read their writing, their work will not improve. If we help children take knowledgeable responsibility in reading their own work, we not only help them to be effective lifelong writers, but we shift the responsibility for their writing to them, where it belongs.

I've stressed the point that children need peer response when they share their work from the Author's Chair and when they publish their writing. Although I still hold to this approach, I've seen a kind of "group think" take over, one that unfortunately fosters conformity to certain ideas and genres. Teachers need to be active in encouraging individuality and in pointing out the risks and the new approaches each child explores.

A Fresh Look is filled with Actions intended to help teachers learn right along with students. The Actions are experiments in learning. As with any experiment, some work and some don't. In this sense, learning is an inexact but joyful journey. My hope is that readers will use what works, adjust what doesn't, and most of all, take time to do what lasts.

ACKNOWLEDGMENTS

Writing: *Teachers and Children at Work* was published over a decade ago. Since then, I've written seven more books and been the co-editor of two others. All of them have relied on countless teachers and children and colleagues to lead the way in learning. I run along beside them on my short, stubby legs trying to scoop up what they are learning in the classroom through my questions and observations.

Some of my colleagues, especially Camille Allen and Jane Hansen, have read chapters of this book as I've completed them, helping me to maintain a consistent flow throughout the two-year process of writing it.

Mary Ellen Giacobbe was of special help with children's spelling and patiently listened to my ideas on the telephone. Nancie Atwell played a similar role. People often don't realize when they are helping with a book, but even conversations about seemingly unrelated topics can contribute to the writing. In this regard, I particularly mention Georgia Heard for our discussions about children, poetry, and learning. Thomas Newkirk at the University of New Hampshire and Bonnie Sunstein, professor at the University of Iowa, have been important thinkers who question both the world of academia and education in the schools. Carol Tateishi, who directs the Bay Area Writing Project in Berkeley, California, was helpful in responding to my concept of "Reading the World."

Carol Wilcox, now a doctoral student at the University of New Hampshire, has responded extensively to texts and supplied sound information about children and portfolios. Margaret Shane Cusack, a teacher from Clarence, New York, commented on several chapters and supplied a poem for Chapter 7.

During the past year (1993–94) I was fortunate enough to be a weekly visitor in the excellent classrooms of Louise Wrobleski and Karen Coyle in Madison, New Hampshire, which provided a valuable laboratory for my ongoing learning.

Ruth Hubbard was especially helpful in her detailed reading and critique of the entire book. She brings a wealth of knowledge from the field and has a knack for reading from the viewpoint of both the author and the audience who will read the book. Susan Stires of the Center for Teaching and Learning posed valuable questions about the text.

I was fortunate to have Jim Whitney do the photography for this book. Jim is that rare artist who is also an educator. He knows literacy, children, and "the moment" when significant learning events occur between children and teachers.

Two years ago, Philippa Stratton got the book moving by asking me "Don't you think *Writing: Teachers and Children at Work* ought to be revised?" At first I didn't want to revise it, because I felt that an entire new book was in order, and I wasn't sure that I wanted to write another book. She said, "Think it over." When I explored the notion, I could see more than ever that I had to write a new book. I could even get excited about it. I am grateful to her for getting the book launched.

Toby Gordon took over as editor when Philippa left and has followed the book through to completion. With a blend of humor and tough questioning, she has transformed an arduous task into a delightful experience.

Through all of my books I've neglected to mention the copyeditor, Linda Howe. I have never met her, since authors seldom meet the people who do this kind of work, but she senses what I am trying to say at a level deeper than I may understand myself and then helps me match my intentions to the conventions of language.

My wife, Betty, has read the whole of this book through its many drafts. Because she is not an educator in the formal sense, she is able to pick up on jargon that might be offensive and the concepts that make little sense. As always, I thank her for sustaining me through the ups and downs of writing this book.

Donald Murray has not read any of this book, yet he has probably been my greatest resource in learning about writing. For twenty years we have spoken daily and swapped poems, articles, and books by mail, by FAX, and over lunch. We have shared the joys and struggles of learning the craft (then we can get into more important and serious matters, like the Bruins, the Celtics, and the Boston Red Sox, politics, children, grandchildren, health, medicine, death, and the University of New Hampshire). When Murray asks "What's new?" he really wants to know. It is the "what's new" of living and learning that have contributed so much to the life of this writer. I dedicate this book to him.

I

MAKE A FRESH START

1 CONSIDER YOUR ROOTS

You are alone reading a book by your favorite author; you are nineteen, twenty-three or forty-three. The words carry you back in time, across the sea, or into a character's personal struggle. The words create vivid pictures in your mind. You want to write words like these, words that make people turn their heads. Just last week someone said, "You could write a book about that. There's a whole book there," and you knew they were right. But a small voice always whispers, "You don't have the talent. Only a few people have the talent to write."

When I observe first graders they are pouring drawings and words onto the paper with relentless fury. When they finish, they rush to the teacher to share their victory. What happens between first grade and the adult years? Children express themselves easily in first grade, but gradually they lose that creative freshness. Audiences of peers, teachers, and parents emerge, but only a few of them really know how to listen to the writers. The writer feels thwarted. In the adult years, the desire to express remains, but it is overshadowed by the sad notion that it is too late to begin.

A number of years ago I conducted a study for the Ford Foundation on the status of writing (see Graves, 1978). We interviewed people from all walks of life about their learning and writing experiences in school. Thirty-eight of the interviewees were professional writers but not one of them learned to write in school: sixty-five percent could not cite a single teacher who had helped them say something worthwhile; thirty percent had one teacher who made all the difference in their writing; no one had more than two good teachers in a lifetime of learning to write. The study also revealed that good teachers of writing were also good teachers. In short, we can borrow skills from any good teacher from our past to improve as a teacher in general, and as a good teacher of writing in particular.

You may have noticed that you express yourself more easily in media not associated with school: you pick up a hammer, brush, egg beater, pencil, or camera, or you turn on a computer or sewing machine. In a corner of your life, you maintain tools for your kind of expression. You savor your medium, whether it is clay, wood, food, flowers, a well-exercised body, paint, cloth, paper, or words in a play, and the smell is sweet.

The thought of being alone in a room with your sewing machine, a new pattern, and a length of beautiful woolen cloth is comforting. The image of a clean workbench, the smell of well-seasoned cherry boards, and the prospect of an uninterrupted Saturday morning for building a bookcase set your shoulders aright.

Perhaps a member of your family or a friend is responsible for your current expressive interest. Or you may have taken a short course with a professional. You have observed how the artist developed her craft, spending long hours alone with her materials, gaining a vision of the possible, and exploring a sense of play as she feels the shape of an idea in her hands. Such creative people are submerged in their creating, and they show you how to join them. They see possibilities in you—and you are surprised that they see more than you do—because they practice their medium, and they know something about you and what you wish to express.

You want to teach. You want to help children create and take pride in their work, just as you have. You see teaching as another kind of authorship, which encourages students to express what they know. You observe them on the playground and overhear them talking. You sense the stories and ideas embedded in a single written line. You witness their expressive potential and help them realize their own intentions. You say to yourself, "This is why I want to teach."

We'll spend a lifetime crafting our teaching in order to allow children to be the authors of their own texts. We lean into the future striving to be the teachers we envisioned when we first chose the profession. But before we look ahead let's take a glance back at your own learning/expressive history. I find it worthwhile to look at my own history occasionally in order to understand my strengths and my potential blind spots in encouraging learning in the lives of my students. I begin with an Action. An Action is something you do that helps you become an active teacher of writing. This book is based on research clearly showing that we need specific experience with children before we can understand what they are writing. I would caution you that it is virtually impossible to become a good teacher of writing simply by reading this book. The Actions are intended to carry you into many experiences that will help you to become the kind of teacher you envision. They serve as a guide to the more important experiences. You will bypass some Actions simply because your experience and background lead you to choose those that address your growing skill as a teacher.

ACTION 1.1:

Recall the teachers in your past who particularly affected your learning.

This Action will help you to look back at your past before you start thinking about the teacher you wish to become. I will do the Action with you to show how I work with this exercise. Make rules on a sheet of paper as shown in Figure 1.1.

In Figure 1.1 I have listed the names of the teachers who affected my learning in any area and in any subject from my early school years until quite recently. In the first column I put down actual teacher names (I've changed the names of those who had a negative effect on my learning). These are all teachers about whom I have conscious memories of good learning or poor learning. In the second column I have listed the names of people who affected my learning outside of school.

Now that you have made up your list, here are some different ways to think about the teachers you have posted. Take your list and do an exercise with me:

> Put an S next to the teacher who was responsible for your learning a specific skill.

▲▼ **Figure 1.1**
Teacher Memory Exercise

	TEACHERS IN SCHOOL	TEACHERS OUT OF SCHOOL
PRIMARY	ms. Jones SK	mom Dad
INTERMEDIATE	ms. adams K	mom Dad
JUNIOR HIGH	ms. Johnson S	Grandpa Hiller mom
SENIOR HIGH	M.s. Dower S+ ms. ditch K+ mr. muller SK+ ms. Valente S ms. mclinus S mr. motyl S mr. Black N mr. Rogers N	mom H Nelson Wilbur Grandpa Hiller
COLLEGE	Prof. Berkleman S Prof. Seward SK Prof. Fairfield K Prof. Rangely N	mom Tip Weeks H. Nelson Wilbur
POST COLLEGE	D. Durrell SK J. Fiore SK m. Barth SK A. Roden K	adv. Stepanoff L. Raleigh Dr. Burack L. Cohen L. Demarest B. Padginton H Porter D. murray m.E. Giacobbe L. Funkhouser

S Learn a skill

N Negative teachers

K Teacher making personal connections

I'll name several of my own teachers and then record the skill next to each name:

Ms. Jones, Grade 1: how to read
Ms. Johnson, Grade 7: math
Mr. Muller, Grade 12: singing and speaking Spanish
Ms. Valente, Grade 9: Latin
Ms. Macklinus, Grade 11: typing
Mr. Motyl, Grade 9, 10: mechanical drawing
Dr. Durrell, Graduate School: how to teach reading
Dr. Fiore, Graduate School: how to do research
Dr. Barth, Seminary: how to read the New Testament

I acquired my skills in a variety of ways. Ms. Jones was encouraging and enthusiastic: she liked the way I read aloud, and I've enjoyed reading aloud ever since. Several teachers were systematic and demanding, as in the case of Ms. Johnson and Ms. Valente, my mathematics and Latin teachers. I did rather poorly, only C's with each, but I am aware that I still remember most of my Latin today even though I had only a year of it with Ms. Valente. In the case of Ms. Macklinus and Mr. Motyl, the skills were of a more "mechanical nature," yet I can still type and do drafting, both of which have been of lifelong importance.

Mr. Muller taught me skills while I had fun. Each week we'd sing in Spanish, and I still carry large amounts of Spanish with me because of my enjoyment of the singing. He also immersed us in the language by speaking only Spanish in class, and he remains an important figure in my teaching today. Learning a subject by immersion from someone who knows and enjoys it is a key approach in my teaching repertoire and my teaching philosophy.

> Put a K next to the teacher from whom you learned because that teacher made some kind of personal connection with you and your existing knowledge and carried you beyond what you already knew.

I find that when teachers speak about memorable mentors they often say, "They knew me outside of class." Relationship was an important factor. When students feel "known," then they learn more easily. This is especially true if they feel that the teacher knows them beyond the subject matter at hand. I have put K's next to the names of those teachers.

Ms. Fitch, my high school biology teacher, learned that I was interested in birds and in hybridizing gladioluses because I told her. The students in her classes were constantly telling her facts about themselves because they knew she'd be interested.

Everyone has had different negative experiences that have shaped their learning history.

> Put N next to the teachers who affected your learning in a negative way. (You may need to add some names as you focus on this phase of the Action.)

Ask these questions of yourself as you record N's on your sheet next to the teachers who affected your learning on the negative side (remember that "failure" is a relative judgment yet an important aspect of learning; for some of my N postings I was simply unable to handle the subject and did poorly, although I didn't fail).

- How have you dealt with school failure? How do you think the failure may have affected how you teach today?
- How much was the failure a result of your general inability to understand the concepts of the subject area?
- How much of your failure was a result of your inability to deal with the effect of the teacher's personality?
- How would you redesign the learning situation so that you might have learned better?

I suspect that I've repressed many of my failures; I can't recall them. But the more recent ones I remember, and the memory of those failures influences my teaching. I say to myself, "I don't want to teach that way," and I give a particular approach a wide berth.

Sometimes I find it difficult to separate my own poor learning habits from poor teaching. In Ms. Black's freshman algebra class I barely skimped by with a C–. I couldn't grasp the concept that letters represented objects that were manipulated mathematically. I'd ask, "What does that *a* or *b* stand for?" Ms. Black would reply, "It won't help you to think that way." I had assumed that learning algebra was like learning to read; all the symbols stood for something. Yet when I stopped "imagining" and tried to link up with her way of looking at the problems, the process and the subject became almost impossible abstractions. Worse, I couldn't go home and use algebra. I probably have students in my writing classes today who find words on a page to be equally abstract. For them, print produces no images and they see little use in writing or books.

I experienced my most traumatic failure when I was a senior in college. I tried to explore my struggle with conscientious objection and death in my senior thesis on Tolstoy's *War and Peace.* A close friend had just been killed in battle in Korea, and I was due to be drafted the following June. The professor wrote a cryptic response: "Please change your typewriter ribbon—D+." The only other marks on the paper highlighted thirty-six errors in grammar and punctuation (there were actually many more he didn't circle). He made no response to the content—my struggle with death, conscientious objection and the death of my friend. I felt humiliated and defeated. The Dean put me on academic probation.

I've built a teaching career on that horrendous event. On the positive side I vowed that I'd be sensitive to the human struggles in my classroom and would "always" respond to the content first. Of course, I've probably missed more times than I realize: some struggles are obvious to the writer but not to the reader.

On the negative side I have failed to attend to my students' errors as well as I should. Final papers should not be filled with the kinds of mistakes so evident in my senior thesis, yet they should not be ignored. If such mistakes affect the meaning of a student's piece, the teacher should respond directly. For many years I tended to avoid teaching mechanics for fear I'd distort the writer's intentions. Only in recent years have I learned how to deal with this issue.

ACTION 1.2:

Post names of any teachers associated with the teaching of writing.

Construct a chart like the one shown in Figure 1.2. Note on your chart the names of any teachers associated with the teaching of writing. (You may find that you need to post new names; I've just added two: Miss Fortin and Professor Angus.) Place a W next to any names that recall strong memories of people who have influenced how you write today. I include the following areas as part of the writing memory profile: spelling, handwriting, grammar, punctuation, reports, fiction writing, poetry, and essays.

▲▼ **Figure 1.2**
Teacher Memory Exercise—Writing

	TEACHERS IN SCHOOL	TEACHERS OUT OF SCHOOL
PRIMARY		
INTERMEDIATE	Ms. Fortin W	
JUNIOR HIGH		miss Thompson
SENIOR HIGH	Ms. Dower W+	
COLLEGE	Prof. Angus W+ Prof. Rangely W-	
POST COLLEGE	J. Fiore W+ M. Evans W-	D. Murray W+ also W+R Natwell W+R J. Hansen W+R B. Graves W+R

W   Teachers who influenced writing
W+R Teachers who influence writing as good readers of my texts
    - negative effect
    + positive effect

You will note that my chart has only a few names, especially in elementary, junior, and senior high school. In fact, we did very little writing in those years. My first minus appears in sixth grade. Although Miss Fortin was an excellent teacher, she finally reached the end of her patience with my handwriting, and delivered a most eloquent sigh in my presence. Generally, however, I was fortunate to have teachers who didn't leave me with the feeling that my poor handwriting affected the content of my writing.

I find that many people, especially those who are poor spellers, end up feeling that they are poor writers because of their struggle with spelling. Although it is important to be able to spell, we should not equate the quality of a person's ideas with good or poor spelling. According to this logic, a person's stuttering would signal mental incompetence.

One high school English teacher, Mrs. Florence Dower, took me seriously when I told her I wanted to be a writer. When I asked what I had to do to be a better one, she said, "Write and rewrite," and proceeded to give me extra work. She might have said, "Based on what you've shown me thus far, you'd better think of a different career."

As you write down the names of teachers who have affected your view of yourself as a writer, consider some of the following exercises:

- List the name of any teacher who recognized that you had something to say and helped you to say it. Can you recall a specific incident? Put a + next to the W.
- List the name of any person who is a good reader of your writing. They may not teach you to write but their response to your text helps you to move ahead as a writer.
- List any recollections of any teacher who thought you had little of significance to write about. What was it like to write in that situation?
- List any recollections you have of your writing being posted on a bulletin board, included in a collection, or published in a school magazine or newspaper.
- List any recollections of your writing being turned down for publication or posting.

Professor Angus, my teacher in freshman composition, jacked my writing up another notch. How I struggled to say something significant as a young freshman writer. Professor Angus wanted us to use writing to think. One day I wrote a piece connecting the image of young and meandering streams from my geology class with Toynbee's theories of young and old cultures. "Now that's real thinking," Professor Angus said. He helped me use analogy and see relationships between ideas in one field and those in another.

As I write these words, I realize how difficult it is to do justice to the teachers in our lives. Only now, at the moment of writing this paragraph, can I appreciate Professor Angus's contribution to my development as a writer. The discovery of our learning histories is an ongoing mining of past experiences for present use. I had to wait until I was forty-three years old to run into a teacher who actually saw value in my ideas and showed me how to express them. I had to wait until I had a doctorate before someone said, "You know things and here's how to go about saying them so other people will understand what you have to say." The teacher was Donald Murray, author of *A Writer Teaches Writing* and countless other books, and my colleague at the University of New Hampshire. He was the writer who actually *showed* in his own writing how to write simply and directly.

There are people I turn to because they are effective readers of my writing. The three people I have listed here, Nancie Atwell, Jane Hansen, and Betty Graves, read my texts in different ways. Jane Hansen has known me and my work over the last dozen years and responds with a long-term perspective and an understanding of how my thinking changed. Nancie Atwell doesn't often read my texts in their entirety but I can read a part of a text to her over the telephone and she responds with both vision and insight. She seems to see more in my words than I do. My wife, Betty, on the other hand, plays the role of no-nonsense critic. She simply says "I just don't get this." Good readers who will tell us what they do or do not understand, without praise or admonition, can be our best teachers.

Look Ahead

Your writing history is important. The Actions in this chapter are intended to carry you back through your learning experiences in elementary, junior high, and senior high school, college, and beyond. You've recalled the teachers who influenced you in a significant way as a learner and as a writer. Some of them may have had a negative effect. Others saw something in you that surprised you: particular skills, ideas, or original ways of looking at the world. They helped you to say what you didn't know you could say.

You aspire to be a good teacher. Some of you are just beginning; many of you may be in mid-career. I've been teaching for thirty-eight years and I still try to teach better tomorrow than I did yesterday. I learn from good teachers in any field and I learn from good teachers of writing. I also learn from poor teachers when I say, "I won't teach that way, I'll teach this way."

ACTION 1.3:

Identify important attributes of teachers in your past to plan the kind of teacher you wish to be in the years ahead.

I'll run through my own past to show you what I mean. What I write here will not be in any particular order; I'll select first those elements that are important to me as a learner and then those that help me teach writing today.

- *Take a writer seriously:* Mrs. Dower, my high school English teacher, believed me when I said I wanted to be a writer.
- *Help writers to have high expectations:* Mrs. Dower took me seriously by asking me to do more work. The extra work was proof that she believed in me.
- *Demonstrate a life with high expectations:* Don Murray, along with Mrs. Dower, helped me to have high expectations because he expected much of himself. Both of them revealed their own hunger for learning.
- *Show students how to write by writing yourself:* I had to wait until I was forty-three before I finally saw a writer in the process of writing. Only then did I understand what writing involved.
- *Give the writer a chance to say something worthwhile:* Professors Fiore and Angus gave me a chance to choose topics I knew something about so that I could write with authority.
- *Get to know the student beyond the classroom:* Ms. Fitch, my high school biology teacher, enjoyed listening to us speak about our lives beyond the classroom. She took what she

knew about us and used it to teach biology. She knew her own subject well enough to include us.

- *Use failure as a way to teach, not punish:* If Professor Rangely had shown me how my mechanical problems detracted from my ideas, I might have ended up with a different view of conventions.
- *Help students to teach others through their writing:* A writer takes on a different identity when his words leave him and are published, put on a bulletin board, or read and responded to by others.
- *Be a learner:* My best teachers taught me most by the way they inquired about the world, toyed with ideas, and expressed their convictions. They let me teach them about what I knew.

Final Reflection

You want to write. In one sense you are no different than first-grade children. We all know we have stories to tell, ideas to share, and opinions to voice. To express oneself is a fundamental characteristic of being human. Yet because of our school experiences, many of us have left writing behind and adopted other forms of expression.

You want to teach. You want to help students to express their thoughts, feelings, and ideas. You want them to use writing to learn. How you teach today is greatly affected by your own learning history, especially learning how to write. Now that you have reviewed your own learning history, repeat your positive experiences with your own students as they write and learn.

When I conducted the Ford Foundation study I found that if students had *one* good teacher of writing in their entire career, irrespective of grade level, they could be successful writers. *Be that one teacher.*

2 LEARN FROM THE CHILDREN

Among the thirty-nine seventh graders in my classroom during my first year of teaching is a boy named David. His former teacher calls him a "grasshopper"; other teachers call him hyperactive. I wryly mention to a colleague, "Hyperactive kids make hyperactive teachers; I can't keep up with him." David's file is thick; I glance through it and find little to help me in teaching him. His disabilities and failures are well documented; a phalanx of specialists have written reports urging more work with skills.

So I do my job: I blitz David with worksheets. David tries to do what the school wants, but he rushes through his work; in ten minutes he announces, "I'm done." My stomach feels weighted down with iron. "Go read a book," I say in desperation. He picks up a book and thumbs through, looking at the pictures. I waste David's time. Day after day, confined to his chair with no help from anyone else, he repeats his failures. I work with him on skills but the skills make no sense to him. Worse, my only knowledge of him is based on his file, which records his repeated failure to deal with print.

Several years later I discover that David worked in his father's greenhouse and knew a great deal about raising roses. He knew about fertilizers, adjustments for light, diseases, and prize hybrids.

He knew his business; I didn't know mine. There is no question that David needed help with skills; I just didn't know him well enough to make them relevant.

My education professors usually tossed the same quick line over their shoulders: "Get to know your students." Easy to say—but I simply didn't know how to go about doing it. Today we know that, although it takes careful work, the process can be one of the most rewarding aspects of the profession. Our research data show that entire years—or even school careers—can be wasted if we don't let our students teach us. I am embarrassed to report that as a director of reading clinics for one city's schools, I never asked students what they thought their reading problem might be. I gave battery after battery of tests yet ignored the "patient's" appraisal of the problem.

Our business in this chapter is to get some experience in finding out what the children in our classrooms know. For the moment I want to bypass learning from children through their writing; we'll do Actions on that important sector in Chapter 7. In Chapter 1 we worked at retrieving our own learning history. In this chapter we'll help children begin to establish theirs. One of our most important roles in teaching is that of being an effective *learning historian*, who works actively to help children become aware of an effective learning history. This means that we look at children's abilities quite broadly. The following series of Actions are intended to help you construct children's learning histories and learn about their abilities.

ACTION 2.1:
Practice listening to children.

Learning through listening is the foundation for all the Actions in this book. Through our active listening, children become our informants. Unless children speak about what they know, we lose out on what they know and how they know it. Through our eyes and ears we learn from them: their stories, how they solve problems, what their wishes and dreams are, what works/doesn't work, their vision of a better classroom, and what they think they need to learn to succeed in math or to complete reports. We transform what we learn from them into the beginning of an effective learning history:

Teachers Let Children Teach Them What They Know

"I see you got that math example just right, Jennifer. Tell me, how did you know how to do that?"

"Hmm, I don't know. Let's see. Well, I read the problem and then I started to multiply. Then it came out right." Jennifer's initial statement about how she did the problem is sketchy at best. Still, it allows me to discover the rough outline of the problem in her head. I reply, "Yes, you got it right. You are on the road to beginning to understand how you do things. That's what good learners are able to do." As this example shows, one of the best times for children to teach us about what they know is when we confirm that what they have already done is accurate. Jennifer has *taught me* that she has a rough approximation of her problem-solving process but needs more specific ways to help her solve problems in the future.

Sadly, the notion that children teach teachers has been misunderstood. Children do indeed know things that we do not, in the knowledge or experience sense, and we have to discover their conceptual constructs through their own demonstrations in order to know how to teach them—in short, through their attempts to teach us.

Some teachers seem to invite children's conversation. Children speak to them constantly; they try something and almost immediately tell their teacher about it. I've tried to observe what these teachers do that makes their students such good informants. I used to think it was their methodology. Now I realize that it is a kind of philosophical stance, which children intuit in the teacher, that inspires their confidence and invites their reactions to their work.

Somewhere, in your stomach perhaps, you have a belief, even a fascination, that children know things, and you can't wait to find out what they are. In fact, you probably enjoy learning from everyone. Children seem to know when we are genuinely interested in what they think. From birth they have learned to read the reactions they see on adult faces and the words they hear.

I have to admit that when I first began teaching, my stance was one of chief informant. As an English major, I was in the classroom because I knew things about language and literature that the students ought to learn. Unfortunately, that's why I went into teaching—to inform my students about what they ought to know. In those early teaching years I did a lot of informing but very little teaching. I was too busy railing against the students who "didn't get it."

But sound teaching means that we show children how to do things through our own demonstrations of learning. Listening to our students helps us to see the inner mechanisms of their learning. Of course, by revealing their learning construct to students, we allow them to see themselves as learners.

Your task in this Action is to place yourself in the position of being informed by your students. Try some of these approaches.

- When students have done something accurately, no matter how small, ask them how they did it. Try to elicit a sense of process if you can. When they explain, repeat their statement back to them asking, "Did I get this right? Is this what you said?"

- Choose a common classroom experience (discussion, problem, experience, field-trip). "This morning we had a discussion about ————. I'd like to get your version of what went on as best you can remember it. What did you think of it?" (I clearly want the child's expression of value in this instance.)

- Choose something the student has constructed (drawing, project, block building). "How did you make that? Take me back to when you first started and then tell me about it from there to when you finished. How did it go? What is your opinion of it?"

- Observe children in the process of some physical activity, on the playground or in physical education. Some children find it easier to speak about physical events than about events involving stories or print. "How does that game work? I saw what you first did . . . take it from there and tell me how the rest of it goes. What do you think of that game? Are there others that you prefer? What do you have to know how to do well in order to play that game . . . [or do that thing]? Can you take it from there?"

There are a number of principles that underlie these approaches to learning from children:

- *There are no right or wrong answers.* What you seek is the *child's version* of events. Of course, the child may think that whenever a teacher asks a question there is only one right answer.

- *Learn what the child values about the event.* This naturally follows from the child's version. Until the child states how something is done or what process is involved, she may not know how she values it.

- *Make sure you have interpreted the child accurately.* "Okay, let me see if I have this right. You said this, this, and this happened and then you thought that maybe this could have been done better?"

- *And what will you do next?* This is optional. When I get rich detail from a child, along with a statement of value, I ask the next logical question: "And now what will you do about it? How will you work on this next?" The ultimate evidence of value is what the child chooses to do with the facts.

ACTION 2.2:

Follow one child and record data about what that child does during a forty-five minute block of time.

For this Action, you may wish to choose the same child you encountered in Action 2.1, where you learned primarily by listening. You want to know more about the child. In this instance you will learn from this child by observing how the child copes with her school environment and the people in it. Your task will be to observe the child's world *through the child's eyes.* This is not an easy task, since it essentially requires that you "become" the child. You continuously observe how the child takes in data from the world and then acts upon the world based on that evidence. Divide a sheet of paper into two columns to record two sets of data: in the first write down what the child encounters and does; in the second, write down what you think may be the child's interpretation of the event (see Figure 2.1).

You stretch your mind to become the child in order to understand the world of the child. When you have completed the forty-five minute observation, choose four areas in order to compare your interpretation with the child's, and ask the child about each of them. For example, if I am curious about this child's first interchange with his neighbor, first, I state the situation: "I noticed that when you first started to read, you'd read for about five minutes, stop, chat, then go on." If I know enough about the child and think he can handle a further question, I'll ask it: "Tell me as best you can what you were thinking when you first started to read. I'm really curious."

Another approach to finding out more about the child's point of view during reading/writing time is more general. To get the child started I ask, "Remember the very first thing you did when you started reading this morning?" If the child remembers it I may tell her, "Okay, tell me everything you remember from that point on." At points where the event seems especially significant to her I might ask, "And what were you thinking at that point?" Since this Action may be a little abstract for the child, remember to look at the child and show as much sincere interest as you can muster. Occasionally you should say, "Let me see if I have this right," and then repeat what the child has said. If your work goes well, you will begin to get a feel for how the child sees her world, and the value she places on what she is doing, so that you can check it against your interpretation.

▲▼ **Figure 2.1**

CHILD'S ACTION	MY HYPOTHESIZED INTERPRETATION THROUGH CHILD'S EYES
8:40 - Looks in desk for something - pulls out a book. Begins to read.	Where is my book? I should be reading.
8:42 - Begins to talk to neighbor "What are you reading?"	I don't feel like reading right now.
"I've already read that one."	I'm a better reader than he is.
"This one here is my challenge book."	I'm reading a harder book than he is.
8:45 - Child reads for 5-10 minute stretches, glances around, sharpens pencil.	I wonder if I will like this book. (Child is just beginning the book.)
9:10 - Reads for a straight 17 minutes. Face mirrors pleasant events on page.	I'm beginning to like this book. It isn't so bad.
9:27 - Puts book away. Gets up and extracts writing folder from rack.	It's time to write now.
"What are you writing Jeremy?"	Writing can be lonely. I wonder what my friend is writing.
"You draw jets good."	My friend draws well. I don't, maybe he will help me.
"Will you draw a jet for my Crash Story?"	

If you have full-time classroom responsibility, ask a colleague if you can observe a child in her classroom during one of your special sessions, such as music, art, or physical education. Although it can be useful to observe a child in your own classroom, the point of this Action is to get practice in viewing the world of school through the child's eyes.

ACTION 2.3:

Ask a child to tell you how his classroom works.

You may find it useful to involve the same child you observed in the previous Action. The purpose of this Action is to find out how children interpret the structure of the classroom and the function and value of the various elements in the room. Tell the student, "I'd like you to take me around the room and tell me how this place works." First, I let the child take me on his guided tour, noting the areas and practices he leaves out, since it is important to understand what the child feels is important. When the child completes the tour, I tell him what I've learned so far. Then I say, "Now there are some other things I wondered about; will you please help me with these?"

During the first phase, as I follow the child wherever he takes me, I ask some questions:

- (Pointing to certain books) "What are these for?"
- (A child is reading, writing, or doing math) "Would you please tell me what she is doing right now? . . . Oh. Why is she doing that?"
- "I see the teacher is working with those children. Can you tell me what she is doing? Why is she doing that?"
- "When the children finish that, what will they do next?"
- What do you do when you get stuck on this?"

I ask questions because I am interested in finding out about the following basic elements:

- The child's understanding of the *purpose and function* of the various artifacts in the room.
- (If the room is decentralized and the children exercise a fair amount of choice and responsibility) The child's understanding

of the limits of things or how she negotiates differences. Here are some examples of questions that get at these issues:

- "Suppose two children want the same book. What do you do then?"
- "I see you choose topics for your writing. Suppose the topic you choose isn't working. What do you do then?"
- "You can choose how you use time. Okay, but suppose you just sat there and didn't do anything for an hour. What would happen then?"

ACTION 2.4:

Find a child for whom words are probably not the easiest means of communicating what she knows.

Most of the data you have gathered from children thus far has relied on their recall of what they have done or their verbal interpretations of the meaning of various events. Words are the common currency of thought in school. Children are surrounded by print and words fill the air of the classroom. But not all children choose to express themselves in words. Americans are particularly anxious about the quiet child. Sadly, we interpret a lack of verbal skills with a lack of intelligence or a sign of some deep–rooted social disturbance. In other instances, children simply don't reflect on past events. In their minds, "what's done is done."

To gather data for this Action, I follow these guidelines:

- I ask children about the meaning of events as they are *in the midst* of doing them: "I see you've just drawn a picture of a knight charging on this horse. Tell me about this right here. And what will happen next?"
- "*Show* me how this works."
- "*Show* me what you did first, then next, and next."

For some children showing is much easier than telling. At the same time, as they show me how they constructed something, they may be able to tell me what they understand about the process.

ACTION 2.5:

Learn about the child beyond the walls of the school.

For better or worse, the lives of children are shaped far more by experiences outside of school than by the limited time we work with them in our classrooms. I have been writing my autobiography as a learner for the past ten years and I am struck by how much my profile as a learner is shaped by events and people outside of school. My values about learning and about thinking, and, above all, my desire for learning were fueled at home.

Although some of us may teach in neighborhoods similar to those we grew up in, few of us duplicate the lives of any of our children. In this Action, the child takes you on a tour of his neighborhood. (You may find it helpful to work with the same child you observed over a forty-five minute stretch or the child who took you around the classroom. The principle here is the same as before: "What is *this child's* perception of his neighborhood?" Our questions, as much as possible, should be free of any remarks that impose our own values on the child's world. In short, we don't comment on the child's perceptions other than to make sure we have an accurate rendition of what he sees.

To carry out this Action you will need to get written permission from the child's parent to walk with him around the neighborhood for about an hour after school. In some instances you may be more comfortable if an adult companion also accompanies you on the tour.

I approach the tour in this way: "I've never been to your neighborhood; I'd like you to take me around and tell me all about it." Above all, let the child speak first. Naturally, I have questions as we go that as much as possible respond to the child's own statements:

- "Where do you play around here?"
- "How far can you go when you play?"
- "Tell me about that store over there."
- "How long have you lived here?" (In some instances the neighborhood may be as new to the child as it is to you.)
- "Are there kids here with whom you can play?"

Further guidelines: you are looking through the child's eyes in order to see what is *important* to the child in the neighborhood. Listen first to the child but also note other items that may loom large in significance but which the child ignores. Ask about those after your tour.

Some children may come from more rural or sparsely populated areas where the neighborhood is less defined, but there are still places the child may be allowed to explore. In fact, the child's own neighborhood may be limited to his or her own yard; be prepared for a child who may not be allowed to venture outside of his home because the neighborhood situation is simply too dangerous.

I fully recognize that it is not possible or feasible to visit some children's neighborhoods. Depending on the child's age or circumstance she may not wish to be seen with you or want you to see her neighborhood. Ruth Hubbard, a professor at Lewis and Clark College, suggests that you or the child construct a map of the neighborhood and then take the tour from the map. Or you may be able to take photos or make a video of the areas near the child's home. Above all, consult with the child on your planned approach.

ACTION 2.6:
Get to know your children through a three-column exercise.

This exercise is the culmination of other Actions for learning from your children. You should have a better idea now about the various kinds of notes you can make about each child in your classroom. I've been using this approach for fifteen years and it is one of the most rapid ways for me to move directly into the role of learning historian.

Take a standard sheet of paper and make three columns, the first an inch in from the left margin and the second an inch in from the right. That leaves a large column in the middle of the page (see Figure 2.2).

Record the number of students in your classroom in the upper right-hand corner and circle the number. Now number down the left-hand column up to that number (for example, if you have twenty-five children you will number from 1 to 25, taking up twenty-five lines on your page).

Now write the names of your students from memory, giving one line to each child. See how many children you can remember. Note which names you remember first. I find that they are often the students I enjoy and those about whom I worry the most. Some children I won't remember. The missing children are often those who just don't stand out, who get lost, or who are noticed only after three days of absence. Draw a line under the ones you were able to remember. Now

▲▼ **Fig. 2.2**
FIRST MEMORY ATTEMPT
February 2

	EXPERIENCES AND INTERESTS	CONFIRMATION COLUMN
1. Fred Gallo	Sharks	
2. Marcella Cowan	Horses	X
3. John Pringle		
4. Allison Goodrich		
5. Norman Frazier	Sister in hospital	X
6. Delores Sunderland	Sea life, birds	
7. Frances Sawtelle		
8. Jonathan Freedman	Prehistoric animals	
9. Charles Lentini	Motorcycles	
10. Aleka Alphanosopoulos	Singing	
11. Jason Beckwith		
12. Jon Finlayson	Football	

13. Joel Cupperman
14. Mark Andrade
15. Patricia Rezendes
16. Betty Oliver
17. Margaret Texeira
18. Marcus Washington
19. Patricia Snow
20. William Frost
21. Paul Gardner
22. Jason Tompkins
23. Ford Park
24. Laurie Kunstler
25. Albert Guimond

All children below the line were not remembered on first attempt on the second day of school.

━━━━━━

write in the missing names until you have listed the rest of the children. (If you don't have a self-contained classroom, choose a particular class period to get to know more about that group of students.)

In the second column record what you know about each child's experiences and interests. You will probably have blank spaces in this column.

Finally, in the third column, check to see if what you wrote down in the middle column about that child has been specifically confirmed ("specific confirmation" means denoting the particulars of the child's knowledge): "Ah, David, I see you know which are the very best roses on the market," or, "Janice, I didn't know you have two children to take care of when you get home and that you sometimes cook their supper as well."

The ultimate objective of this column exercise is to be able to fill in all three columns, to carry a unique landscape of information for each child in memory as well as to confirm something in their lives that will *begin* to make them aware of their own effective learning history. Of course, the students over whom we struggle most are the ones who need this acknowledgment of what they do well the most. Naturally, I am continually striving to go well beyond a single item in a child's profile. This exercise is merely an initial way to become aware of what children can do. Figures 2.2, 2.3, and 2.4 reveal the gradual emergence of children's learning history over several weeks.

Final Reflection

You have made a start at entering your student's world. You have shifted your point of view to see through her eyes as she observes her world, describes her classroom, and shows you her neighborhood. Unless we begin to understand what our students know, how they know it, and what they value about it, we waste their time. Worse, if our students think we don't know something special about them, which they value, they may find learning to be an isolated and meaningless exercise.

You may recall from your own learning history how important it was that you be *known* by a particular teacher. This shouldn't be misunderstood as a gooey, cuddly feeling; it is rather being known in the sense that the teacher possesses specific information about you that helps you learn.

You and your students will create effective learning histories together. It begins when you call a student by name . . . and from memory ("He cared enough to call me by name"). You deliberately memorize an entire roster of names before your first class hoping to match a face with a name you already know. Soon you will add more specific information to each name you carry in your head. The joy of teaching is contained in the mutual building of effective learning histories.

▲▼ **Fig. 2.3**
Second Memory Attempt
February 9

	Experiences and Interests	Confirmation Column
1. Marcella Cowan	Horses, birth of foal, 4H	X
2. Norman Frazier	Sister well, fishing	X
3. Jonathan Freedman	Tyrannosaurus rex, bronto-saurus, draws well	X
4. Marcus Washington	Athlete, kick ball	
5. Delores Sunderland	Any craft especially painting, sea life	X X
6. Jon Finlayson	Football, collects cards of athletes	X
7. Betty Oliver	Takes care of little sister, cooks	X
8. John Pringle		
9. Frances Sawtelle	Cat and kittens	
10. Ford Park	Works with father on road moving equipment on Saturdays	X
11. Joel Cupperman		
12. Jason Beckwith		
13. Fred Gallo	Sharks, movie "Jaws"	
14. Aleka Alphanosopoulos	Collects records	X
15. Charles Lentini	Collects motorcycle bro-chures, brother has cycle	X
16. Allison Goodrich		
17. Mark Andrade	Fishes with father	
18. Jason Tompkins		
19. Paul Gardner	Traveled to dog show	
20. Margaret Texeira	Cares for little brother and sister; this angers her	X

21. Albert Guimond		
22. Patricia Snow		
23. Patricia Rezendes	Knows something about weaving	
24. William Frost		
25. Laurie Kunstler		

All children below the line were not remembered on second attempt one week after school started.

▲▼ **Fig. 2.4**
Third Memory Attempt
February 16

	Experiences and Interests	Confirmation Column
1. Delores Sunderland	Anemone, various seaweeds	X
2. Jon Finlayson	Collection of 250 athletic cards—knows statistics on each one	X
3. Marcella Cowan	Caring for a horse	X
4. Jonathan Freedman	Prehistoric animals, cave dwellers, lake people	X
5. Aleka Alphanosopoulos	Folk music, also dances	X
6. Marcus Washington	Brother—outstanding athlete, watches track meets	X
7. Betty Oliver	TV mysteries, bakes bread	X
8. Fred Gallo	Is into "fright" type mysteries, builds huts	
9. Margaret Texeira	Mother works, knows how to do some cooking	X
10. Ford Park	Collection of brochures on heavy equipment, operates a bulldozer	X
11. Charles Lentini		
12. Norman Frazier	Got Ford Park to collect brochures, follows cycle races, describes fish equipment, process of catching fish	X
13. John Pringle	Into leather crafts—father has tools which he can use	X
14. Joel Cupperman	Likes to keep records but knows nothing beyond that	X
15. Patricia Snow	Interested in fashion— not very specific	X
16. Paul Gardner	Canoeing, dogs, caring for dogs	X
17. Mark Andrade	Knows different kinds of trout and how to catch them	X
18. Laurie Kunstler		
19. Jason Tompkins	Agility as observed on playground	X
20. William Frost		

21. Allison Goodrich	Has kittens—not much into them	
22. Jason Beckwith	Picks up quickly on choral speaking	X
23. Frances Sawtelle	Cares for kittens, took cat to vet with mother	X
24. Patricia Rezendes	Samples of weaving, brought in loom, can use	X
25. Albert Guimond		

3 WHY WOULD ANYONE EVER WANT TO WRITE?

A few years ago I was asked to give an address at a well-known New England prep school during morning assembly. Sensing that the audience might be more than a little intimidating, I delivered my first lines from the very edge of the stage apron: "I hate writing," I thundered. The entire audience of nine hundred instantly leaped to their feet and cheered. Though somewhat taken aback at their unanimous declaration, I finished the line: "but I love *having written*." Those weren't my lines; I stole them from the famous writer Dorothy Parker.

Although they were used to spoofing and a good time, I suspect the prep school students shared a basic sentiment about writing that is universally felt by most students in this country: writing is a sweaty business. The act is so painful that most delay writing a class paper until pure terror takes over. We pile references on the table next to us and simultaneously read and write, hoping our references will impress our teachers. "I hope this is what they want," we say to ourselves.

We write a few paragraphs, but the language doesn't sound like us. On the one hand we fear that if the language sounds like us the professor won't like it; on the other, we know how hard it is to actually make the stuff sound as though we are the confident person who is in charge of the material. In effect, we write while looking back over our shoulder to see if there is an approving look on the face of the teacher. It is hard to walk straight ahead while looking back, and when we look back as we write, our voice is passive.

A Bit of History

A quick historical overview of writing will help us understand its place in our life today. "He has a good hand and can spell well" was a compliment coveted by our forebears. Back at the turn of the century, when few people went to college, the well-educated person was someone with good handwriting and spelling. Glance at an old text-book and you'll find many exercises in forming letters. At the same time, the spelling bee was a popular social institution in school and community life.

The educated person spoke with good diction and used proper grammar: the intrusion of a double negative in writing or in speech quickly marked a person as "poorly educated."

These standards are still the measures of social and educational station. There is enough of the human in all of us that we apply this shorthand in judging people according to the surface features we first encounter in their oral and written speech.

Teachers and school administrators feel pressure from a public that worries about handwriting, spelling, and grammar. Behind parental complaints lurks the anxiety that their children will be marked by the educated class as socially unacceptable. Thus, such practices as inventive spelling are worrisome to parent groups, especially in middle-and upper-middle-class communities. Yet rarely do parents complain about the inability of their children to formulate and express ideas in a clear and logical fashion.

Those reform movements in America that emphasize *meaning* before conventions and mechanics get into trouble. The teaching of reading has long been marked by the meaning controversy. One group claims that children need to learn phonics, the basic building blocks of reading, before getting to the question of meaning. First learn the fundamentals, they say, and meaning will follow soon enough. Another group urges an emphasis on meaning from the start: children acquire the skills of reading just as they learn to speak. Capitalize on the child's urge to extract meaning from symbols; show her how to make sense of the text.

This debate has raged in an "either-or" fashion for well over a hundred years. Each group has a vision, highly colored by philosophical, social, and political views, of what kind of world the child is to join. At the heart of the debate, although seldom discussed, is each person's view of what constitutes a democratic society.

In 1980 I was interviewed by a national tabloid newspaper following the publishing of my report to the Ford Foundation on the status of reading and writing in the United States. One sentence in that interview provoked a deluge of mail (which I haven't quite understood until I started writing this paragraph today). The sentence read: "In a democracy it is important for the governed to be able to respond to the government in writing." The reaction came from two groups, the liberal left and the conservative right (the readership for this type of tabloid). The mail from the left said, "What democracy?" The mail from the right said, "You can't trust the people." Both groups, though somewhat extreme, were dealing with the issue of the place and function of writing in a democracy. Consider the following example of a community's reaction to children's attempts to explain to adults why their Summer Institute on critical thinking ought to be retained in the school budget. The author, Rebecca Rule, a parent at the meeting, explains the incident:

> I watched and listened as three sixth graders attempted to save a program they loved, and I thought: It's working. All the writing these children have been doing since kindergarten, all this emphasis on thinking for themselves, taking in and responding to the ideas of others: Here is the payoff. They have learned how to think and they have learned how to communicate their ideas effectively. They are actively engaging in a democratic process that demands clear thinking and communication if it is to work well.
>
> For a few moments I basked in the glow. Then darkness descended in the form of a large angry budget committee member with a quivering handlebar moustache who announced that it was obvious the children had not written their own speech, that this was a political ploy orchestrated by an adult to play on the emotions of the committee. It was in essence, he said: "A cheap shot."
>
>   * * *
>
> After their presentation, the children left the town hall. I stayed, seething. A friend—who could see how angry I was—whispered: "Don't say anything. Let it go. Let the kids handle it."

* * *

When I got home a couple of hours later, Susan and Adi were in my study working on the word processor. They were writing a letter to the editor. They called Ethan for his contribution too.

In the letter they thanked the budget committee for allowing them to speak. They also criticized their critic—rather thoroughly. They didn't use the word prejudice, but obviously they had felt its sting. "On behalf of us and our families," they wrote, "we cannot believe that an adult would put three children on the spot and accuse us of lying with no evidence whatsoever, except for the fact that we are in sixth grade. (And, by the way, we *did* write this letter as well as our speech.)" (*Christian Science Monitor*, February 13, 1991)

These children clearly understand the power and function of writing. They view writing as one way to make a point to a group of people outside their usual sphere of communication—the school. But when children overstep their traditional "meaning boundary," adults often have a hard time adjusting to their active use of the medium. In this instance, the children see writing as a tool to transcend themselves and to affect other people, an act that redefines writing as a political tool. Indeed, it brings writing closer to what I feel is one of the major functions of writing: to transcend oneself in space and time.

Sadly, for most of us, throughout our school careers—from first grade through advanced degrees—writing was used to check us out: Did we know what someone else thinks we ought to know? "Write a term paper, an exam, a theme; answer questions at the end of the chapter; fill out this form." There is a place for this kind of writing, but when it constitutes nearly the whole diet, students lose sight of what writing is *for*. Worse, they lose their political birthright as well as a valuable means of finding out what writing can do.

Of course, writing serves functions other than politics. My daughter is in her third year of medical school with a surgical clerkship that requires her to live away from home for two months. She entered medical school after marrying and starting her family. Her husband runs the household and maintains home base in addition to working a full-time job as supervisor in a plant. But their youngest child, Gregory, an energetic ten-year-old, misses his mother. Gregory attends a school in Deerfield, New Hampshire, that provides countless opportunities for children to use writing in an authentic way. Nevertheless, he is not as interested in writing and reading as one might expect. He writes under protest and only occasionally reads.

Gregory surprised his father one day when he announced, "I miss Mom and I'm going to write her four poems." And he proceeded to do just that. One of his poems reads:

> When you are gone,
> I am a fawn or mouse,
> but when you are back
> I'm a bear or a lion.

Although his use of metaphor is appealing, I find his spontaneous understanding of what writing is *for* more exciting. Gregory knows that writing transcends a situation and a relationship, that writing can define his feelings and connect him again with his mother. He will never lose his understanding of the function of writing, just as he will never forget how to ride a bicycle. The constant provision of authentic opportunities to write in school finally connected with Greg, and he was able, when circumstances required, to elect to use writing to suit his own needs.

A Late Learner

I didn't begin to find out what writing could do until I was about forty-four years old. Up to that time I thought I *might* have something to say, but I needed a teacher who could show me the fundamentals of good writing. Thanks to Donald Murray, I was able to break out of my writing limbo and begin to put one word in front of another.

"Know your subject and say it. Say it your way and say it quickly," he directed. At one particular dodgey moment when I was facing an impossible deadline, he told me to put my references away, write rapidly, change nothing, and when I came to the end of a page, to put the page in a box where I couldn't read it and then go on to the next page. "You know your subject, just write it," he said. It worked. I've often used this approach to break out of writer's block.

Since most of us associate writing with what schools have taught us about it, we lose out on learning about the purpose and place of writing for ourselves. Writing is a highly personal medium through which we communicate the facts and the meaning of our experience. The hard part is realizing that we actually have something to say. I've found that learning to write means first discovering where writing comes from, then seeing how it gets onto the page.

ACTION 3.1:
Begin to learn to read the world.

Writing comes from the events of our daily lives, from what appears at first glance to be trivial. A student once said to me, "I have nothing to write about; I haven't been anywhere and nothing tragic has ever happened to me. In fact, my life is boring." The writer's first act is to listen and observe the details of living. As an example, I'll take the stuff of my life from the last twenty-four hours to see what may be there to write about. Most of all I'll be looking for unanswered questions. I'll be "reading the world." I'll write for about fifteen minutes to see what is there (the text in roman type is what I recall from yesterday, the text in italic is my questioning of and reflection on those details).

8:30 A.M. I begin to write this chapter, Chapter 3. Will anything be there? I still fear, but not as badly as in the past, that the page will be empty. I just write drivel for a while, then take a look. *Question: Will this worry ever go away? Is it the state of the human condition that we worry that our words will fail us?*

8:45 A.M. Call from our daughter Alyce in Georgia. She has something to FAX to us. It is a Christmas memory from when she was ten years old. She wonders if it is a collage of memories or just from that year. No matter, her writing is just beautiful. She worries about writing to her writing father. Heavens, she writes so well, she has nothing to worry about. *I realize that a simple letter about a Christmas memory evokes more of the spirit within me than a purchased present.*

11:00 A.M. Snow starts to fall. We live in the White Mountains and there has been no snow this year. They say we are out of the jet stream that could bring it. Seems as though the weather is always atypical. There is no such fish as typical weather. *Ah, that's a piece I'd like to write. I keep weather records and none of it is typical. This is the wettest month, the dryest month, the month with the least snow, the coldest August on record. Why are Americans so fascinated with weather? When I was in Scotland the weather report was two minutes long and that was it. We portray the full drama of weather as if we are being invaded by forces from another planet. When there is a storm the weatherman is in his glory. Why is weather such an American phenomenon?*

11:30 A.M. I finish writing and I don't like it. I have a funny, depressed feeling inside. It is snowing and I should be elated. Oh well, I need some exercise. When I get down, exercise is the way out for me. *Why is that so? What is there about being in motion, doing something physical, that gives me a lift?*

1:15 P.M. To the fitness center to work out on Nautilus equipment. I've been working out on nine Nautilus machines for the past two weeks. I'm wondering what kind of conditioning this will add to my running. I observe the various people working out in the gym. I wonder why there are so many mirrors around and I note that one woman lifts bells and checks the mirror every other moment to observe her upper arms (so it seems). Another man who has been in the barbell area just walks around feeling big in the chest; he doesn't work out, he just looks at himself. Another young man just works; he doesn't look. *I just want to get in shape but I have to admit that I take a peek every once in a while. Now I see mirrors everywhere—in the locker room, going out the door, in the gym. What kind of narcissistic deal have I gotten myself into?*

Well, that's twenty minutes of rapid reflection. First I just state what happened as quickly as possible. Then I deal with the embedded meaning.

I didn't notice the number of mirrors until I wrote about the health club and my own reaction to what those mirrors might mean for me. Working on the body involves quite a bit of ego; can I admit just how much there is? Two words fly off the end of my tongue at every turn, "How come?" These words are followed by other questions: "What does that have to do with me? with people? with the world?" Until I write more extensively I have only teaser questions. I try to add the answers to the page.

ACTION 3.2:

Go back twenty-four hours and begin to record the details of your day. When you have finished, jot down some quick questions about yourself and the world.

University Professors Write with Their Students

You may not be used to looking for details or asking questions. "So, who cares?" you say. Writing helps me to understand myself in relation to the world. As I write, the world becomes a richer place, even when I concern myself with its most depressing elements. When I write, I feel as if I have claimed some turf. Writing gives me a solid place to stand and speak with some authority.

Notice that, although I am writing about "reading the world," my initial sentences sound more like a personal journal. Now I move on to write about the occasion I've just observed. I am going to take the episode in the gym and write for ten minutes to put more flesh on the bones of my first observations.

A young man/woman? curls a ten pound barbell; she's turned sideways looking at herself in the ten-foot-high mirror that runs the full length of the end of the weight room. She curls twice, pauses, looks, checking her bicep for size and form perhaps. I decide now she is a she. She reaches for a full lift with maybe one hundred pounds and facing the mirror. As I write this I realize that maybe balance and form are more important than I'd first thought.

The neophyte projecting his own bias sees ego. She sees form, balance, and beauty. I've been working in this gym for the past two weeks and I realize how little I know about the world of weight and mirror, the world of condition and physical beauty. I'm a 62-year-old man who worried my instructor with age and the danger of heart attack. He has me sign two pages of forms to make sure the place couldn't be sued. He seemed to relax after that. I've got more questions to ask of him next time we meet. I need to talk with the people who work out, find out what they have in mind, why they are there, what gives them satisfaction. "How do you feel?" I'll ask on occasion. "How long you been at this? How did you get started?" Maybe I'll learn about myself.

An old New England puritan like myself is scared to death of mirrors. A full look in the mirror might reveal a part of myself I've denied for years. It might reveal someone who actually enjoys body and form and Pride. Can I say the word, pride? Puritans regarded mirrors like original sin. Therein lies the problem of Adam; he looked in the mirror and saw God. Eve looked in the mirror with him and said, "Yes, you do look like God."

Well, that quick, unedited piece turned out quite different from what I'd expected. I still embed a lot of questions in the text; that usually means that there is a lot more to explore. I started with details about the woman on the weights, then realized that I was projecting my own problems with mirrors onto the woman. I just kept adding details and questions, and any shift in thought, to the piece. I wrote rapidly, changing nothing. That's the way it is with a first draft. Allow everything into a first draft. Listen to yourself and what you see in the shadows and sense just around the corner of thought. As you let the information in, include all the questions and doubts that go along with it.

ACTION 3.3:

Take one of the elements from the list you made when you "read the world" and write a ten-minute piece from it.

Circle three or four items or questions that interest you. Remember, it is the question, the fuzzy details, the *unknown* that moves people to write. If I already understand something, what's the sense of writing about it? Unfortunately, many of our students have already had too big a dose of writing about what they are already supposed to know.

There are several guidelines you should follow when you write this piece:

- Write rapidly, changing nothing.
- Allow thoughts and questions to enter your writing even though they may not be related to the topic with which you

began. Add them right into the text. (Notice how many shifts I made in writing my text, any one of which could have been a new subject in itself.)

- Lower your standards. Do not try to sound literary. Do not even try to write well.

ACTION 3.4:

Continue to write short pieces until you feel relaxed about what is on the page.

I find it is easier to learn to write by starting with short pieces. I need so much practice in seeing, observing, and questioning—in reading the world—that if I were to set out to do a large project I would lose touch with what I have to say.

This Action requires that you write two ten-minute pieces over the next seven or eight days. You will actually start to look for occasions that merit more attention to detail. "Hey, I'll write about this," you'll say to yourself when you are in the midst of something interesting. You will see something that merits a question: "how come?" you'll say to yourself and you'll begin to observe. Occasionally, the significance of the event won't strike you until the next day as you're writing.

ACTION 3.5:

Take a photo from your wallet—or any artifact that means something to you—and write about it for ten minutes.

Writing is one of the best ways to remember something. As I follow a line of words, scenes start to come to me from yesterday or years ago. Writing is an act of self-hypnosis in which you follow thoughts and images, one after the other, until you begin to see a pattern you wish to pursue. Let me show you what I mean. I'll take a photo from my wallet and look for the details that may be there and write for ten minutes (the photo is a shot I had taken in an instant photo booth while I was in basic training in the U.S. Coast Guard in 1952).

> A smiling young man with a white sailor hat tipped just so over the eyes to impress my sweetheart back in Boston. Basic training is a lonely business, new guys, new demands, new surroundings, no one I'd ever known before like my freshman year in college. The thin, shallow line of letters coming and going kept me alive.

I gave her my picture and she sent me two of her which I'd prop up at the end of my bunk when I wrote to her. One of the photos smiled just so and I'd flash it at the other guys. "Just got a letter from her today," I'd say like I was trying to prove she was for real. "Could anyone believe I'd have a girl as lovely as she?" Of course, looks were everything if you wanted to show your girl.

I knew she was a presidential scholar at the college I barely graduated from. She could read anything and understand it and over the miles and through the letters we'd discuss art, music, and psychology. I so wanted her to think I could think and knew things that were important. I loaned her my record player and records when I was sworn into the military so we could talk the same music while I was away. I loved opera, especially La Boheme and Tales of Hoffman, and my favorite tenor, Richard Tucker. Sharing music is like sharing poetry; you share much more of yourself than if you shared a book. Music reaches way down deep to what makes your soul tick. Later she told me that we fell in love through La Boheme.

We still share opera though not as much as in those days when the thin thread of a letter declared her deep feelings over the death scene of Mimi in La Boheme and Rodolfo, played by Richard Tucker, which reaches the heights of pain in his tenor voice.

That was a quick eight-minute first draft. I began with the photo and nothing much in my head but a question: "What will I do with it?" I quickly moved to the next question: "Why did I have it taken?" I wrote a little about that, and in the writing further questions came to mind: "What was the place of the letters?" I quickly switched from the letters to the photos and wrote down some details about the photos on my bunk. I used them to show off a little but really there was so much more to it than the mere flash of a picture. I then wrote about my great respect for her as a thinker and that quickly led to our real sharing through music. I made my real discovery in this piece when I wrote the line, "Sharing music is like sharing poetry; you share much more of yourself than if you shared a book." I have a hunch that music, no matter what kind, is very important when two people are in love.

John Jerome, one of my favorite writers, speaks of his early days as a professional writer. He wrote for a skiing magazine. His editor said to him, "If you are going to cover skiing, you've got to cover the mountains. Skiing is more than runs and mechanics." In short, always bring in the context. In that short, ten-minute piece I kept reaching for context, not worrying about following my initial line of thought. I put in as many details as I could—the photo propped on my bunk . . . the names of our favorite operas and singers. The details help me to see what is there more vividly; in the details I sense the actual feelings we knew in those days.

Write down the details of some of your memories and let your thoughts travel where they may. Use the same guidelines as in your last ten-minute Action: write rapidly, change nothing, and don't try to be perfect.

Throughout these last few Actions, you have been discovering what writing can do. You have practiced reading the world and in your reading you have listened to and observed specific details from your own experience. You wrote about events. Writing is first of all for us. I write short pieces about particular occasions and events regularly, in addition to writing books, to keep in touch with the rich world around me. I write for myself. A secondary benefit is that my students are able to learn from someone who is a practitioner of the craft. Writing with your students is probably the single most powerful thing you will do to help them learn to write.

ACTION 3.6:
Work to find out what children think writing is for.

This Action is intended to help you find out more about children's understanding of the function of writing in your classroom. It requires you to think carefully about the questions you ask children and about your analysis of what they have to say.

Find a child engaged in writing, point to the writing, and ask, "What's that for?" Another way to phrase the question is, "Why do you write?" Children's responses will be shaped by the way writing is taught in the classroom as well as by their own stage of development as writers. The following responses give a composite picture showing how children answer questions about the function of writing such as "What's that for?" Use the following categories to examine the statements for each of the four children:

- the child's overall understanding of the function of writing;
- the child's understanding of the role of audience;
- how writing may be taught in the child's classroom.

FIRST CHILD

- That's a boat. (I'm doing this because I wanted to draw a boat.)
- I like boats. See the boat; it is going fast.
- My teacher likes my boats. My friend draws the boats and I do the writing.

SECOND CHILD

- We have to write about boats.
- This is for the teacher. She said we had to have something done by Friday.
- Today is writing day and I need to get it done.
- My teacher said we had to write about stuff from the summer.
- It's for writing time. I need something to share at share time.

THIRD CHILD

- I am into boats. I write about them all the time.
- This is mine. This is for me. I like to write.
- The kids in the class like my boats.
- I want to publish this one. This is one of my best and I'm going to make it my best and then the teacher will publish it.

FOURTH CHILD

- I am going to read this in the other teacher's class. She's my teacher from last year and she said she'd like to hear some of my stuff.
- My mom likes everything I write. This is for her.
- Everyone is writing about Teenage Mutant Ninja Turtles. [Implies it's for all the kids since they are all writing about these now.]

You may have noticed that most of these responses don't get at function. Very young children tend to say, "I am writing this because I am writing it" (I simply like boats). But gradually, you notice a sense of audience emerge in children's explanation of the function of the piece. "This is for the class, my mother, my former teacher, etc." I listen very carefully for this sense of authorship in children's responses. At first the "What's it for" is basically "It's for me!"

Experiment as well with the question "Why do you write?" which is more direct and may prompt more abundant responses. Extend the question to include others: "Why does that boy over there write? "Why does your teacher write?" Make note of whether or not the children change their notion of the function of writing from person to person. Does the child perceive that the teacher's use of writing is different from his own or that of other children? Does the child see other children using writing for different reasons?

This next question, though more academic, leaves out the personal, yet it may reveal a clearer picture of the child's understanding of writing: "Tell me all the different ways people use writing." You can follow up by turning the question back to the child: "Okay, now tell me which of these you've tried. On this one, why did you happen to be writing here?"

The main purpose of these questions is to discover children's understanding of writing. I look forward to the day when children see writing as a powerful tool they can use to influence others and to clarify their own thinking. I am very sensitive to children's notions of whether they have the power to initiate a text.

Final Reflection

Why would anyone ever want to write? Most of us are burdened by so much required writing that the notion of initiating writing on our own behalf is far from our thoughts. Look back to your histories in Chapter 1; think of your current situation. How much of your writing do you initiate? How much of your writing attempts to affect the thinking of others?

In 1978, as part of my Ford Foundation study, I reviewed UNESCO funding patterns for literacy programs in various countries. Virtually all the literacy programs were geared to helping people learn to read. None of them stressed the importance of a citizen's ability to write. I find it curious that the great debate in America still centers on how to teach our children to read, not on their learning to write. Unless children see themselves as authors with something to say, as writers with the power to initiate texts that command the attention of others, they may remain as sheep both in the classroom and later in the larger society.

Our own sense of authorship as teachers and citizens will strongly influence the way our own students view writing. I constantly review my own literate practices: how I read the world, how I use the craft of writing as a tool for thought. The Actions in this chapter focused on reading your own world and then writing short pieces to explore your own literacy.

You carried out Actions with your children that gave you a sense of their own authorship as well as where they are on the road to their own independent exercise of the craft as a genuine tool for thinking.

The next chapter will follow one day in the life of very young writers to demonstrate ways you can encourage them from the start to regard writing as a vital medium for thinking.

4 DAY ONE: HELP CHILDREN TO WRITE AND KEEP WRITING

Writing is a studio subject. I invite children to do something I am already doing. Just as an artist in the studio paints alongside her students, I write along with the children. A piano teacher may show his student how to play a particular passage, but occasionally, he plays an entire piece so that his student can experience the beauty of it.

This chapter will focus on the simplest of beginnings—Day One in the teaching of writing. My invitations to the children will be similar to the invitations I extended to you in Chapter 3. I will show them where writing comes from, how I begin to write, and how I keep on writing. And I will demonstrate how I circulate through the class while the children are writing, first with kindergarten and first grade, then with second through sixth grades.

Kindergarten and Grade One

Depending on how much experience you have had with children, you will need to decide which of several approaches will work best for you. Some teachers begin with the entire class. They invite children to sit on the rug or pull them together on the floor and chat with them as a group. An invitation to write begins almost as an intimate conversation.

Other teachers, especially those who are beginning to teach writing for the first time or want to listen more carefully to the reactions of individual children, will find a small group better. Whether with an entire class or a small group, your conversations with children will be similar to the ones I share in this chapter.

If you choose the cluster route, begin with five or six children who show some sign of using letters, who can write their name, or whose drawings are beginning to show more extensive content than a simple drawing of one object or contain far more than random lines.

I'll probably use experience chart paper or the chalkboard in working with my small group. Here is a sample dialogue:

Teacher:	Let's talk about yesterday afternoon when you went home from school. What do you remember?
Carolyn:	I had to go next door to stay at my friend's because my mother was still at work.
Teacher:	And then . . .
Carolyn:	Well, I played over there. My friend has a puzzle. We put it together.
Teacher:	It was hard?
Carolyn:	No, it was her little brother's. So we tried to do it real fast and we got to laughing.
Teacher:	Anyone else?
Tenisha:	I played with my cat. She's just a kitten and she's crazy! I had to change my shoes and I couldn't do it because she kept playing and hitting my hands when I tried to tie them.
Jennifer:	I've got a canary and she's noisy. I cover her up when she's noisy. Then she shuts up.
Andy:	I had to go to the doctor's and get a shot.
Group:	Ohhhhh!
Andy:	Yeah, and I didn't cry either.
Teacher:	You felt like you wanted to?
Andy:	Not really, but I was still afraid I would.
Teacher:	I don't like shots. Anyone else ever have a shot?
Brendan:	I got a lot in the hospital. I cried. I got sick of 'em.
Carolyn:	I had a 'fection and got one. The needle was this big! [shows with hands].

Teacher: I had one last summer when I stepped on a nail. When the nurse comes with the needle, I look the other way so I can't see it.

The first entry point into writing is simple conversation. In this instance, the teacher has chosen to open discussion about what happened yesterday afternoon after school. She listens carefully to what the children say and extends their comments with a few questions. Her language is responsive, and not until much later—during the discussion about shots—does she interject her own experience. When the discussion turns to shots, she sees that this is a common discussion topic for all the children and lets the discussion run its course. Then she observes:

Teacher: I've learned all different kinds of things from you. Some of you played like Carolyn with her puzzles; Tenisha had her cat, Andy had a shot and we've all had shots, Brendan too, and Jennifer has her canary. We've done lots of things and things have happened to us. I would like you to take this paper and write about one of the things we've talked about or anything else that comes to mind. I think I'll choose my dog, Billy.

   Billy and I go for walks together when I get home. I'll quickly make a sketch of him here—the two of us walking. This is the lead I snap onto his collar [quick sketch].

   Now I'm going to write something to go with it. What do I want to say? Let's see. "Billy and I go for walks." Help me.

   B . . . il . . . ly [She says the word very slowly].

   Help me with the first sound "B." What letter do I write here?

Brendan: "B." I've got that one in my own name. It's easy.

Teacher: Right you are. Listen for any other sounds you hear in the word. I'll say it again slowly.

Carolyn: I hear an "l."

Jennifer: I hear an "e."

Teacher: Actually it isn't an "e." But it sounds like one. Good going.

The children continue to help the teacher compose, volunteering the names of the letters that go with the sounds she needs to represent. She "invents" the sounds that go with her text after drawing a quick sketch. Data show that a drawing often helps the child to think about what might be said in the text that follows. In this demonstration the teacher is showing:

- where writing comes from (actual events in their lives)
- that drawing can be helpful to writing by serving as a rehearsal for the text that follows. Soon children will be placing more information in their drawings than exist in their text, but the drawing serves to help the child contextually with the text when they read the words.
- how to invent the words and write them:
  - slow the text down by saying it slowly and aloud
  - help children use the resources of the letters in their own names
  - place spaces between words to help with rereading
  - compose from left to right
  - show how particular letters that go with particular sounds are formed
- how to make the transition from oral to written discourse

Many skills are involved in demonstrating writing and for this reason, many successive demonstrations are needed to help children become more independent writers. (You will find further help in teaching very young children who are emergent spellers in Chapter 16.)

ACTION 4.1:

If you are teaching kindergarten or first grade, choose a small group of children who exemplify the criteria mentioned on page 48 and introduce them to writing through your own oral discussion and demonstration.

When the children set out to put their notions on paper, you may notice some of the following:

- Some just draw. Some may draw only one object, a few, many, or even an entire scene.
- Some draw and put one letter, an initial letter, to go with the drawing.
- Some write whole words by using primarily the initial and final consonants only.
- Some have sight words.
- Some of the children may not be responsive to a "retelling." Narrative doesn't interest them.

- A few children are afraid to invent. They are sophisticated enough to know that words have only one spelling. They *demand* your help and want you to supply them with correct spellings for all that they write.

This is the short list of what may happen when children write. Since you can't supply all the words children need for full spellings, resist the temptation to respond to the child who wants you to spell all of them. You can help this child by supplying the full spelling of *one key word* in a sentence. I say to that child, "Okay, you choose one very important word; I'll give it to you, but you need to invent the others on your own or get help from someone else. I don't have time to do all of them."

There are some children who do not find a story-type discussion helpful. Making a list and giving commands or directions is closer to their communication and thinking needs.

Here is how I would demonstrate this type of introduction:

Teacher: Sometimes I like to make lists of things.
Watch, here's a kind of a list. I know different kinds of animals [if children are at the point of learning how to invent, I say the word slowly and they help supply the letters to put on the board]
bear
deer
cat
dog
Help me with my list.

Child: Tiger.

Teacher: Good, another . . .

Child: Lion.

Teacher: Right. You can make a list, draw them, or even draw them first and write afterward. These pages are for doing the list kind of writing. [The paper children use for this type of writing is much smaller, allowing for a drawing and a label to go with it.] I'll do the first one on my list.

Teacher: We can make another kind of list. How about cars?
Here's a start:
Ford
Toyota
Mercury
Tell me some more cars I could put down here.

Child: Subaru.

Child: GMC truck.

Teacher: Of course, another list could be different kinds of cars like
sedan, pickup. Give me some others . . .

Children are naturally inquisitive and like to think they know a lot
about certain subject areas. The discovery of different areas is as
important as the lists that go with them. Inventing with the children
during the list-making also seems to help them build up associations
between drawings, sounds, and the letters they place on the page.
Again, many children who may not feel the urge to begin to explore
narrative enjoy listing. The point is to begin to help children to find
out what writing and print can do for them—today.

ACTION 4.2:

*Choose a small group of children who don't seem to be as interested in the
narrative side and try exploring lists. (If appropriate, have them help you
invent the spellings of the words.)*

Remember that some children are not yet ready to make letters to go
with objects or drawings. They may still be scribbling and making
random drawings that have not yet reached more traditional forms
(see Harste, Woodward and Burke [1984]; also Temple, Nathan, Burris
and Temple [1988]). The two examples given as introductory modes
thus far (story-telling about yesterday and listing) are for children
who already have a general sense of sound-symbol correspondence
and are ready to communicate. In short, each of these examples is
intended to open the door to the mode of communication preferred by
particular children.

One last example of an entry point into writing is the sign or brief
command. Thomas Newkirk (1989, 23) shows that children embed the
rudiments of argument in the signs they compose. His six-year-old
daughter composed this sign:

Desin-a-button

only 75 cents   the desin
chuck.E.cheese
Unicon rainbows

and much much more

it's a better pric
than last year
75 cents

Newkirk points out the complexity of the sign's content:

- Major assertation: Buy a design-a-button
- Major reason: Low cost
- Evidence: The cost is seventy-five cents
- Major reason: The many designs (implied)
- Evidence: Chuck E. Cheese, unicorns, rainbows, and much, much more.

He also notes that young children's first use of print may be in brief signs like "Keep Out," "Stop," "Stay Out," or in short messages intended to influence others. Indeed, these may be the more elemental forms of essay and exposition.

Teacher: There's a kind of writing that can be pretty useful. See that sign over there? What do you suppose it says?

Child: Go out.

Teacher: Good. That's what it means. It says "Exit." That's where you can go out of the building. It shows you where to go. Have you seen any other signs that you know?

Child: Out front it says "stop" for the buses.

Child: My brother has one for his room that says "keep out."

Teacher: Let's have some signs you'd like to make to help others or have them do things.

Child: I'd like a "quiet" sign. It gets pretty noisy sometimes and I'd like to hold it up when that happens.

Teacher: I like that one. That's a hard one to write though. I'll say it slowly and then write it.
    Qu i et
Okay, I have one for you. Let's see if you can read my sign: "Can you help me?" [*She helps the children to read the message and to quietly leave the group and go to their seats.*]

The teacher goes on to help children observe other signs that are displayed in the building. She stresses the communicative nature of signs or short requests: they exist to help people—sometimes the writer and sometimes the people the writer wishes to address. They go on to discuss signs the children might like to make or those they notice in their classroom, school, or community.

ACTION 4.3:
Experiment with making and reading signs and messages with a small group of children.

Notice which children first understand the *function* of sign and message making. Until children have a rough approximation of the meaning of sign and message making, writing won't make much sense. We explore, explain, and demonstrate over and over what print can do as a communicative medium. One of the best ways I have found to help children extend their understanding of print as communication is to write very short messages to them.

"Come see me."

"I saw you tie your shoe."

"Good work."

"Come to the small table."

If I wish to have a group come to the table, I'll pass out small slips to those children I wish to meet with me. If they can't read the message they may consult with another child.

ACTION 4.4:
Practice writing short messages to children and note how they make meaning out of them.

Second Through Sixth Grades

My starting points for older students do not vary a great deal from those from grades two through six. I begin with a demonstration of "reading my world" for the previous day (see Chapter 3). I select elements from my day that will be of interest to older children. I match the complexity of my observations to their age, experience with writing, and sophistication.

ACTION 4.5:

Demonstrate where topics come from in the everyday experience, selecting incidents from your own life that will interest your students.

Don: I'd like to show you how I "read the world" around me in order to use what I see for things I might write about. I'll tell you about what happened, show you how I think about it, and then it would be helpful if you'd ask questions about what I say. You might be curious to know more about something; if so, raise your hand and ask the question. Okay, I'll start and then I'll put some notes on the board as I talk.

Let's see, about 4:00 P.M. I was in my study and I was on the telephone. You know I've always liked to have a place to go to that was mine. When I was your age I got a table and I made believe it was my desk.

It had a little slide you could pull out and one small drawer. I thought I was big stuff. I shared my room with my brother. The desk was on my side of the room. I'll put a few notes here to help me remember:

in my study
when I was a kid
wanted a place of my own
a desk, drawer
be alone

I was lucky because my brother didn't like to be alone in the room; he liked to be outside. Well, I liked to be outside but I also wanted to be alone and just think. How many of you like to be alone in a room? How many of you would rather be outside? See, we're all different in some ways, the same in others.

I remember once my mother sent me to my room because I hadn't done my chores.

Child: What were your chores?

Don: Oh, we had to take turns doing the dishes. I was a boy and I didn't think that was right. My mother just said, "Get busy." She was pretty strict. Any of you have chores or jobs around the house?

Child: I have to walk my dog.

Child: I have to help my dad mow the lawn. I also have to make my bed every day and take out the trash.

Child: I have to take care of my little brother. Every day after school!!

Don: Just a minute, I've got to get some of this down.
> *Mow the lawn.* (I had to do that too.)
> *Do dishes, not fair.*
>
> Anyway, as I said, I got sent to my room. That was a way my mother punished me sometimes. Got a spanking once too.

Child: What did you do?

Don: I'll never forget it. My brother and I took our dog, Rags, for a walk and we didn't come home until after dark. We just forgot what we were doing and how late it was. Our parents were frightened out of their wits. When we got home they were glad to see us and very angry at the same time. Both my brother and I got turned over my Dad's knee and spanked real hard. I tried not to cry; I think I just yelled a little.

Okay, I'm going to stop there. Now watch what I'll do with what I've written (see Figure 4.1). I'd like you to try something and see how it goes.

Notice that I simply started by going to my study. "How come?" I said to myself. And I got an answer inside my head, "I've always enjoyed going there. Even as a kid." That sent my mind way back to when I was your age. Then I remembered something else, how I got sent to my room for not doing my chores. You asked questions about what I'd done wrong, and then I remembered still more about other punishments. See how one thing leads to

▲▼ **Figure 4.1**
Demonstration

WHAT HAPPENED?	REMINDS ME
4:00 to my study →	always wanted place of my own as a kid / my desk
Chores → / sent to my room / spanking	had to do dishes / enjoyed being alone / walked dog too late / didn't want to cry

another. I let my mind run; I listen to myself and find lots to write about. So much of writing is connected to just remembering and being curious about what's there.

The basic objective here is to help students learn how to *listen to themselves.* I need to show them how I do that; and, of course, some of my reflections have been prompted by their questions. For many children, learning to listen to themselves is a new experience. Much of our education says, "Listen to me" (the teacher or the parent). There is little teaching that shows our children how to do this. I used to say to my sixth-grade students, "Think for yourselves. I want to know what you are thinking." The trouble is, I never showed them what I meant by that or where original thinking comes from.

Sadly, most students do not know how to find topics in the common everyday events that surround them. At this point in their lives

The Teacher Writes with the Class

they can only seize on major events: a trip to New York or Disney World, or *someone else's experience* on television or motion pictures. Unless we show them how to select topics from the ordinary events of their own lives and expand them into fiction, an essay, or a personal narrative, they can only draw on the experiences of others, which they do not necessarily understand.

I would mention too that one demonstration, like the one portrayed here, will not go very far. Our children need to see us do this many times: once a week at least in a short mini-lesson. Further, recognize that only a few children can start writing in this way. Still, it opens the door to many other topics for those children who are ready.

ACTION 4.6:
Show children the options for writing topics from an everyday reading of the world.

I return to the content of my demonstration to show children the origins of various genres. Here is some sample dialogue that demonstrates what we might discover:

Don:	Let me show you where fiction comes from. Fiction comes from people wanting something and the journey they take to get it. Let's go to what I've just reviewed here. Let's create something that somebody wants.
Child:	Well, you said you wanted a place of your own. Well, we could have this kid who wanted to be a scientist and he wanted his own laboratory.
Don:	Got it; yes, that's it. Now the story comes from maybe things that got in his way to getting it.
Same child:	Well, maybe he was poor and he found some boxes and he made one up in his basement and he just can't find boxes.
Don:	Right, that's fiction: A boy who wants his own place to experiment and he works really hard to find boxes and there are all kinds of adventures on the way to finding boxes.
Don:	Let's have another.
Child:	Well, maybe there is this girl and her father has remarried and she has lots of chores. Her stepmother just picks on her. She wants to please her father because she misses her real mother but her stepmother wants to keep her out of the way so she can have her father all to herself.

Don:	Okay, let's see if we have fiction here. Do we have someone who wants something?
Child:	Yes, a girl who wants her father.
Don:	What's in the way?
Child:	A stepmother who gives her chores to keep her out of the way.

In Chapter 18 I will discuss how you can be of greater help to children writing fiction. Here I only show the basic ingredients inspired by what I experienced the previous day: a character who wants something and the kind of conflict that gets in the way.

ACTION 4.7:

Conduct a series of writing conferences in which the children teach you about what they know.

The purpose of the writing conference is to help children teach you about what they know so that you can help them more effectively with their writing. When you showed children how to "read the world" in Action 4.5, you showed them how to discover what they know, choose those areas for topics, and then write about them. Thus, as you move around the room conducting conferences try to note what children write in their texts and help them to speak to you. I usually come to each student with these notions in mind:

- what the topic is about
- where the topic came from
- what they will write next

For your first conferences choose three to four children who are already writing. Get the feel of the writing conference by working with children who find it easier to talk about what they are doing. The unspoken guideline in the conference is "You know things that I don't."

Don:	What is your piece about, Jennifer?
Jennifer:	It's about my cat and how she plays with me.
Don:	Oh, tell me about a time she played with you.
Jennifer:	Well, she likes to stick her paws through the up and down things under the bannister (I forget what you call 'em) and when I put my finger up she hits it like she's a boxer. She doesn't use her claws.

The Child Initiates in a Conference

Don: I can almost see her doing that—her paws darting in and out. What will you write next?

Jennifer: Hmmm, maybe I'll write about that. I was just finishing a part here about how she plays with my toes under the covers in the morning.

Don: Looks like you have lots to write.

I notice that Jennifer can say what her piece is about in one sentence. This is an important ability that writers of all ages need to acquire. She focuses on the central characters (herself and the cat) and the essential action (we play). I quickly ask Jennifer to tell me some *specifics* that relate to her essential topic: "Tell me about a time she played with you." I listen carefully to what she says the piece is about, and then I ask a question she is mostly likely able to answer. If Jennifer is unable to handle that question I would ask one that may put her in touch with why she chose the topic in the first place: "How did you happen to write about you and your cat playing, Jennifer?" Sometimes children lose touch with the reason they chose their topic. When Jennifer remembers why she decided to write about her cat, she may also recall episodes and memories about the cat.

I try to restrict this type of conference to about two minutes and to keep my comments to a minimum. A rough profile of a good conference shows the child speaking about 80 percent of the time, the teacher 20 percent. You may wish to tape-record your conference to get a sense of the ratio of your talk to the child's talk and to assess how well you are able to prompt the child to tell you about what they know.

I end each conference by stating what the child will write about next or what to do in order to move forward on the piece. Of course, the child may already have told me what she intends to do, and this is especially important for students who find it difficult to write.

Another conference might involve a child in the midst of a dilemma: he is wondering about the right topic for his piece.

Don: What's your piece about, Jeff?

Jeff: I don't know. It's all over the place. I'm afraid it will be boring. See, I want there to be good action here. I want it to be about these people who are fighting off the space invaders but maybe it's about just the space invaders.

Don: I'm curious about how you decided to choose this topic to write about, Jeff.

Jeff: Well, when we were doing that thing you did with us, I got to thinking about space and weapons; it's what I think about a lot, the ultimate weapon, so I wanted the ultimate weapon in here.

Don: Tell me about the person who uses it.

Jeff: Well, there is this mad scientist who is in charge of it. He developed it.

Don: Why is he mad?

Jeff: Oh, hmmmm. His mind snapped because he was treated badly by the other scientists.

Don: Okay, let's stop there, Jeff. I've learned quite a bit about your scientist and what you had in mind. He is mad because he was treated badly and now he has a weapon he will use. My last question is, What does he want? What does the mad scientist want? Something is bugging him because he can't get what he wants. Take this piece of paper and just write for five minutes about what he wants and why.

This conference turned out to be longer than most. Jeff has a sense of what he wants to do, but it doesn't match what is on his paper. In addition, he has lost sight of what he is doing because he is worrying so much about composing a piece that is boring. Children often lose sight of what they've set out to do, especially with fiction. The solution to most of their problems is character, like Jeff's mad scientist. In fiction, character is all. Things happen because of what characters want and how they get stopped from getting what they want. I left Jeff writing on another piece of paper in order to develop a character with some substance. Once he has a central character, his fiction will be more successful. (Chapter 18 will discuss more ways to help this kind of student.)

Remember, the main purpose of the conference is to encourage the student to show you what he knows and gain a clearer picture of what he will write next. I concentrate on *flow* for the student and *learning* for me.

In this next conference, I encounter a child who is writing fiction more closely rooted in personal experience. Too much of children's fiction is far afield from what they know, and therefore it is more difficult to help them show you what they know.

Don: What is your piece about, Andy?

Andy: Well, it's about this team that's undefeated and they are going to play the best team in the league.

Don: I see. And what's going to happen?

Andy: They are going to win in overtime even though their star player has gone out on fouls.

Don: I'd gather this is basketball. Is there a main character in the piece?

Andy: Yeah, it's the boy who fouled out and he's so disappointed that he has let the team down.

Don: And what are you writing about right now? What's next?

Andy: He's just fouled out and he's sitting on the bench wondering what he's done. But one of the subs comes through; that's what's next.

Andy has a good sense of where he is in the piece, of his character, and of who will save the day. This is a short conference because Andy knows just where he is going. I have learned from him and he knows what's next.

As you move around the room conducting conferences, the other children are listening. It is easier for them to write if they catch your encouraging tone: "You know things that I will learn from you." This allows them to learn from themselves and each other more easily. You set the standard for learning through your attentive listening.

ACTION 4.8:

Conduct a writing share session with a small group or with the entire class.

For this Action, gather the children in a circle or on the floor in one section of the room. The share session comes at the end of the writing time. For your first share session you may wish to select certain children to share what they have written thus far, or ask for two or three volunteers. This is how I introduce the session:

Don:	Two people will be sharing their writing this morning. Danny will share first, but before he reads his piece he'll tell us the one thing it is about. Then it will be our job to listen very carefully, because when he finishes we'll tell him what we *remember* from it.
Dan [reading]:	Last Saturday me and my Dad went to the science museum in Boston. I remember the owl especially because of the way he turned his head. It was like he could turn it all the way around. When the man held him he told us about his sharp claws. They were long.
	Then there was Tyrannosaurus Rex. If you lived when he did he would be able to eat you with one bite.
	He was very tall—about fifty feet high.
	We had pizza for lunch. We got home about seven o'clock.
Don:	All right, Danny, you are in charge. You call on the children whose hands are raised. They will tell you what they remember. You'll need to listen carefully too in case we forget some things that are in your piece.
Child:	I remember the Tyrannosaurus Rex. How big he was.
Child:	You had pizza.
Child:	The owl had long, sharp claws.
Child:	Tyrannosaurus Rex was fifty feet high.
Child:	You went to the science museum.
Don:	All right, Danny, what did we forget?
Dan:	The owl can turn his head almost completely around. And we got home about seven o'clock.

The first thing children need to be able to do is to listen carefully to a classmate's text. I call this *receiving the text*. Further, children need to learn how to listen to a text so they remember before they ask questions. I find that, unless children work hard to listen to what a writer has written, their questions border on the trivial. Just for practice, you may wish to allow the children to ask a few questions of the author after they have received the piece.

Final Reflection

In this chapter you have introduced yourself and your students to three basic elements in the writing classroom: discovering writing topics, writing conferences, and sharing. The Actions I describe are useful to teachers throughout their entire careers. They work to refine them virtually every day of their professional lives.

You *demonstrated* the sources of your own writing for the children. You showed them how you learned from your world and from their world during your conferences with them. You made it possible for them to learn from each other by sharing their own writing.

I suggest that you try each of these Actions *on successive days for at least one week* in order to begin to be comfortable with them in the writing classroom.

As you moved around the room conducting conferences or demonstrated topic origins with the children you probably noticed that children are at different points in their development. This will be the focus of the next chapter.

5 UNDERSTAND CHILDREN WHEN THEY WRITE

"Yes, but what I want to know is what I can expect of my children as writers by the end of fourth grade," the teacher, her voice rising, asks after our workshop. It is clear that she wants an answer—perhaps she has been commissioned by her district to ask the question. Principals, teachers, and school districts all want to establish benchmarks in order to know what to expect of their students. This is a good political move, but it doesn't necessarily help us to know what to do when we teach individual children. Benchmarks sometimes go beyond what some children can do at a particular moment or underestimate what to expect of them at another.

Teachers do need to know how to get a rough sense of where their children are on a learning continuum in writing, and they need to know what expectations are realistic. This chapter will explore the developmental aspects of writing and look at some of the factors that are involved in the act of writing. The Actions will give you a chance to see how well you understand the children with whom you are working.

Notions of Children's Development as Writers

When I first began to explore children's writing development, I harbored a strong Piagetian bias. I believed that careful research would reveal certain inviolable sequences in children's growth and that clear, identifiable stages of development could be established. What I didn't count on was the power of the determined young writer and top-level teaching, especially by teachers who demonstrated highly literate thinking and had big expectations of their children. After the dust of disappointment had settled, however, I could see that a *general understanding* of how children change as writers could be useful for our teaching.

A Quick Profile

How does a child change as a writer as she increases in age and sophistication? Let's consider successive pieces on the same event, "The Wedding." The first example was actually written by a first-grade child, but I have written examples 2 through 5 to show how the same topic might be treated as the child grows older. Although I can initially indicate the approximate age of this writer, it becomes increasingly difficult to do so, since such factors as maturity and, above all, instruction, have much to do with how a young writer develops. Each example is followed by an interpretive description of the child's behaviors during composing each passage.

1. Thr wr lts uv pepl thr. Atrth waz prety we hd lets uv cakniccrm. [There were lots of people there. Aunt Ruth was pretty. We had lots of cake and ice cream.]

This child is in the second half of first grade. She finished the written portion of this piece in about ten minutes. The greater part of her effort went into a drawing of her aunt in a wedding gown, which took about fifteen minutes. Much of the early writer's work often goes into the drawing, which can serve as a rehearsal for the text that follows. That is, while she draws, a text begins to grow in her mind, although she isn't conscious of a text to come. If she shares her writing, the other children are usually more interested in the drawing. For quite some time, there is more information in the drawing than in the text.

The text is "invented" in that it evolves from the child's early understandings of sounds and symbols. The consonants are more accurate than the vowels, and some of the words run together because this is how she "hears" them when people speak (cakniccrm: cake and ice cream).

The piece has a beginning (lots of people there), a middle (the wedding itself: Aunt Ruth was pretty), and an end (We had lots of cake and ice cream). In short, there is a rough sequence to the text.

The child observes many conventions: the text moves from left to right and proceeds from top to bottom. She knows that words should have spaces between them. She has vowels (though many inaccurate) in places where vowels belong. She uses two periods correctly (first and last sentence.) Her story follows a logical temporal order that shows an early sense of narrative.

2. Ther wer lots of peple ther. My Auts, Unkls, gradmuthr, gradfadr, my sistrs. Ther wer cars ther wer flowers. The day was nic. Aut Ruth was pretty. She had ona white gowd and cared some flowers. She wet dowd the ile. Everyone looked at her. Then we had lotsof cake and ice cream. It was hot then we wet home.

About six to nine months later, the child's piece would look more like this. There are more full spellings (flowers, white, cake, ice cream, then, she, was, everyone, looked). Invention still is dominant but the vowels are much more precise than before. She still doesn't have a strong visual memory of what words look like—these systems come more from extensive reading than from writing—when this is acquired, her spellings will be much more complete. She has just about learned where most words are separated. Her sentence sense is growing, although some still run together and she is using periods and the serial comma. Knowing when to place a period to end a sentence will become more difficult for her over the next several years as her texts become more complex.

Her sentence structure uses repetitive structures: "there were" and "then." These are narrative markers that help her story to progress from start to finish.

Her language is much more specific (detail on members of the family, the appearance of Aunt Ruth, and the actual moment of the wedding itself). The ending is also characteristic of so many endings at this age (Then we went home). It won't be long before she also writes "The End" following "Then we went home."

Drawings may still accompany this text, and at times they may follow the writing. One will probably be of Aunt Ruth coming down the aisle, capturing the most important moment for the writer. Instead of the single figure in 1, additional detail will show the aisle, flowers, and some of the people seated in the church.

3. We got up early in the morning to go to Northampton. Mom said we beter eat a big breakfast cuz there wouldn't be anything to eat until the reception. I got my clothes all laid out, then put them in the suitcase. Wen my Dad strted the car it wouldn't go. Mom said, "Oh no, not again." They had a big argument. My Dad banged around and it started. We got there just in time for the wedding. There were all kinds of cars. My cousin got them parked in the right place. We sat next to my other cousin Kathy. The organ music played and Aunt Ruth came down the aisle. She was beautiful. She had on a jeweled band across the front and the gown went way down behind her. My other little cousin walked behind her to see that nothing happened to it. They got married and my new Uncle Tom

kissed. Then they came down the aisle and they were smiling. Then we had a reception. You could hardly move there. There was lots to eat. I had cake, ice cream, pop, sandwiches, salad. Then more ice cream. It was so hot I had to eat lots of ice cream and coke too. My dad said we've got to go now and my mom said let's stay. My dad won and we got into the car. It was a long trip. It was dark when we got home. My mom said we didn't need anything to eat because we ate so much junk. What a day! I went to bed about ten o'clock.

This is the classic "bed to bed" story in which the writer reports all the details starting with the beginning of the day when she gets up and continuing until she retires in the evening. Such a piece, depending on maturity and instruction, could be composed between the ages of nine and fourteen. Children, even adults, seem not to be able to start with the wedding; they have to write down the details that get them to the wedding. This type of writing can even last beyond high school as an example of the narrative form. There is little selection or highlighting of one section over another; each part of the day has equal value. This author, however, now brings in her mother and father. Once other people appear and their actions are detailed, we can be confident that comments about relationships will soon follow. This is where instruction is particularly important.

Full spellings are evident throughout with only a few holdover inventions. The author is reading more and is also concerned with the audience's reception of her piece. Further, in reporting the actions of her parents, she seems to have a sense of what will interest others in her class. She even includes a small reflection on herself: "It was so hot I had to eat lots of ice cream and coke too."

4. Family weddings—I love them! Cousins you haven't seen for a long time, aunts, uncles—lots to eat and fancy clothes. My Aunt Ruth's wedding was something special. We've always been close and I wouldn't miss hers for anything. My new Uncle Tom danced with me at the reception.

Note how quickly the writer gets off the mark. She knows what her subject is and quickly pursues it. She may have written an earlier draft that included some of the "bed to bed" elements, but she has learned how to delete once she knows what her piece is about. The author also notes relationships: "We've always been close and I wouldn't miss hers for anything." It seems that her last line, "My new Uncle Tom danced with me at the reception," is tacked on almost as an afterthought. The fact that she danced with him was very important, but she didn't quite know where to put it. Depending on maturity and instruction this piece could come from a child as young as ten and as old as sixteen.

5. Aunt Ruth and I have always been close. As she walked down the aisle, regal in white gown and tiara, I wondered if we would still talk. Just that morning my parents had an argument, not a big one, but enough to remind me I might not have Aunt Ruth to run to anymore.

Note how the same author in 4 and 5 is able to extract essential meaning from the wedding. She is now dealing with the meaning of relationships from a much broader time frame ("I used to talk to her but I might not be able to anymore"). She notes the

conditional nature of human relationships—Life is "iffy." She reflects on human relation-
ships in the world and puts those reflections into her text. She uses writing to understand
life. As professionals, we don't often reward writing that extracts more penetrating
insights in a short text. We crave length *because that shows the writer has worked "very*
hard." Indeed, we may have assigned a piece of a certain length, thus encouraging
inflated thinking rather than penetrating revision and insight. This piece would follow
the same age profile (ten to seventeen) as 4.

This is a very rough picture of what children's texts look like from about first grade through the secondary years. Now I want to examine the process writers use when they compose.

What's Involved In The Act Of Writing?

In *Thought and Language,* L. S. Vygotsky (1962) gives us the clearest theoretical picture of what happens when children actually write. Of course, children—and we ourselves—are usually unaware of what Vygotsky describes. In *Writing: Teachers and Children at Work* (1983), I took Vygotsky's paradigm and used a young child's writing to show how his theory becomes manifest in what children do:

> Alison reread her first sentence. She frowned and bit into the soft wood of her pencil; a tear formed in the corner of her eye. Glaring at the paper she muttered, "Stupid," and rumpled her paper into a ball. Alison was in sixth grade and wanted to write about the death of her dog, Muffin. The first line didn't do justice to her feelings.
>
> Each day Alison writes in class. Today is Wednesday, and since Monday she has known she would write about the death of her dog. Since then, a series of images and impressions have rehearsed their way to the surface for inclusion in her story about Muffin. Last year she would have poured a torrent of words and sentences onto the page. This year she is a dissatisfied writer. She is paralyzed by her range of options as well as the apparent inability of her initial words to meet her personal expectations.
>
> What Alison doesn't know is that what reaches the page is the end result of a long line of reductions from an original swirl of memories about her dog. The chart on page [70] shows the progression of Alison's reductions to the words that finally reach the page.
>
> Since Monday, Alison has been rehearsing a host of images and memories. But when she writes, she can only choose *one* to work on at a time. Alison chooses the image of Muffin on the bed next to her. Since Alison's communication will use words, she now converts her image to words. The words swirl in telegraphic form and in no particular order. Her final act is to put the words in an order that others will understand: "I felt him

THOUGHT	ONE CHOICE REDUCTION	TELEGRAPH WORDS	CONVENTIONAL ORDER
image: play with Muffin on lawn			
image: Muffin next to her on bed	*image:* Muffin on the bed	*image:* Dog on bed	
smell: wet dog hair after rain	*new image:* hand across Muffin's head	*words:* bed, lump on the bed; he's there, feel him nice, pat	"I felt him on the bed next to me."
texture: feel of fur			
image: combing the dog			
image: hugging the dog			
words: nice, miss him, cry			

on the bed next to me." Compared with the range of images and words Alison has entertained in the process of writing, the sentence is but a ghost of her impressions. A year ago Alison would have assumed the missing material was represented in the sentence. Not now. She knows that words are inadequate. Worse, she does not see any promise in them for reworking. Alison is stalled.

Alison's frustration could be that of a seven-year-old, a doctoral student, or a professional writer. All go through the same process of reduction. The only difference between the amateur and the professional is that the professional is less surprised. Writers who compose regularly have stronger links between the part (sentence) and the whole (the overall story or article) and expect that first attempts will probably represent poor choices. They rewrite for focus, to make better choices, and to rework other images, until words match that inner "yes" feeling. Then they write *to add* what is naturally subtracted through the very process of writing itself.

What teacher hasn't heard these words: "I'm stuck. This is dumb. It's no use. Now what do I do?" Essentially these writers are asking, "Where am I?" They feel the lack in their words, which have been reduced from richer images and intentions. They don't know where the sentence before them fits in with their original, overall story. Fear even blurs the images and words that once seemed so real in rehearsal.

Teachers can answer children's questions only if they know the writing process from both the inside and the outside. They know it from the inside because they work at their own writing; they know it from the outside because they are acquainted with research that shows what happens when people write. (219–220)

ACTION 5.1:
Interview three children while they are engaged in the writing process.

Thus far in this chapter we have examined how children show their writing growth in both their text and their process. We added a further dimension by referring to Vygotsky's paradigm of what is involved in the act of writing. Now we will move in more closely in order to learn from children while they are actually writing. I stress *actually writing* because that is when children's memory and understanding of what they are doing are much more vivid. This is especially true of children in the primary grades. My first objective is to discover how the child is oriented to the piece. This means that I try to get a sense of its past, present, and future dimensions:

- *Topic origin (past):* I'm curious about what triggered the topic. Possibly another child suggested it or something about it was quite important to the child.

- *Topic focus and depth of information (present):* I'm curious about how focused the child is on the topic (Can he state in one simple sentence what the piece is about?). In addition, I'm curious about her knowledge of the details connected with the topic.

- *Topic direction and final disposition (future):* Does the child know what she will next write? Finally, is there a notion of a specific audience or what will happen to the piece when she has completed it? Specifically, is there someone she has in mind for a reader (another child, a teacher, a parent, or the entire class)?

Children may not necessarily be able to handle all of these dimensions, although more advanced writers do have a rich sense of past, present, and future. Their rehearsal periods are longer; that is, they think about the piece well before starting it and they usually know where the piece is going. Of course, there are times when any writer is uncertain about both focus and audience.

Jennifer

Here is an interview with a fourth grade girl in the process of writing:

Don: Excuse me, Jennifer, can you tell me what your piece is about?

Jennifer: Oh, it's about my new baby sister.

Don: I see. And where are you in the piece right now?

Jennifer: I've been working on this for two days. I'll probably finish it tomorrow. I need to write the part about how she's screaming bloody murder right now. Maybe I'll be done about then.

Don: Screaming bloody murder? Gosh, what happened to make her scream?

Jennifer: Oh, she's got this thing called colic. She's in a lot of pain. I don't like to hold her when she's like that. She gets real stiff.

Don: So, you have to take care of her sometimes?

Jennifer: Yeah, and sometimes I can't do it very well cuz she screams so much. Then my mother comes over and takes her. I wish the baby wouldn't do that.

Don: How did you happen to choose this topic to write about, Jennifer? Tell me about when you first decided to write this.

Jennifer: Let's see, it was Monday night and my mom was real tired from work and she wanted to take a nap, so she asked me to keep an eye on her, but just after she was fed and my mom put her head down she just started yelling. It's an awful sound. She isn't doing it on purpose, Mom says, she really has pains in her stomach. So, I knew on Tuesday morning I'd write about it. Maybe I'd feel better if I did.

Don: Sounds as though you didn't mind taking care of her, but when she screams it really bothers you. So that's how you decided to write this, to see if writing it would maybe make you feel better. Is it?

Jennifer: Sort of, I guess.

Don: If you finish this piece tomorrow, Jennifer, what will you do with it? Who will read it?

> *Jennifer:* Oh, I don't know. Maybe my mom. I don't think I'll publish it or share it with the class. I have another friend who has to take care of her little brother, so I'll probably show her. I don't think it's too good a piece but I'm glad I wrote it.

In this conference I pursue the dimensions of past, present, and future (see my field notes in Figure 5.1).

Jennifer has a fairly well-developed sense of her piece. It is significant that she thought about it well before she actually sat down to compose. For Jennifer, writing is clearly a means to an end. Although she won't do much with the piece in the future, she has a sense of the few persons with whom she'd share it.

When you interview the children, choose three who represent a wide range of personality and ability types so that you observe the differences from child to child. In addition, if you have the opportunity, interview the same child about three different pieces; you will notice differences even with one child. On this last piece, for example, Jennifer did not have a high personal involvement in her account of her sister's colic. I call it a "wait and see" piece.

Alex

Alex's time frame is very different for his piece about "Marauders from Outer Space." He knew on the day he started it that he would do still another piece about "Marauders." Some children stay with the same topic for a variety of reasons: in one case, the child enjoys "playing" with the same subject; in another, the child is known by the class for writing in a particular genre; in still another, it would be difficult for the child to shift. It is also possible that the child continues to learn by working in one genre. You will discover this by saying to the child, "Put your pieces about this same topic on your desk; look them over and tell me how you think you've changed as a writer. What will you be working on next to be a better writer, to say more about your topic?"

When I ask Alex about the future, he is quite indefinite. The audience is a vague entity to him; in one sense he himself is his only audience. For students who are highly critical of their own work or write only to please themselves, the audience factor may not be a problem. But, if students are uncritical or have only a vague sense of what an audience needs, their work will not move ahead.

Figure 5.1
Field Notes

	Jennifer	alex	carol
Past	monday night when baby was screaming maybe I'd feel better if I wrote — sort of	this is my fourth one so I decided today to do another one	Just now, I knew I'd have to write so I just thought "Why not write about going to the mall?" I couldn't think of anything else.
Present	about my new baby sister Details understands colic	about the marauders from outer space	about my trip to the mall
Future	I need to write about how she's screaming. audience: mom Friend who takes care of brother Not much happens to it.	Next I'll write about the new weapons they invent to kill the creatures. I don't know who will see it or whatever	Next I'll write about having lunch. I don't know what I'll do with it. I won't Know till I'm done. maybe it will just be boring.

Carol

Carol has a low-level investment in her piece. She decided only a few minutes before class that she would write about yesterday's trip to the mall. Her sense of an audience for her piece is vague. And since it is just going to be an account of going to the mall, her rendering will be matter-of-fact in tone. She already has a hunch that it will probably be boring—at least to herself.

Of these three students, Jennifer appears to have the strongest investment in her piece. She is writing to find out; her writing fulfills some need, some wanting to know. Alex may be in a learning situation; further questions might reveal his investment in the piece. Today Carol is putting her time in; she'll write, but her choice at this point seems a weak one.

Beginnings: Choosing a Topic

The writing process has many beginning points. It might begin as unconscious "rehearsal": a person observes a child at play, sees two dogs fighting, or recalls a humiliating moment in college while reading a daughter's paper. The more a writer writes, the more the processes of choice and rehearsal occur, and at unpredictable moments. Facts restlessly push their way to the surface until the writer says, "I'll write about that."

For the last five years my eighty-six-year-old mother has been in declining health because of Alzheimer's disease. At the onset of her illness I wrote one short poem but I have written practically nothing about it since.

Nevertheless, through those five years I've been looking for a way to say what I think straight out. The other day I finally got some words on paper. Maybe this is the piece I've been waiting to write. Compare six-year-old Mary, who goes to the classroom writing center, picks up a piece of paper, and murmurs, "Let's see, what'll I write about? I know . . . a wedding." She murmurs "The wedding, the beautiful wedding" as she reaches for a crayon to draw a bride with veil, tiara, and flowing gown at the top of her paper.

Conscious rehearsal accompanies the decision to write. Rehearsal refers to the preparation for composing and can take the form of daydreaming, sketching, doodling, making lists of words, outlining, reading, conversing, or even writing lines as a foil to further rehearsal. The writer ponders, "What shall I include? What's a good way to start? Should I write a poem, debate, first person narrative, or short story?"

Rehearsal may also take the form of ego boosting. "This will be magnificent. Surely it will be published. My friends will think I am super. I'll work every day on this. The kids will like it and laugh."

Mary rehearses for writing by drawing. As she draws, she recreates visually her impressions of the wedding: colors, dresses, hair styles, the actual persons in the wedding party. She adds jewelry to the costumes. "This is what I'm going to have when I get married," she announces to Jennifer, who is writing at the desk next to her, "lots of gold and diamonds." If Mary is asked *before she draws* what she will write about, her response is general, "I don't know, something about a wedding." If she is asked the same question further along in her drawing, her response will be more detailed.

John is nine and wants to write about racing cars. Last night he and his father tracked their favorite cars and drivers at the raceway. John can still feel the vibration of the engines as they roared into the curve where he was sitting. Dust, popcorn, the bright lights overhead, the smell of exhaust and gasoline are all part of his subconscious memory. John is so sure of their reality he thinks he merely has to pick up a pencil and the words will pour forth. Without rehearsing, John pauses for a moment, and with mouth slightly moving writes:

The cars was going fast.

He rereads the words. "Agggh," he bellows, "this is stupid." No images come to mind from his simple sentence. There are no details to build on. John's reading abilities are strong enough to let him know the sentence says little, but he doesn't know what to do with his words. John thinks, reads, but doesn't go on. He can't . . . alone. He has not yet written regularly enough to learn how to retrieve images and information from previous events.

My mother has been in a nursing home for three years. Each time I visit her, her expression has seemed more and more vacant. Now she no longer recognizes me. I knew that some day I would write about her and about the disease. The event grew to such importance, however, that I couldn't. I simply didn't know where to begin. In one sense, I was chosen by my topic.

Mary, John, and I were hardly aware of making a choice about a writing topic. Topics pushed their way to the surface until each of us said, "I'll write about that." For writers who compose daily, other topics come to them in the midst of writing about another subject, especially if they know they can exercise control over their choices. If a child has to wait for teacher-assigned topics, rehearsal is not useful. The very act of writing itself, though heightening meaning and perception, prepares us both consciously and unconsciously to see more possibilities for writing subjects. Writing that occurs only once every two weeks limits the ability to make choices because it limits both the practice of writing and the exercise of topic selection. Rehearsal cannot occur since the writer usually doesn't know what he will write about that day. Under these circumstances, teachers have to come up with topics for the children, which rules out both choice and rehearsal.

Composing refers to everything a writer does from the time the first words are put on paper until all drafts are completed. Sometimes when a writer must rehearse by writing, there is overlap between the two, composing and rehearsing.

About four years after my first tentative poem about my mother and her illness, I began to compose again. Where to start? I worried that such an important subject might bring nothing to mind. Then I decided to describe my mother as I last saw her in the nursing home dayroom. She sat there with her eyes closed and leaned to one side as if she might fall over. I wrote:

> Mother lists to the starboard
> in the dayroom chair

The verb "lists" set up the entire poem. In fact, it contributed to the ship imagery that follows. Suddenly I saw my mother as a sinking ship, with no one on the bridge to help her through the storm. I finished the stanza:

> Mother lists to the starboard
> in the dayroom chair,
> her superstructure too heavy
> to support this dying ship;
> the windows on the bridge
> are dark; no commanding officer
> there to bark orders

to deck hands. There
will be no more ports of call,
no journeys planned.

These words felt right but I knew more had to come. The line "windows on the bridge are dark" suggested that the person I knew just wasn't there. In one sense her eyes *were* gone, since she did not recognize the people or the world around her. I wanted so much to say with a kind of controlled rage just what the disease had done to her. It was as if all her wiring mechanisms had been torn apart; nothing connected with anything else. I wrote another stanza:

Sinister technicians tinker
behind those vacant windows,
ripping out instruments
of depth and direction;
they leave nothing
but empty black wires
which hang like devil's
claws in the dark.

I sent the draft off to Don Murray, who questioned "sinister." He was right, of course; I'd already shown "sinister" by describing what the technicians were doing. In another rereading I spotted "empty" and knew that wasn't the right word to describe the wires. They were broken, torn apart, and left hanging. I changed it to "broken." Normally poems do not come to me in a rush like this piece about my mother. Even so, several words needed work and, I suspected, I'd still be tinkering with the poem over several months, maybe even years.

Gradually I have come to trust my writing: if I stay at it, something will come of it. Time is my greatest ally. I try to listen to the words to find out which way they will lead me. In the case of this poem, listening and observing the image behind the verb *"list"* allowed me to find a way to understand my mother's illness.

I have tried to move from the poem about my mother to writing about the death of my grandfather, whom I never knew. I guess I figured that working on the first poem would help me to tackle another big subject. After three days of writing I'm not much ahead of where I began. Still, I put my time in. I take comfort in the words of Flannery

O'Connor: "Every morning between 9 and 12 I go to my room and sit before a piece of paper. Many times I just sit for three hours with no ideas coming to me. But I know one thing: If an idea does come between 9 and 12, I am there ready for it" (cited in Murray, 1990, 60).

Mary finished her drawing, paused, glanced at the wedding party in stick figures and costumes, and spoke softly to herself, "When." She scrawled "Wn" on the line below the drawing, spoke "when" again to confirm what she had done and to establish where she was in the writing, and added "we." "Wn we . . . " As Mary writes she feels the words with her tongue, confirming what the tongue knows with her ear, eye, and hand. Ever since she was an infant, eye and hand have been working together with the mouth, confirming even further what they don't know.

Mary composes so slowly that she must return to the beginning of her sentence each time and reread up to the current word. Each new word is such a struggle that the overall syntax is obliterated. The present is added to a shaky, indistinct past. The future hardly exists. Beyond one or two words after the word under formulation, Mary cannot share what will happen in her story about the wedding.

Mary may borrow from her internal imagery of the wedding when she writes, but she also uses her drawing as an idea bank. She does not appear to wrestle with word choice; rather, she wrestles with the mechanics of formation with spelling and handwriting, and then with her reading. She wants the spelling to be stable enough so that when she tries to share it later with her teacher, she will be able to read it.

After writing one sentence, "Wn we wt to the wdg we hd fn," (When we went to the wedding we had fun), Mary's composing has ended. In her estimation the drawing is still the more important part of the paper. This is not surprising since her drawing contains far more information than her writing. Other children will also respond more to her drawing than to her writing. For Mary, the writing adds to the drawing, not the drawing to the writing.

John impatiently taps the eraser part of his pencil on the desk and glares at his paper, empty save for the one line, "The cars was going fast."

"What's the matter, John?" inquires his teacher, Mr. Govoni.

"I can't write. I don't know what to do. All I have is this."

"Turn your paper over for a minute, John. Now tell me, how did you happen to write about cars?"

"Well, you see, last night, me and my dad, we went to the Raceway out on route 125. We go there every Saturday night and you should see those guys drive. Charley Jones is the hottest thing right now. You should see him sneak up on a guy, fake to the outside, and just when a guy looks in the mirror at the fake, Charley takes 'em on the inside. Nothin' but dust for the other guy to look at. Charley makes top money."

"Slow down a minute, John. You've said enough already. You know a lot about Charley Jones. Put it down right here and I'll be back in five minutes to see how you are doing."

John begins to write: "Charley Jones makes a lotta money. He's the best driver around. He has won two weeks in a row. Me and my Dad we saw him drive and he's our favrit." John rushes the words onto the paper, hardly pausing between sentences. A look of satisfaction is on his face. Triumph. At least Charley Jones is in print. John doesn't give the details about Charley passing the other driver. Even though this is good information, John picks up on his last statement. For John, talking has provided the needed rehearsal, a means of hearing his voice and intention. He orally selects, composes, and with a quick rereading, notes that the writing is satisfying since he has been able to include Charley Jones in his draft.

Composing Patterns

All writers follow a simple pattern: select, compose, read; select, compose, read. Both Mary and I had to select one bit from a mass of information in order to start writing. First I selected the image of my mother seated in the dayroom of the nursing home, but until I hit on the ship image the words just "floated" in space. That image allowed the words to flow quickly onto my computer. I don't have to worry about handwriting and spelling during the composing process. I can concentrate totally on the poem emerging on the screen before me. I see each sentence in relation to the total image: my mother's head becomes the bridge of the ship. But the windows on the bridge are vacant; no one is in command. Further, this ship will sail no more.

Each line emerges through a select, write, read, write, reread, and rewrite sequence. Most of my rewriting has focused on my struggle with two words.

Mary uses the same cycle in her writing. She selects information, but from her drawing, chooses words to go with her selection (voicing them as she goes), composes (still voicing), reads, selects, and composes again. Handwriting, spelling, and reading dominate her conscious process. Letter formation, thinking of what sounds will be right with letters, nearly obliterate her message. Mary's reading is different from mine. We both read for orientation but Mary reads exclusively to know where one word fits in relation to other words. She rereads from the beginning after every addition. If she has to struggle with a difficult sound-symbol arrangement in the middle of a word, she may have to reread from the beginning to find each word anew. Under these circumstances, revision for Mary means only the adjustment of handwriting, spelling, and some grammatical inconsistencies. Mary is not yet reworking her information.

Voice

The writing process has a driving force called *voice*. Technically, voice is not a process component or a step in the journey from choice-rehearsal to final revision. Rather, it underlies every part of the process. To ignore voice is to present the process as a lifeless, mechanical act. Divorcing voice from process is like omitting salt from stew, love from sex, or sun from gardening. Teachers who attend to voice listen to the person in the piece and observe how that person uses process components.

Voice is the imprint of ourselves on our writing. It is that part of the self that pushes the writing ahead, the dynamo in the process. Take the voice away and the writing collapses of its own weight. There is no writing, just word following word. Voiceless writing is addressed "to whom it may concern." The voice shows how I choose information, organize it, select the words, all in relation to what I want to say and how I want to say it. The reader says, "Someone is here. I know that person. I've been there, too."

Our data show that when a writer makes a good choice of subject, voice booms through. When voice is strong, writing improves, along with the skills that help to improve writing. Indeed, voice is the engine that sustains writers through the hard work of drafting and redrafting.

Voice should breathe through the entire process: rehearsal, topic, choice, selection of information, composing, reading, and rewriting. Although this suggests a general order, in fact, many of these steps occur simultaneously. For some writers a new topic may emerge while they are in the midst of writing about another. The writing process is an untidy business. In the years since *Writing: Teachers and Children at Work* was published, I've found that some teachers have misunderstood the writing process. They deliberately take children through phases of making a choice, rehearsing, composing, and then rewriting. Of course, these processes do exist, but each child uses them differently. We simply cannot legislate their precise timing.

It is a writer's voice that gives me the best sense of his or her potential. Although John was frustrated by his inability to write about his trip to the raceway with his father, his frustration was born of voice that couldn't find its way to paper. John's frustration was evidence of his potential. We turn now from learning about the process and children's development as writers to a closer examination of their potential in order to expect more of them as learners.

6 EXPECT MORE OF YOUR WRITERS

"Be tough and expect a lot of your students." This was the universal advice I received during my first year of teaching. I tried to teach thirty-nine seventh grade students; I tested, expected, demanded, gave homework, and assigned readings, all with little result. Sometimes I expected too much; at other times I expected too little. I simply didn't know enough about my students or about the teaching of writing to know what to expect of them. Worse, I didn't write myself. I took false comfort in the top four to five students, put in my time with the average group, and ignored those students who struggled most.

I've since learned that high expectations are based on real knowledge of the student and the subject at hand. When both the student and teacher have a high sense of potential, both have the energy for teaching and learning. The most difficult teaching/learning situation is that in which the student believes he knows nothing and the teacher simply doesn't know how to find out what he does know.

How well I remember a statistics course in which I struggled to make sense of various formulas and the theories that lay behind them. I couldn't distinguish between what I knew that was accurate and what was misguided information. I felt the professor's embarrassment at my presence. When he asked the class a question and searched for eyes alert enough to promise good responses, he passed me by. He had to ignore me; he didn't know what to do with me. Eventually, I went to him and together we hammered out a sense of what I knew and what I needed to learn. I began to have a sense of my own potential and to welcome his expectations.

Unfortunately, our students usually do not come to us when they are confused. If they have poor learning histories or don't understand their work, they try to go unnoticed or disrupt the classroom. This is why teachers need to learn as much as they can about students' potential in order to help them expect more of themselves. This usually means that both need to construct a shared vision of what students know and what and how they will carry out that vision.

You began to work on this sense of shared vision in Chapter 2 when you interviewed children about the class and their interests outside of school, and then constructed a three column exercise, which helped you to link their names with their knowledge and potential. This chapter will focus more specifically on the writing process by looking more closely at children's writing. From these data, you will have a better sense of the child's potential as a writer and how to confer with the child to consider her goals.

The Interview

ACTION 6.1:
Study one child's potential by examining one piece of writing the child selects for review.

You may wish to carry out this Action with one of the children interviewed about the writing process in Chapter 5 or their understanding of the classroom in Chapter 2. I will demonstrate how I observe and interview a child to help you see how to begin to understand a child's potential and then move to some notion of a shared vision of that child's future as a writer. I asked Jason to select a piece for me to read. "Choose one you'd like me to read because I want to look at all the different things you know. I'll meet with you afterward to let you know what I've seen; then I'll ask you a few more questions so I can learn still more what you know about your subject and your writing itself." Here is the text he selected:

MY HIKE

Me an my freds went for a hike last Sadidy. I had a canten, pack an lunch. It was cold an we made a fire. We hiked up the river to a cler plas were we put up a tent. We didn't stay overnight we just wanted to see if we could put the tent up. When we made a fire I had to stay so the smoke wouldn't blow in my face. I kept moving and the smoke followed me. We laughed. We were cooking hot dogs an they tasted good.

We didn't see nothing on the hike. There was a dead tree with lots of holes in it and sawdust on the ground. But some of the sawdust had big chips in it an we figered it was done by a big woodpecker the way he knocked them out.

Figure 6.1 shows the data I gathered when I had read his paper.

Content—Text

There are two phases to examining what Jason can do. First, I carefully read Jason's text without having him present and jotted notes on the left column under the heading "Content—text." Then I interviewed Jason basing my questions on what I have learned from looking at his paper. During our interview, I add information to the right column.

Content—Interview

I try to connect what Jason knows, as shown in his writing, with where his knowledge comes from. I try to elicit the history behind his knowing. Children need to know the roots of their knowledge.

Don: Jason, I noticed that you knew what to take on your hike—the canteen, pack, and lunch. I'm curious to know how you knew that and roughly how long you've been taking hikes.

Jason: Well, me and my friend, Joey, have been doing this all spring. Well, no, we did it last fall. And he went to camp last summer, so that's just what you take. You should have water, something to eat, and something to carry it in.

Don: I see. So, you know what to take. Anything you forgot?

Jason: Yeah, my raincoat. It rained and next time I won't forget it.

Don: I noticed you built a fire. How did you know how to do that? Especially if it was raining.

▲▼ **Figure 6.1**
Worksheet for Writer Potential Based on Paper and Interview

WHAT DOES THE STUDENT KNOW

Context—text	Content—interview
Generally *what goes into a hike, How to build a fire, outdoor cooking*	Generally *About friend, Joey. Hiking—not an isolated event*
Use of specifics *smoke followed me, holes in tree, sawdust, wig-chips*	Use of specifics *Forgot raincoat—the details of the whole process of building a fire.*
What has child observed? *what a woodpecker has done, Noticed size of chips, How smoke travels from a fire*	What has child observed? *Carefully observed and learned from Joey*
Process—text	Process—interview
Can handle a narrative appears as though he thinks he has finished	*Jason writes to relive his experience*
Stories or information I suspect student knows but has not yet written	Stories or information child can tell but has not yet written
How to plan what to take on the hike. How do you build a fire in the woods? How do you know so much about birds? Does smoke really follow you? Tell me about the others who were with you.	*Details on fire Birds from Joey*
Use of conventions—text	Conventions known but not used
Indent, left to right, spaces between words, potential serial comma, good sentence sense, use of titles	*Periods go when you have something new. a general sense*
Language—Text	Language—Oral
Verbs *hiked, wanted, stay, blow, followed, cooking, tasted figured, knocked*	Verbs elicited *good process verbs when talking about building the fire. Good detail of sequence here.*
Use of time/space markers *last saturday overnight looks back on trip*	Use of time/space markers *good sense of what happens when he builds a fire.*
Individual language use *"figured it was done by a big woodpecker the way he knocked it out"*	Individual language use *Didn't notice any*

▲▼ **Figure 6.1 (continued)**

1. Find the best part here and tell me about it. *The part where I try to get away from the smoke.*
2. Anything you learned in writing this one? *(Notes from following section appear in narrative in text.)*
3. How is this piece different from other pieces you have written? (Have the child take out four to five pieces he has written and place them in front of him as you ask the question.)
4. Look for something the child has done correctly. E.G. "I see you got this period in just the right place. How did you know how to do that?"
5. As best you can, give an oral summary to the child of what he knows from the data you have gathered thus far. Then ask, Now that you know all this, what else would you like to learn order to be a better writer?

Jason: We built the fire before it rained but Joey was the one who actually built it. I helped him get the wood.

Don: Is building a fire dangerous?

Jason: I suppose it could be. Joey told us we had to push back all twigs and leaves. We built the fire in some rocks in the middle of the clearing. We had to haul the rocks in—about six of them. He's pretty good.

Don: I had to laugh when you told the part about the smoke following you. That happens to me when I'm cooking outside; I keep moving and smoke keeps stinging my eyes.

Jason: Yeah, it was stinging my eyes too. The wind was tricky like.

Process—Interview

In this section I want to understand the origin and future direction of Jason's piece and to elicit some of the reasons he wrote it and his feelings as he wrote. How "alive" was the piece for him?

Don: Jason, I notice that your piece goes right along. You start by mentioning the hike and then you sort of just tell what happened. Can you tell me how you got the idea for writing this? Then would you tell me anything you remember about writing it?

Jason: It was a neat time so I wanted to write it.

Don: I'm curious Jason. Did you experience any of the same feelings when you wrote this as you did when it actually happened?

Jason: What do you mean?

Don: This may be a little hard, but sometimes when I write I feel it all over again. I don't actually feel the sting of the smoke, but I sort of experience it all over again. It's like I'm right there. Were there any parts that made you feel like you were right there as you wrote?

Jason: Oh sure, when we were building the fire and then putting up the tent. That part was a little hard but we felt good when it got up and then we could duck into it when the rain came. We had a good laugh inside the tent.

Don: So, where are you in this piece now? What will you do with it next?

Jason: I guess I'm done.

Don: How can you tell when you are done, Jason?

Jason: I don't know. I just am, that's all. I wanted to write about the hike and I did. That's all. I want to write something else now.

Stories or Information the Child Can Tell

For this part of the interview I refer to the questions I noted on the left column of the sheet while I listen for still more stories that might be embedded in Jason's comments.

Don: How do you build a fire in the woods, Jason? How did you know how to do that?

Jason: Like I told you before, my friend knew how to do it better than I did. First, you have to clear the area out so nothing will catch fire. Then you get rocks to keep the fire in. Then it's small twigs and dry bark when you can get it if it hasn't been raining too much. Get wood and dead branches up off the ground. Then you get the bark and twigs and put yourself so the wind can't blow out your match and you start it up; that's all.

Don: But suppose the fire starts up. You need more wood than just bark and twigs.

Jason: Oh right, well, you've got to have your other wood right there to put on when it does start. You had to have that all set ahead of time.

Don: One more question on this part, Jason. I was struck by your observation that you knew it was a big woodpecker when you saw the chips instead of just sawdust. How did you know that? That's pretty good.

Jason: I didn't really know it. I didn't think it was a beaver or something like that. Joey learned it at camp from his leader maybe. He said it first but I never saw the bird. It had to be really big. Joey said the bird's name but it was long and I've forgotten it. You should have seen the pile of stuff at the bottom of the tree.

Understanding of Conventions

In this part of the interview I choose a few of the conventions Jason has used correctly and ask him how he knew how to get them right. I will also choose a few that are inaccurate to see if he knows how he might go about getting them more accurate.

Don: I notice that in these first four sentences you get the periods in just the right place *[pointing to the period after "lunch" in the second line].* How did you know how to put this one here?

Jason: I don't know. Geez, it just seemed like it was time the period went down. The next part was about the fire and not about what I took on the hike. I don't know.

Don: You are right, Jason, you did start something new. You have a good feel for when a period goes down. Here's a comma after "canteen." That's pretty good. How did you know to put that one there?

Jason: I don't know. I never think about this stuff. Commas separate stuff. It just seemed like it belonged there.

Don: It's true, Jason. Commas separate things. And right here your comma separated the canteen from the lunch you packed. Commas keep words organized so you can understand the words better. Good thinking. You spell quite well, Jason, but this word up here, "Saturday," is spelled incorrectly. What would you do to give it a correct spelling?

Jason: Look it up. Ask a friend.

Don: Actually do it. Show me how you'd get it right, right now. *[Jason visits with his friend Teddy, who shows him the correct spelling.]* You seemed to know just who to ask, Jason. That's good, but suppose you were all alone, now what would you do?

Jason: On this one I'd go to the calendar cuz it's written there. I shoulda
looked there in the first place; I knew it wasn't right but I forgot.

Language—Oral

I am particularly interested in the specificity of Jason's language as I
try to elicit more details about his hike. Children usually know more
than they have written if they have made a good choice in their topic.
The most difficult word to make specific is the verb.

The notes in this section come from the remainder of the interview. I notice that he uses good verbs and a logical sequence when he
explains how he builds a fire with Joey, who actually taught him all
those details. If pressed for further details he can share more process
information. If time permitted, I might have asked him how he put up
his tent. The following section fills in the material from the second
page of "Worksheet for Writer Potential."

1. Find the best part here and tell me about it.
"I like the part where I try to get away from the smoke and it kept
finding me. That was funny. The other kids laughed."

2. Anything you learned in writing this one?
"Yeah, I learned a lot from Joey. I want to go to camp like him."

3. How is this piece different from other pieces you have written?
[Have the child take out four or five pieces he has written and place
them in front of him as you ask the question.] "Well, this is one about
hiking. It isn't too funny except for the smoke. I had a real good time
on the hike. The others weren't as much fun." [Note that Jason doesn't
distinguish the event from the writing. The quality of the experience
determines the quality of the piece.]

**4. Look for something the child has done correctly: "I see you got
this period in just the right place. How did you know how to do
that?"**
[As is often the case in an interview of this nature, this question has
already been asked. It is here for you to use if the child has not
already answered it.]

5. As best you can, give an oral summary to the child of what he knows from the data you have gathered thus far. Then ask, "Now that you know all this, what else would you like to learn in order to be a better writer?"

Don: Jason, this is what I have noticed that you know so far. Listen to my list and then be thinking about what you'd like to learn next. *[I will focus on two general headings: his knowledge about content and his knowledge about writing itself.]* I've noticed that you know about what you need on a hike, how to build a fire, and maybe put up a tent. I didn't ask you about putting up the tent. Maybe you even know something about cooking because you did cook over a fire.

Jason: Yeah, I know how to cook a hot dog on a stick. You cut a green stick about this long *[motions with hands]*, take your knife and make a point, then stick it in the hot dog and put it over the fire.

Don: Yes, I guess you do know that. Although you learned about that special bird who knocked out chips I was impressed that you remembered and noticed the difference in the sawdust. That's good looking.

　　When you write, you start at the beginning of the story and go right through. I can understand what may come next. You use a title, indent, and do a pretty good job of getting the periods in the right place and you pretty much have a good sense of where paragraphs go. You started to use a serial comma and you had a way to get the correct spelling of Saturday.

　　After knowing all that, are you prepared to tell me what you'd like to learn next to be a better writer?

Jason: I didn't know I knew all that. I know my spelling could be better and I wish I could write longer pieces.

Don: Why is that?

Jason: Like lottsa stuff happened on the hike and I'd like to get it into a piece but I get tired and I don't know what happens. I get to thinking of something else, a new piece.

Don: What do you think would help you to learn how to do that?

Jason: I don't know.

Don: Why don't you think of having a conference before you start, get a list of what you might want to put in? Or, set it up where you could share a piece with a small group you'd like to share it with. Sometimes writers get to feeling alone with a piece and they need

> some other people to give them a reaction; then they can go back to work. Which of these sounds like it would help?
>
> *Jason:* I think it's the one where I could share. I get tired of the piece, get bored with it, and I think no one wants to hear this stuff.
>
> *Don:* Okay, next time when you are about halfway through, decide who you'd like to listen to it at that point. Thank you, Jason. One last thought before we end our interview. In a few days I'll be interested to see what you remember from this conference—what I told you you knew about content and writing. I'd like you to think about other things you know about besides the ones we've talked about here. I'll ask you about those, too.

In one sense, the most important part of this interview is when I share with Jason all that I have noticed about what he knows thus far. Then he can think over what he wants to learn next. Unfortunately, in the past I've asked children what they wanted to learn next without helping them to have a sense of what they knew already. Some children languish in school for years without being aware of what they know. I can challenge children who *know* they know things far better than children who flounder, wondering if they know anything at all.

You certainly don't have the time to interview many children this extensively, but even one interview can help you become sensitive to the potential children possess. You will begin to spot details in children's writing that reflect knowledge of both content and process. You will note strong verbs in children's speech and spot them in their writing.

ACTION 6.2:

Within two days, re-interview the same child and ask her what she remembers about what she knows, as well as what new things she can add to her list.

You may wish to ask the child if there are new things she'd like to learn in order to be a better writer. Here is one option: leave a photocopy of the interview sheet with the child and ask her to add the various things she knows on the sheet itself.

If you have an experienced writer, you might pass out a blank copy of the interview protocol and ask the child to fill it out before the interview. I have never done this, but I can see how it might be beneficial for children who are in a classroom where they share learning experiences. In this instance, I'd suggest showing the class how you'd look at your own writing to discover what you know (you can display your piece on the overhead). Children need to become proficient in saying to themselves, "I know that. I'll list it here."

The Content of Expectation

I've already suggested that we need to have a rich sense of children's potential before we can help them to set high expectations for themselves. Spotting children's potential in their knowledge and their writing creates a different mood in the classroom: "We know . . . and we want to know more."

But there's more than knowing to the "expectation game." There's also the "passion game." Neil Simon writes (1992), "In every comedy, even drama, somebody has to want something and want it bad. When somebody tries to stop him—that's conflict." All our students want to learn. They want to be known for what they know. There are stories and conflicts inside them they want to understand. Many of them can't believe that their wants and feelings have anything to do with school.

Nudging: The Specifics of Expectation

The word *nudge* has been an important part of my teaching vocabulary for the last four years. I overheard Mary Ellen Giacobbe use it when showing teachers how to raise students' expectations of themselves. *Nudge* was just the right word to clarify what bothered me about much of my own teaching and what I observed in classrooms. Sometimes children get stuck in one gear, writing about the same topic or the same personal experience five or six times in a row, or engaging in endless drawing before writing. When this occurs I have the same feeling about my teaching: the children are not changing or improving their work. We are all stalled in a stale sameness.

A nudge suggests a slight push in the right direction. Nudges are based on sound observation, on listening to children, and on a careful reading of their texts. To make the nudge more specific, I carry what I call "nudge paper" with me—paper of sufficient size to accommodate five to ten minutes of writing.

Nudges fall within the context of an overall classroom philosophy: we all try new things in order to be better writers and thinkers. I nudge the children; and often, when I write on the overhead projector, I'll invite a nudge from them. Here are several examples of nudges, the first from *Explore Poetry* (1992, 55).

The Wreck

The car *hit* the rail
went down the bank,
and the man *climbed* out.
He *was* okay.
The wrecker *came*
and *took* the car away.

In a conference, the teacher nudges Mark to help him with his verbs. She listens carefully to the verbs he uses in his speech to help him with his written language.

Teacher: Mark, I get a rough picture of what happened with the man. He climbed out of the car. Maybe he came out through the window, I'm not sure. But I was wondering about some of the other things that happened. You said the car hit the rail. Can you tell me more about that or what actually happened?

Mark: Well, the car hit some ice and skidded left and hit the rail and then shot right and rolled down the bank.

Teacher: Stop right there, Mark. Already you've given me some good verbs, words that show more clearly what actually happened. I've written some of them on this piece of paper here: *skidded, shot, rolled*. I'd like you to take these and experiment with putting them into your poem. When you used them in your account of the accident, I had a clearer picture of what happened than when I first read your poem. See if you want to use them after you've experimented here on this piece of paper.

The second example is from *Portfolio Portraits* (1992, 87–88).

Teacher: John, I see you have a new character here. What does he look like?

John: I'm not sure. I want him to be about sixteen, kind of big.

Teacher: Tell me some more about him. What kind of person is he? If I were to meet him, what would he be like?

John: He gives people trouble. He picks on smaller kids.

Teacher: I get a feel for him now. He is kind of big and he picks on others, especially people smaller than himself. Tell me about his face when he picks on someone.

John: Oh—hmmm—he has kind of snaky eyes. He squints when he looks at you.

Teacher: I see him. Take this piece of paper and experiment quickly with what he looks like, John. He's important to your piece. Just experiment for about five minutes. You may not want to use this, but experiment anyway...

Teacher: Mark, look over the verbs here on your first page. What do you see?

Mark: [*after a pause*] Got, got, was, went.

Teacher: What kinds of pictures do you get from those words?

Mark: Not much.

Teacher: Okay, take this small sheet here [*the nudge paper*] and try this [*writes each of Mark's verbs on a separate line*]:
1. got—"picked up"
2. got
3. was
4. went
Experiment with some different verbs that will create a clearer picture for you and the reader of what is going on here in the piece. Try the first one: *got*.

Mark: How about *picked up* the newspaper?

Teacher: Do you get more of a picture from that?

Mark: Yup.

Teacher: Experiment with these others for a little while. See how it goes.

ACTION 6.3:

Look through the current writing the children are doing. Think through some appropriate nudges that will help them become better writers. Leave nudge paper to allow them to experiment.

I'd suggest starting with five or six children who you think may be ready for nudges. Keep these principles in mind:

- If you are asking the child to supply new information about a character (as in the second example about John), allow sufficient time for the child to respond to your questions. Remember, he may be formulating answers to your questions for the first time.

Teachers Nudge and Expect

- If you have a series of questions, make sure they are based on the child's last response. This shows you are listening.
- If possible, summarize what you've learned before you leave the nudge paper.
- Don't leave nudge paper if the information the child supplies is brief and the nudge you've tried seems ineffective.

ACTION 6.4:
Practice directives.

Someone once said to me, "Do you ever tell the student to just *do* something?"

"Heavens, yes," I replied. "Where did you get the notion that I didn't tell students to do things?"

"Well, you listen so much and set yourself up to learn from the child, I just didn't think you'd actually tell a student to do something like, say, 'buckle down and get to work.'"

Later, I pondered her words and could understand how she had arrived at her conclusion. We do stress listening to and learning from students. I'll often nudge a student into trying new things. In some cases the nudge is a very strong suggestion.

But there are times when I'll say straight out, "Andrew, I want your piece revised and completed by tomorrow afternoon. Now get busy!" Sometimes children have to be saved from themselves. Sometimes a little prodding is needed to get them out of their lethargy and on with the task. But if I find myself giving one directive after another, I know something is wrong with my own teaching.

Being able to direct a student is an important part of your teaching repertoire. If you feel that you have not been able to direct students into productive work, or your listening is disproportionate to the nudging and directing you think is required to foster successful writing, then you ought to consider this Action.

Sometimes when I direct the child to do something it means I've overruled her judgment about what the situation requires. Before I do so, I want to be sure I have as much information as possible. Here is an example of that process:

Don: Tell me about your piece, Jason. What's it about?

Jason: It's about these robots that are taking over the earth.

Don: I see. Where are you in the piece and what will you be working on next?

Jason: I just got started and this part here that's coming. See this picture up here? This robot here is made of a special metal that you can't destroy and he's coming here to take things apart. See the army here with their laser beams can't do nothing about this robot here.

Don: This sounds familiar to me, Jason. You've written on these robots before. Take out your last four pieces from your folder and let's take a look.

Jason: Yeah, these are all on robots. I like robots; they're indestructible.

Don: Put these all out here on your desk, Jason. How have these changed from the first to the last, the one you are working on right now? I'm curious to know how you sense you are getting better at writing these.

Jason: Well, I know my drawings are getting better. And more exciting things are happening. The kids like these.

Don: I have another question for you, Jason. Who is controlling the robots? Tell me about the people here.

Jason: There's an evil one from the robot's planet.

Don: Tell me about him then.

Jason: He's just evil. He wants to take over the universe.

Don: Why?

Jason: I don't know. He just does.

Don: Jason, if your piece is to be more believable you've got to know more about this "evil one." You need some help on this if you are to keep writing about "evil ones" and robots. Later I'll be having a workshop on characters for kids who are starting out with characters. I expect you to attend, but I think you'll enjoy it.

Without help in developing characters, Jason is going to keep writing fiction that is primarily plot centered, with thin, one-dimensional characters reminiscent of Saturday morning cartoons. I could easily say to Jason, "Look, these robot pieces are going nowhere; it's time now to switch to some other topic." Inwardly, that's just the way I feel. On the other hand, Jason needs help to develop his characters. Therefore, I will do a mini-lesson which I expect Jason to attend. (See Chapter 6 of *Experiment with Fiction* [1989a] for ways to help students develop characters; and Chapter 18 of this volume.)

For students who possess information and need to use it in their writing, directives can be useful. I also try to tie in the nudge or directive with how the student seeks to improve as a writer.

ACTION 6.5:
Interview five children to find out what they are working on to become better writers.

Interviewing is a useful diagnostic tool for finding out how specific the children can be about what they need to do to be better writers. My experience shows that writers from first grade through college usually know how they need to improve to be better writers. You can help them be more specific in several ways:

- Demonstrate writing a piece of your own work. State how you are trying to improve as a writer.
- Use the books the students are reading to point out good writing.
- Use nudges that are appropriate to the individual writer.
- Offer focused mini-lessons to improve student writing.

Students need to see how their writing is improving in order to know how to proceed. A discouraged writer often feels that nothing can help him improve.

If time permits, you may wish to ask the students a follow-up question: "If that's what you need to learn, how will you go about learning it? What kind of help do you think you will need? How long do you think it will take to be able to learn this . . . to be better at it?"

Students may know what skills they need to learn, but they will be unrealistic in what it takes to learn them or how long it takes to acquire them. Again, this is useful diagnostic information.

Final Reflection

Every study of young writers I've done for the last twenty years has underestimated what they can do. In fact, we know very little about the human potential for writing. Yet, the teacher who has a rich sense of children's potential approaches them differently. And children can see what the teacher thinks they can do from her facial expression.

A teacher says to a child, "You can do it; I've just learned that you know all about the black bear, how they get hungry this time of year and bother a lot of people because of it. In fact, I didn't know that bears eat young animals in the spring." The child knows from the teacher's recycling of her details that "You can do it" is not an idle comment.

Children need to be nudged to try new things and experiment with new skills. The teacher who writes understands what skills are necessary for improvement: indeed, she may occasionally ask the children to nudge her about her own writing.

Children who know how they ought to go about learning are easier to nudge than those who believe the teacher's job is to push them to do everything. They have a more assertive approach to their future as writers. They know what they need to learn.

II

ESTABLISH THE ESSENTIALS
FOR CHILD RESPONSIBILITY

7 CONDITIONS FOR EFFECTIVE WRITING

I've often been asked, "What is your method for teaching writing?" I think in my earlier books I tried to respond to the question by giving specific instructions—first this, then that . . . Granted, there are some systematic and highly structured elements to teaching writing, but I didn't realize until I wrote the introduction to Nancie Atwell's *In the Middle* that good writing doesn't result from any particular methodology. Rather, the remarkable work of her students was a result of the *conditions* for learning she created in her classroom. This chapter is intended to give you an overview of the *conditions* that encourage good writing (most of them will be explored in greater depth in subsequent chapters).

Time

My best recollections of learning to write are connected to the "theme a week" in junior and senior high school. The essay was due on Friday and that ruined my Thursday evenings. I moaned, I struggled, I asked my parents for help, but most of all I procrastinated. Only the late night terror and embarrassment of having nothing but a blank paper to hand in to my teacher the next day coaxed words onto the page.

But people don't learn to write that way—at any age. Fifteen years ago students wrote an average of one day in ten. By "write," I refer to compositions in which the student presents new ideas on a specific topic. Although the amount of writing has increased in recent years, we are a long way from having both the time and necessary conditions that make it possible for our students to learn to write.

Professional writers experience near panic at the thought of missing one day of writing. They know that if they miss a day, it will take enormous effort to get their minds back on the trail of productive thought. In short, it is extremely inefficient to miss a day. In addition, as our data on children show, when writers write every day, they begin to compose even when they are not composing. They enter into a "constant state of composition."

A fashionable educational dictum these days is "time on task." We look to see if every child's mind is on the book, on the paper. We want to see minds engaged, pencil and pens moving across the paper. What we don't consider is the most significant "time on task" of all, what students choose to do beyond the walls of the school. Only when children read and write on their own because they have experienced the power of literacy can we speak of the significance of time on task.

If students are not engaged in writing at least four days out of five, and for a period of thirty-five to forty minutes, beginning in first grade, they will have little opportunity to learn to think through the medium of writing. Three days a week are not sufficient. There are too many gaps between the starting and stopping of writing for this schedule to be effective. Only students of exceptional ability, who can fill the gaps with their own initiative and thinking, can survive such poor learning conditions. Students from another language or culture, or those who feel they have little to say, are particularly affected by this limited amount of time for writing.

When a teacher asks me, "I can only teach writing one day a week. What kind of program should I have?" my response is, "Don't teach it at all. You will encourage poor habits in your students and they will only learn to dislike writing. Think of something you enjoy doing well; chances are you involve yourself in it far more than one or two times a week.

How well I remember the seventh-grade students I had in my first year of teaching. I taught writing once a week on Friday afternoons—

just as I had been taught in public school and at the university. All my teaching was compressed into that one day, and that meant that I had to correct every error on student papers. Today I know that correcting errors is not teaching. Teaching requires us to *show* students how to write and how to develop the skills necessary to improve as a writer. And showing students how to write takes time. They need daily writing time to be able to move their pieces along until they accomplish what they set out to do.

ACTION 7.1:

Examine the amount of time your students have for writing. Rethink the way time is used in your classroom in order to have at least four days a week when they can write.

If you have trouble finding time, consider some of the following ways of carving out the necessary block of writing time:

- Bring handwriting, spelling, and language skills into the writing block. You will be able to teach these subjects through mini-lessons. (See Chapter 12 for further help in this area.)

- Start the day with writing. The minute children come into the classroom in the morning, have them get out their writing folders and start to write. I find that a great deal of time is wasted in handling lunch money, taking attendance, and attending to other daily matters that students should learn to take care of themselves

- If you have a departmental structure and students change classes, then time is certainly at a premium. In this case have students pick up their folders and begin writing the minute they enter the classroom.

- Combine the teaching of reading and writing into a ninety minute language block. These two subjects ought to be taught together since each contributes so much to the development of the other.

- For older students, combine the teaching of literature with writing. This works particularly well if students learn to read as writers read. (See Jane Hansen's *When Writers Read*, Donald Murray's *Read to Write*, and my five book series, *The Reading/Writing Teacher's Companion*.)

Unless you are able to find time for students to write, there is little this book can do to help you to assist your students in learning what writing can do.

Choice

Children need to learn how to choose their own topics when they write. When I began teaching, I wanted my students to have challenging, morally uplifting topics, so I assigned them. I thought I knew what would engage students' minds. How well I remember the moment every Friday when my seventh grade students returned from lunch. Behind the Denoyer-Geppert map of the Soviet Union I had written the topic of the week—something like "Should there be capital punishment?"—on the chalkboard. To make it more challenging and increase the dramatic tension, I would suddenly release the catch on the map, which would roll up to reveal the topic for the week. My students had no chance to read, interview, or gather material, to do what professional writers do before writing. I invited poor writing—and got it. I should have realized how confused my students were when one asked, "Does this mean we capitalize everything?"

Several years later I moved into what I call my "creative phase" in teaching writing. I still assigned topics, but this time they were intended to release the spontaneity of students' minds. I had the students write on topics like "If I could fly," "If I were an ice cream cone or a baseball glove," "If this glove could talk, what would it say?" I thought the writing they produced was cute, artsy, imaginative. It wasn't. It was gushing and nonspecific. Worse, it had little to do with what writing is for: to help students learn to think through the issues and concerns of their everyday lives.

When students write every day they don't find it as difficult to choose topics. If a child knows she will write again tomorrow, her mind can go to work pondering her writing topic. Choosing a topic once a week is difficult. The moment for writing suddenly arrives, and the mind is caught unprepared.

How well I remember Amy, a fourth-grade youngster in our research project in Atkinson, New Hampshire. The researcher, Lucy Calkins, kept asking this remarkable young writer how she wrote but got little response. Finally, Amy announced that she knew how she wrote: "Last night I was sitting in bed wondering how I would start my fox piece. But I couldn't come up with anything. My cat, Sidney, sat on the bed next to me. I said 'Sidney, how am I going to start my fox piece?' but I still couldn't come up with anything. Finally, at about 10:30, my sister came home and turned on the hall light. Now over my doorknob there is a round hole where you'd have a turnlock. When my sister turned on the hall light, a beam of light came through the hole and struck Sidney in the face and Sidney went squint. Then I knew how I would start my fox piece." The piece goes something like this: 'There was a fox who lived in a den beneath a stump. At midday a beam of light came through a crack in the stump and caught the fox in the eyes and the fox went squint.' That's how I knew I'd start my fox piece."

Here is a child in a constant state of composition: she knew that tomorrow she would write (*time*) and that she could write about the fox (*choice of topic*). The time she devoted to pondering the best lead for her piece was time well spent.

When children choose their own topics, I can expect more of their writing. "What did you set out to do here? Did you have an audience in mind for this?" From the beginning in our conference I can focus my questions on their initiative and their intentions. I am reminded of how important it is that a writer choose his own topic by Donald Murray's recent workshop experience at a New Hampshire conference. The workshop participants sent Murray out of the room while they chose a topic for him to write about. When Murray returned they announced their decision: "Write about your favorite place in New Hampshire." Murray began writing on the chalkboard: he wrote several leads, erased them, began again, made some notes, started again. Finally, he turned to the group and announced, "I can't write this piece; I have no favorite place in New Hampshire."

Murray could have produced a false choice or decided, although he had never thought about it before, on a favorite place in New Hampshire. But as a professional, he knew that dishonest writing is not good writing. How easy it is to teach our students to write dishonestly to fulfill curriculum requirements. Indeed, a student's entire diet from first grade through high school can be a series of one dishonest piece after another. Sadly, the student can even graduate without learning that writing is the medium through which our most intimate thoughts and feelings can be expressed.

Although students can choose a topic for most of their writing, they are expected to write. They must produce. Sometimes topic assignments are helpful and even necessary. Students do make bad choices and experience writer's block, or they need to shift to new topics after exhausting their usual few. When you show students how to "read the world" by writing with them, you also demonstrate how to deal with many of these issues. You may even find it useful to ask students to assign you a topic in order to show them how you work on assignments.

Response

It is important that you take children's choices seriously. Your response to a child's text helps him to realize what he set out to do when he started to write. When I began to teach—and for many years afterward—I only responded to students' work when they had finished writing. At that point I corrected their papers and made a few comments lauding or condemning what they'd written. But that wasn't teaching, and what is worse, I was the only person responding to their texts. The students wrote for me, and only me.

Students need to hear the responses of others to their writing, to discover what they do or do not understand. The need to help students know how to read their own work and the work of their classmates provides further teaching and demonstration opportunities (see Chapter 13).

How well I recall my first attempt to initiate peer response in my seventh-grade classroom. I simply said, "Okay, I want you to exchange papers and respond to each other's work. Listen carefully, take the paper back, and return to your writing." What I got was a massive blood-letting: first wails, then silence. My students went into shock. Their responses were not helpful. At the time I couldn't understand why peer-response didn't work. In retrospect, I realize that they responded to each other as I responded to them—with nit-picking criticism. My approach in those days resembled an old-time, New England hell, fire, and brimstone method; I tried to stamp out the sin of error.

My first response to student work comes in the form of short conferences (see Chapter 5) as I move around the classroom during writing time. Each class session I rove among the desks, connecting with perhaps six to ten students while they are engaged in writing. Students are constantly writing; as soon as they finish one piece they begin another. Some may be just starting to write, while others are beginning a second draft, and still others are considering final copy. I recognize that since students are constantly writing, it is not possible to respond to all of their work. I keep careful records on which students I visit so that each student, over time, gets a response.

At the end of each class, time is set aside for sharing students' writing and their learning experiences during their writing. One or two students share a piece while the rest of the class listens carefully, first stating what they have heard and remembered from the piece, then asking questions to learn more about various aspects of the piece. This general sharing can also include talk about practices that worked and those that didn't, new verbs, quick profiles of the genres in which children are writing, and brief introductions to fictional characters. This end-of-class experience reaffirms the essential conditions for writing: *in this class we experiment and learn.*

Demonstration

You, the teacher, are the most important factor in creating a learning environment in the classroom. Your students will observe how you treat writing in your own life, how you learn, and what is important to you through the questions you ask of the world around you. How you demonstrate values, how you knowledgeably show the meaning of writing as a craft, will have a profound effect on their learning.

When I began teaching, I didn't show my students how to work with their writing. I merely corrected. I didn't know any other way. When you actually take your own text and put it on the chalkboard, an overhead projector, or experience chart paper, and show your students how you read it, they will receive the clearest demonstration of what writing is all about. (Chapter 13 will discuss in greater detail how to demonstrate reading writing with your students.)

Students can go a lifetime and never see another person write, much less show them how to write. Yet it would be unheard of for an artist not to show her students how to use oils by painting on her own canvas, or for a ceramist not to demonstrate how to throw clay on a wheel and shape the material himself. Writing is a craft. It needs to be demonstrated to your students in your classroom, which is a studio, from choosing a topic to finishing a final draft. They need to see you struggle to match your intentions with the words that reach the page.

To demonstrate the meaning of conventions, you offer "meaning lessons." You show your second-grade children where quotation marks are placed and what they are for: "I'm going to put these marks here because I want to know where my person starts to speak . . . see if you can tell where this person stops speaking. Come up here and put your finger in that very place where they stop speaking. . . Good. These are the marks I put here because they help me and the reader to know where this person speaks."

Every mark on the page is an act of meaning. The words march across the page from left to right. Words are spelled the same way every time they're used. Spaces go between words. Periods go at the end of the sentence. The conventions are as much for the writer as for the reader. I won't know what I mean until I have set my thoughts on the page in a conventional text.

In my writing with the class I demonstrate a mood of discovery and experimentation. "Hmmm, I wonder where my writing is going to go. I'm not sure if I'll write about the way people use the mirrors in the weight room, or my own reaction to the mirrors (see Chapter 3). I've got two things here; I guess I'll keep writing about my reaction to the mirrors." I demonstrate curiosity about what thoughts are around the next corner.

Expectation

I have high expectations for every one of my students. To have high expectations is a sign of caring. Perhaps you have been in a class or a learning situation in which it is clear that the teacher wonders how you got in. When the teacher's eyes scan the class, they seldom rest on your face as if you knew something. Of course, there are times when you might wish to remain unknown and undiscovered. But when you teach, your task is to find out what your students know, to show them how to put what they know into words, and to expect them to do it.

"What are you working at in order to be a better writer?" This familiar question is one I ask a lot because I assume that everyone develops objectives in order to improve as a writer. I expect young writers to experiment, and I nudge them into trying new things in their writing.

Room Structure

The writing classroom requires a high degree of structure. When children face the empty page, they suddenly feel alone and want to talk or move around the room. But if children are to choose topics or figure out how they will solve writing problems, they need a highly predictable classroom.

Teachers help the room to be predictable when they:

- Have students write each day. If students miss a day or don't know when they will write again, they are losing a sense of structure and predictability.

- Establish a basic structure for the student to follow at writing time, such as, "First, get your folders containing all your writing, write, then share writing."

- Set up procedures for solving problems. Basic procedures have been posted telling students what to do when they don't have the right supplies, are stuck for a topic, need to confer with another student, need help proofreading their writing.

- Circulate among the students. The teacher contributes to structure by moving through the class conferring with students, so that students feel the teacher's listening presence.

- Negotiate class management problems with students. When issues such as noise or how to work with others arise, the teacher discusses new ways to solve these problems with the students.

The classroom is not structured for writing alone. Indeed, if writing is the only structured time in the self-contained classroom over an entire day, then the hope that students will learn to make choices and take the initiative is an empty one. Teachers can help to ensure the conditions for effective learning by carefully delegating the jobs necessary to maintaining the classroom and *showing children* how to do these jobs. As the year advances, the jobs become more and more sophisticated. (Chapter 8 talks further about how to develop a structured classroom.)

Evaluation

When children choose their own topics, they need to know how to decide if their choices are good ones. They need to know how to evaluate their own work. Here again, the teacher can show children how to read their own work—by reading her own. Indeed, the teacher's entire effort is geared to helping children learn how to examine their own work at a level appropriate to their developing abilities.

For aeons learners of all ages have passed their work on to someone else for evaluation without participating in the process themselves. Yet children spend 99 percent of their time alone with the topic they are writing about or book they are reading. During those long hours they need to know how to say to themselves, "This is what this is about . . . no, it isn't about that, it's this." Teachers do have an important role in evaluation, but it consists primarily of helping children become part of the process.

A child comes to the teacher and says, "I'm done."

"Oh, how did you decide you were done?" responds the teacher. When I began teaching, I used to pick up the child's paper, read it over, then give it back, and tell the child precisely what needed to be done to make the piece better. Now, when I move around the classroom conducting writing conferences, I expect the students to respond first:

- This is what my piece is about. (It can only be about one thing.)
- This is where I am in the draft. (I'm just getting started. I'm finishing up. I'm ready to publish.)
- This is what I'll write next or this is where I need help.

I expect them to be prepared to tell me about their work and how it is going. This gives them practice in dealing with the structure of evaluation of work in progress.

From the beginning of the school year students keep collections of their writing in folders or portfolios (see Chapter 11). This gives them a sense of their writing history and what they have accomplished that stays with them throughout the year. When a student is blocked on a particular piece, I find it helpful to have him stop for a moment and regain a sense of his history as a writer. Children also need practice in examining and evaluating their work from a variety of angles, and collecting their writing in one place allows them to do that. In all of these ways, children gain practice in using the language of evaluation in reading their own work and that of their classmates, language that has traditionally been viewed as the teacher's property.

Final Reflection

When you decide to focus on the conditions that make for sound, long-term literacy, you enlist in a lifetime venture. Cultivating a classroom that encourages and sustains writing takes far more work than methods because it forces us to look first at ourselves and our own writing. In one sense, teachers are the chief "condition" for effective writing.

You provide time for writing, the first fundamental condition. If students can't write at least four days out of five, they will make little headway or have too little time to listen carefully to a piece that is going somewhere. Four days of writing also give you more access to your students through conferences, mini-lessons, and demonstrations. You have worked to carve out the necessary time for writing because you recognize that unless individuals gain the power to think and express their thinking in a clear manner, they lose part of their birthright as citizens in a free society. Writing is not the property of a privileged elite.

Your students write about what they know. They choose a majority of their topics in order to discover what moves them and what they think. And they share what they write with a variety of audiences—through small groups, whole class groups, and publishing their work. You enable the students to become an effective writing community where they all help each other express what is important to them.

When you write with your students, you show them what writing is for. You show them the "why" of writing and how to negotiate the journey from the germ of an idea to final copy. You demonstrate constantly with the mini-lessons that pinpoint the specific skills writers need in order to write well.

You set high expectations for each writer. You can do this because you write yourself, and you know how the process unfolds. You nudge your students to try new things as you move around the classroom and huddle in conferences.

The conditions in your classroom are highly predictable. Well before students begin to write, they are aware of how the room works. The first and most predictable condition is that each day they will write and exercise choice in their topics. They know what to do when they run out of ideas or need a response to a passage, and they know how to help each other.

8 BEGIN TO ORGANIZE YOUR CLASSROOM

In the classrooms I've described thus far, children exercise a wide range of choice. They choose their own topics, they write continuously, they consult with each other, and they move around the room to pick up supplies or use the dictionary. All of these activities occur without a direct signal from the teacher; the child initiates. But this approach only works if the teacher helps children to learn how to take responsibility.

Responsibility is the key to classroom organization. Children need to have a clear sense of what is expected of them during writing time. There should be no question in their minds about what they are to do when they write. (Easy words to say, I know.)

One of the most common questions teachers ask is: "When I move around the room conducting conferences or listening to children, the noise level jumps, and some of the children get unruly. What am I to do when that happens?" It is not unusual for children to test the limits of their decision-making powers. Yet all the choices you introduce to them are important if they are to learn how to function as effective writers. Choice requires responsibility, and responsibility is taught and learned. Thus, you need to clarify the meaning of choice within definite limits. If limits are indefinite, then children will push them (and you) to the edge. If you establish a limit, but that limit is not constant, children will not treat it as a limit, and they may lose the essential state of mind that says, "This is a secure place in which to work, and I know just what is expected of me."

Children enter the classroom in the morning from households that may differ broadly in their rules about using space, time, and materials, and about how one relates to other people. Some children are allowed to choose when they go to bed, what they eat at meals, how much television they watch, and where they go to play after school, and some of these choices have limits. But many do not, and a child with no limits lives in a frightening world where he may easily become the victim of his own poor judgment.

Children whose limits are indefinite or quixotic find it difficult to use their time well or to function on their own. If you say, "You need to write now, and I expect you to have something completed by 10:00," the child may not be used to doing something right away or know how to use thirty minutes for sustained thinking on her own. You have stated your objective clearly and precisely, but the child simply doesn't know what you mean, at least not yet.

When you demonstrate what you do when you write, you not only show children how to write, you show them how to use their time. You enable them to figure out what to do when they get stuck or need to get help.

Some children will misinterpret your listening as a shift in authority. They will believe that when they control the topic, you have also handed over all responsibility to them. A few children are frightened by this; many others push to find out just how much authority you have delegated to them.

I'll make a list of some of these new choices and show what I mean by the limits that go with them:

- *Choice of topic:* "I expect you to decide what you will write about. This means that you will need to be thinking about your topic *before* you come to class. Remember how to come up with topics from my demonstrations."

- *Children living by their own choices:* "Sometimes you will find that your choice wasn't a good one. After working with it for a while, you may want to change. You can do that."

- *Continuous writing:* "When you finish writing about your topic, when you have looked the piece over and decided that you've done as much with it as it merits, then you can start on a new topic without delay."
- *Delegated responsibility:* "Since this is your topic, I expect you to know as much about it as you can; if you need more information, you will get it. This means you may need to speak with someone; if so, you may quietly leave your seat, discuss your problem or idea with one person for a few minutes, then go back to your seat.
- *Children waiting turns for attention:* "When I am working with someone else, I am not to be disturbed. If you run into a problem, try to solve it with the help of at least two other people before seeing me, and then you must wait until I have finished with the student I am talking to at the moment."
- *Room mobility:* "If you need paper, materials, or supplies, you may get up and get them. You do this by going directly to what you need and then returning promptly to your seat."

Other Limits

Each class has its own particular need for guidelines. When I sense that some of the guidelines are not working, or that additional limits are needed, I'll call the class together. First I state the problem: "I notice that some of you are not starting to write again after you finish a piece." Then I open the discussion very broadly. "Before we get into a discussion of the problem, let's talk about how you feel or what you do when you finally finish a piece. What did you want to do when you finished?" Quite possibly some children may need to shift to reading a book, doing math, or trying something else; still others may need to start a new piece right away. The children know I am listening carefully to their experiences in order to discover the best way to handle the transition after they have completed a piece.

ACTION 8.1:
Hold a small group or class meeting to find out children's sense of limits and their understanding of the various guidelines you have established for the class.

OPPOSITE and ABOVE: Writing Classrooms Don't Look the Same

I suggest choosing three or four guidelines that you feel are essential. Find a way to state them in the form of a problem. That will give you and the children a clear sense of how to handle them:

- Someone has just finished a piece but can't think of anything to write next. What's a good way to solve that problem?

- Someone has finally finished a piece and the teacher told him she wanted to see it when he finished, but right now the teacher is meeting with someone. What's a good way to solve that problem?

ACTION 8.2:
Check the predictability of your time for writing and work to structure your use of the time.

Try to select a set time in the day for writing. This decision alone sets up a rhythm and a predictability that is invaluable to the day's structure. Writing itself is an unpredictable act; one never knows what will emerge on the page—if anything.

I often think of writing as an act of self-hypnosis: I leave the external world in order to visit an interior world of memory, where I search the various caves of experience and recollection. Sleep is also an act of self-hypnosis; for many people, conditions have to be predictable or they can't leave the external world of consciousness for the world of sleep. Consider these conditions: amount of light, firmness of mattress, sounds, room temperature, access to air, weight of covers. Change any one of them and some people can't sleep. The routine has been disturbed.

Thus, I approach the rhythm of writing time systematically. Each writing period follows a similar rough sequence:

- I say, "Quietly get your writing folders and/or portfolios." Sometimes I have three students pass them out.

- I move quickly to the four children who seem to find it most difficult to start. The blank page is menacing to them, or they don't know how to connect today to yesterday; yesterday hardly exists. My job is to bring back yesterday and help them teach me a little about what they are writing. I might ask them what they will write next (generally) or even what the next line will be (specifically).

- Option: I may write first myself, for five minutes, and tell the children a little about my topic.

- I conduct further conferences with six to eight children, remembering that the purpose of the conference is to help the child speak first and to orient her to where she is in her piece and what she will write next.

- I offer a short mini-lesson of about ten minutes on a selected skill (see Chapter 12 for more details).

- We all share our writing—about five to ten minutes maximum. Be sure to bring your own writing to the share session at least one day in ten.

What I have set forth in this Action is quite mechanical. These predictable procedures might be called the bricks. What is missing is the mortar to hold them together.

Humor

One of the essential kinds of mortar is humor. Writing is such a serious enterprise that laughter is needed to break the tension. I speak of laughter from the belly borne of the clear recognition that my performance and my ambitions may not match. It is a laughter that witnesses the folly between our aspirations and what has occurred on paper.

I find the richest laughter in rooms where children are taking risks along with their teachers and are struggling to answer big questions.

A Sense of Humor is Important in the Classroom

High purpose and seriousness are laughter's most favored companions. Laughter comes from the knowing, presumptive question.

A teacher in one of our research projects tells of an incident that occurred as her class was in the midst of taking the annual nationally standardized tests. Her students read widely and knew how to read their own texts as writers would read them. They took risks and enjoyed pushing to the edge of their ambition and skill. Just after she had finished giving directions for taking the reading comprehension section, a child popped his hand into the air. Not wanting to disturb the class, she nodded her head negatively and gestured that he'd better get busy, because the test was timed. He nodded his head indicating a definite "no." Not wanting the rest of the class to be disturbed, she moved to his side and whispered into his ear, "What?"

"Who wrote this anyway? This stuff doesn't have any voice."

"I know, but do it anyway," she whispered back. High seriousness, but still a moment to chuckle together, and laughing, to prevail over difficult circumstances.

Invitation

"I invite you to do something I practice myself. Writing is a time of discovery and exploration. Writing helps to answer my questions. I invite you to write with me." These phrases set the tone of our writing classroom. How can I ask children to be responsible during writing time unless I demonstrate why writing is important in the first place? This tone also serves as essential mortar in holding together the moments and the activities of the day. When children have a sense of where they are going because they see the high purpose of your writing, it is easier for them to be responsible when they write alone.

Individual/Group

Children need to feel that they have *a place* in a group, and for some, finding a place is difficult. Indeed, some children do not wish to be part of a community. They are content to remain quiet, alone, and comfortable with their own thoughts. Americans have a tendency to believe that such children are maladjusted. Our image of the well-adjusted person is someone who is outgoing, vivacious, and the center of attention, in short, popular with the rest of the class.

At the same time, each child possesses unique capabilities that are worthy of attention. I try to carry the uniqueness of each child in my head (note the Actions in Chapter 2). One of the potential weaknesses of the writing process approach, especially where children share their work with each other and with the entire class, is the force of "group think." Most groups seem to have a common standard of what constitutes "good" in writing, or anything else, when values are shared. Group think tends to encourage children to select certain acceptable topics and ways of expression. Thus, the child who explores new ground for him- or herself may be ignored when sharing with the large group. In the face of these normal group forces, I have to work to call attention to children's individual uniqueness, to look for undiscovered potential in their writing, and to encourage experimentation. For some children, it is helpful to call their explorations to the attention of the class; for others, it is detrimental and only makes them feel conspicuous. I try to identify what the child has done that is new or unique to that child. Only then do I ask, "Would you mind if I shared this with the class?"

When the class takes responsibility for their own writing and the managing of the classroom, it encourages individuals to do the same. They say, "We can do these things. Look at what we've done. We're a good class." Children need to write for others as well as themselves, and to do this as a class. Here are examples of this kind of writing:

- Writing to the elderly: One seventh-grade class visited and wrote to elderly residents in a nursing home.

- Class publication: A fourth-grade class published their own newspaper, which was distributed to other classes in the school.

- Pen pal exchanges: A fifth-grade class exchanged letters with a class in Honduras. Each worked to learn both Spanish and English. Translators helped.

- Sharing with younger classes: One sixth-grade class met regularly with first graders to exchange and respond to writing. The classes alternated the setting for sharing: first to the sixth, then to the first-grade classroom.

- School Block study: A third-grade class studied the block on which the school was located. They walked down the sidewalk

noting the various houses, gardens, and stores. They wrote to
the people who lived there and collected their information into
a book about their block, which they shared with the people
who lived there.

When children write only for themselves—*my* trip, *my* piece of fiction,
my poem—their preoccupation with their own needs and wants
obscures the notion of responsibility to others. The class loses out on
one more element important to group structure and solidarity.

Build a Shared Structure

When I first started teaching, the room I taught in was *"my" room*. It
didn't dawn on me until much later that the children spent nearly as
much time there as I did. I worked hard to have tasteful displays and
bulletin boards, to gather paper and materials in just the right place.
The room was organized—I thrived on organization. If the children
messed something up, they were trespassing on my territory. I worried that they wouldn't respect my things. Unfortunately, I overlooked an important element in learning to take responsibility—the
sense that *together* we build a worthwhile place and community in
which to work.

I remember a friend who began one school year with a rather star-
tling idea. When the children walked into the room on the first day all
the art work, books, desks, science materials, cartons of paper, and so
on were heaped on the floor in the center of the room. He motioned to
the children to come sit with him on the rug in the corner, and for the
next two days they dreamed about what they might do as a class that
year. Together they planned how the room would be arranged, and
where the desks and tables might be placed. They discussed guidelines and then delegated tasks—to make bulletin boards, take charge
of displays, and organize the books and art materials—to various
committees. Everyone had rotating responsibilities in making the
room work, all resulting from their shared vision of the kind of classroom they wished to have that year.

When something didn't work out as planned, they took time to
negotiate new directions, reorganize the room, and assign new
responsibilities. Once they had their own shared vision secured,

almost immediately they looked beyond themselves to others in the school and community. In my experience, classrooms without identities, which lack a sense of group power, often turn on themselves and begin to scrap over minor issues, territorial rights.

The next Action concerns two types of responsibilities, first, general room maintenance, and second, interpersonal responsibilities. I phase in both types gradually to make them an ongoing part of classroom operations.

ACTION 8.3

Teach a small group of children (two or three) to take on a classroom responsibility. Keep records of their progress for a week. Conduct two short sessions to trouble-shoot as well as celebrate their progress.

This Action helps you to begin, slowly and deliberately, to understand how children learn to take responsibility. Approach it like a researcher, deliberately gathering data on just how the children learn to work together. This Action will serve as your laboratory for learning how to delegate more responsibilities throughout the year. I'll take one example and show how you can work with this Action throughout the week.

For this first job, I have chosen two children who I know can work together and probably sustain their work for a week without needing too much supervision. Later, they will be responsible for introducing this job to two other children. Then I say, "All right, this is the area where the writing folders are stored. We have twenty-eight people in our class, so there will always be twenty-eight folders in the box when the folders are not being used. At the end of each day, I'd like one of you to make sure the folders are all here with a quick count. The two of you will also be responsible for passing these out at writing time. Over here is the stapler, ruler, two different kinds of paper for writing, and large erasers, and over here are the dictionaries. These are, of course, all tools for use during writing. I want you to make sure this area is kept neat, and please keep a rough count of how much paper we are using. I have this area organized for the class to use, but you may see some better ways we can set this up so it will work better. Today is Monday; I'll see you briefly on Wednesday to talk about how things are working."

Children Assume Many Responsible Roles

Before I meet with the children I carefully think through how I want the materials to be organized and how they might do it. Of course, I am not sure what the children will encounter as they go about their job. But I have discussed the use of the area with the entire class and the job that the two children have to oversee how the area works. The class knows that they will assume more responsibilities as the year advances. I also invite the entire class to make suggestions for other jobs that will make the room work more effectively.

On Monday and Tuesday I observe how the two children handle their tasks and make notes. I try to maintain as much distance as I can (a hovering teacher doesn't help children learn to take responsibility). Unless there is a complete breakdown, I seldom intercede. On Wednesday we meet for a few minutes. My question is a simple one: "How did it go?" I want to know their perceptions. I may ask, "Tell me about all the things you have done." I'm interested in their sense of detail. Of course, their answer to my first question, "How did it go?", may cover everything I need to know. My final question is, "All right, how can this job or system be improved?" or, "How can we shorten the amount of time it takes to do this job? Eventually, I'll want you to teach someone else to do this job, so I'll want you to be thinking about good ways to shorten the time it takes you to do it." These children will stay with this job for five to eight days, and then they will introduce a new team to the responsibility.

Other Types of Jobs

I try to start children with responsibilities that are easy for them to handle and for me to observe. As the class grows in experience, the jobs increase in difficulty. Here are examples of some of the jobs children often handle (Graves 1991, 37–38).

- *Weekly papers.* Papers that are reviewed by the teacher on a weekly basis are passed back by an individual child, who sorts them and delivers them to the children on Friday to go home.

- *Library.* Someone keeps the classroom library books in order for a week. If books are coded by type and go in certain bins or on certain shelves, then that person also double-checks the placement of the books.

- *Messenger.* This weekly task involves carrying notes to other teachers and the main office or handling any other type of communication.

- *Milk tickets.* Simpler to handle than hot lunch, this job requires only a minor amount of math. Rotates on a weekly basis.

- *Hot lunch money.* This is a little more difficult, but it can be handled by a responsible team. Younger children can serve as assistants to older students who come in on a weekly rotating basis.

- *Boards:* Caring for chalkboards is done at the end of each day if any need cleaning.

- *Attendance:* Daily attendance is handled in weekly shifts. A slip is sent to the office daily and is double-checked by the teacher, who lists absentees.

- *Bulletin Boards:* The design and layout, as well as the actual mounting of materials on the bulletin board, is handled by a rotating committee of children.

- *General room cleanliness:* A weekly job in which two children see to the general order and cleanliness of the room. Messy desks and cubbies, stray papers, and other problems are noted and cared for as needed.

This is the short list. You will think of many other responsibilities that children can assume in your classroom. I find it useful for teachers to share the responsibilities their students have assumed at grade-level meetings and discuss how they introduced each responsibility and how they solved the growing pains that go along with each.

Interpersonal Responsibilities

Children need practice in gathering information from other people and using it to help the entire class. These responsibilities are more difficult to introduce than the ones of a more mechanical nature because they require interpersonal skills. On the other hand, these responsibilities contribute strongly to a sense of community. Here are several examples of interpersonal responsibilities (Graves 1991, 38–39):

Host or hostess: Children escort visitors and help them to under- stand how their classroom works. They must be up to date on room procedures, materials, and some of the reasons behind various areas and activities. This is a weekly assignment and begins as soon as you feel the children are ready to handle it. When children have to talk about "their home," a sense of nat- ural responsibility begins to develop.

Visitor invitations: There are occasions when it would be helpful to invite various experts or parent helpers to the room. This per- son handles the letters or phone calls to make the invitations. The precise details must be worked out with the child in advance.

New children: If you know in advance that a new child will be joining your class, you can ask a member of the class (preferably on the same bus as the new child) to get books and supplies for the child and introduce him to the principal and special teachers. She can also help him with class routines, describe the classroom areas, and guide him in using materials for the first couple of days. There are many times, of course, when the new child arrives without warning and the designated child must begin work on short notice. Although this job can be rotated, the first child you ask to take on this assignment should be one you feel can handle it best. The experienced child can then help another child to take on the responsibility.

Sharing in other rooms: It is often helpful for children to share their work in progress or final work with new audiences. One child organizes the sharing, working from a particular child's request, consulting with you, and contacting other teachers. This responsibility requires strong ability and experience and doesn't begin until later in the year.

Scheduling conferences: This responsibility can be delegated later in the year when children are effectively helping each other and know each other's writing and reading, and the room structure is working well. One child queries other children in the room about their sense of when a group or individual conference will be helpful. This child then schedules conferences for all the children for one week. Naturally, there will be times when the teacher changes the requests, but our experience shows that children can handle the main part of the scheduling quite well.

Final Reflection

Teachers work hard to teach children how to manage the wide range of responsibilities in a writing classroom. When children choose their own topic, decide how to use their time, consult with others, and move about the room, the teacher plays an active role. He consciously helps children to learn limits, demonstrates purpose, and creates an atmosphere in which children take responsibility for running the classroom as they do for their writing. Thus, teaching responsibility is not a matter for individual children alone, but for the classroom as a whole.

Not all children come to school wanting to write. Many are not used to initiating thinking or to creating anything in a specific time period. When such children are allowed to choose, they are bothered by the openness of the opportunity. They are used to performing in a box, being forced to do something and having little choice about their future. For these children, limits are a necessity, along with many demonstrations from both their teacher and the other children about what writing can do.

Teachers work hard helping children know what they can do and leading them to become a vital part of the writing/learning community. Children who feel they have a *place* in the classroom find it easier to take responsibility for running it. Children learn to take responsibility when certain intangibles are in place. The teacher set the tone of the classroom when she demonstrates the power and meaning of writing. When children and teachers can laugh together because both are taking risks in a secure and structured environment, writing moves ahead.

Of course, children don't learn to be responsible only during writing time. They learn throughout the day or during those periods when they are in your class. The teacher works hard to build a classroom community with the children. All pull together to make the room work. When something goes awry, the teacher usually gathers the children together to decide a new course of action.

Ultimately, we want children to have a sense of what "we" can do. Their writing expands to touch others in the community, they share their material with other classrooms in their school, and when visitors come, they are able to explain how their classroom functions. A visitor entering their classroom may see no structure at all, but the children are well able to explain what they do and the purpose behind their actions.

9 HELP CHILDREN TO SHARE THEIR WRITING

Jennifer is in fourth grade and can't wait to share her piece about her new baby lamb. Before she reads she thinks about what she wants the group to attend to during her reading: "When you listen to my piece today, I'd like you to remember the part where my new baby lamb is born, then tell me if you can actually see it there after it is born," she announces to the class, now assembled to share writing.

> I just got a new baby lamb. The mother's name is Bertha. We don't have a name for the baby yet. I think it will be Cleo. We are talking it over in my family. When she was born it was a mess. She was sticky with blood and other stuff on her. And she was all black. Bertha licked her all over until she was clean. Cleo looked like she had been for a swim. She blinked a lot like it was too bright. When she stood up she was shaky.

"Okay, just say first what you remember," Jennifer directs the class, who are seated on the floor and ready to respond.

"I remember she was a mess and there was blood."

"She was sticky."

"You want to call her Cleo."

"She's black."

"The mother name is . . . now I forgot what it was."

"Bertha."

"The mother licked her off. Yuck!"

"She was shaky."

"Okay, you got most of it. Is there something you need to have a better picture of her after she got born? Yes, Mark."

"Well, how big was she? "

"Oh, yeah, she was this big." Jennifer holds her hands apart to show the lamb's size. "Yes, Ms. Pritchard."

"Jennifer, when you hold your hands apart I can see how big she is, but you'll be writing this. How would you do it with words?"

"Oh, uh, I need to get a ruler."

"What's another way?"

"I can't think."

"Give her a hand . . . anyone. Andrea . . ."

"You could say she was the size maybe of a small dog. I've seen her at Jennifer's house."

"Yes, that is one way to do it. I could see a good picture in the words you chose, Jennifer. It was messy and bloody. I had a kind of gooey picture, though you didn't use the word *gooey*. I could see the mother licking and licking until her baby lamb was clean."

Jennifer's reading in Ms. Pritchard's class was preceded by many classroom share sessions in which she had guided the children in responding to each other's writing. First they focus on details, the actual words in the piece. Later they turn to comments and questions. In this instance, Jennifer knew from a previous mini-lesson that she could ask the children to concentrate on the language she used to describe the new baby lamb. The teacher participated by helping Jennifer realize that she needed to convey the size of the lamb in words. Ms. Pritchard also summarized the details from Jennifer's piece to show her that she did create a successful picture of the baby lamb. With this kind of guidance, it won't be long before the children themselves will be able to come up with a suitable summary.

Writing is a social act. People write to affect the lives of others. If Jennifer's writing was addressed only to the teacher, the other children would not be able to participate in the excitement of her story, or to ask questions to satisfy their curiosity. At the same time, Jennifer does need help from the teacher in understanding more clearly what she has accomplished in her writing. Ms. Pritchard teaches by showing the children how to look at the text.

Share Sessions Around the Country: A Critical Review

Since the publication of *Writing: Teachers and Children at Work,* in which I advocated using share groups for children's writing, I have sat in on literally thousands of small-group class sessions. I came away not feeling very happy with the results of my recommendations, which needed to be more specific than "help children to share their writing." These are the most common problems:

- Questions: Children ask questions before they have thought long enough to understand the text, and most of their questions are of the pro forma type: "What's your favorite part? What will you write next? How did you happen to choose to write on this topic?" It is almost as if the children have adopted formulaic questions irrespective of the actual piece the author is sharing. Such sessions are quite boring to the children, particularly the one who is sharing at the time.

- "I like": Each utterance a child makes in response to the sharing is preceded by "I like." In this instance, "I like" becomes meaningless, and comments trivial.

- Clapping: After each child shares a piece, the entire class claps. Once again, this becomes a pro forma ritual. But if the class claps after *each* session, once again their approval means nothing. Naturally I'm not recommending that some children receive claps and others don't. I'm simply saying that clapping is unnecessary unless it is truly *spontaneous* and celebrates an obvious victory for the author.

I'd keep the same format, which has children reading their selections from the "author's chair." It is also valuable for the author to feel some manner of control in calling on others to respond to the piece. But changes are needed so that the author receives the kind of help that will move the piece forward.

For Young Children: Grades One and Two
What authors of any age need most is attentive listeners. Before they ask any questions, the children need to "remember" what Jennifer wrote,

what it is in her writing that is easily recalled. I tell the class to try to remember as many of the actual words the author used as they can.

A natural outcome of this approach in the early grades originated with the children themselves, who developed their own nomenclature for it. After a child finished reading, he'd say to the class, "Okay, remembers, reminders, then questions . . . and only two reminders!" "Reminders" are the stories the author stimulated in his readers. For example, a child might write a piece about losing a tooth. Suddenly, everyone has a story about losing a tooth, and the poor author becomes a bystander listening to all these "reminder" stories. Of course, "reminders" are an important part of sharing with an audience, but they often need to be limited, especially in the early grades.

Sometimes I will turn to the child who has just read and ask, "Are there some 'remembers' that we left out? Are there some important parts of your piece that we missed?" The author ought to be listening as carefully to the group as the group does to the author.

After the children work at remembering, I may introduce the "comment." Comments serve to "connect" information. Notice how Ms. Pritchard commented on Jennifer's piece: "I could see a good picture in the words you chose, Jennifer. It was messy and bloody. I had a kind of gooey picture though you didn't use the word *gooey*." In some cases, the children will be able to connect the text with their own lives—the "reminders." But not all children can make connections, since it requires a certain degree of reflection. The child needs to see the small picture along with the big picture; sometimes the big picture is the world and sometimes it is the author herself.

I deliberately have children work through the "remembers" and "comments" before I allow questions. Good questions come from first thinking about a text, and that reduces the number of questions asked just for the sake of asking. Children will discover gaps as they reconstruct a text, and these gaps often lend themselves to good questions. Once children have a sense of this format, I don't necessarily adhere to it strictly. Otherwise, we'd end up with another "pro forma" structure in which form is more important than text.

Older Students

Share sessions with older students follow the same basic format as those with younger students. The main distinguishing element in their participation is quality of their reflection. They should be able to notice more of the elements that make good writing and using more of their reading in literature to help them connect various aspects of their classmates' writing. Two of the Actions in this chapter, one on elements and the other on sharing other discoveries during writing time, will help students learn to see more of these connections during share time.

ACTION 9.1:

Try sharing with a small group in which group members remember, make connections, and ask questions.

If this is your first venture into conducting a group share session, start with five to eight students. Choose children you think will want to share their work. It will be easier to get the bugs out of sharing by starting with children you sense will handle the session more easily

Children Share Their Work

than others. Sharing is always voluntary. After you have found two students who wish to share, review the guidelines with the group:

- "John is going to read a short selection. During his reading our job is to listen so well that when he finishes we'll see how much we can remember. Authors need to know what their audiences can remember. See how much of his actual words you can remember. Next, we'll comment on what strikes us in the piece. We work to make connections. Finally, you can ask questions of John to learn still more about his piece." (With younger children you may just focus on the remembering and introduce other procedures later on.)

- John reads a short selection from his piece. (I try to limit the reading time to no more than five minutes.)

- John calls on the other children who raise their hands to report (1) what they remember; (2) the connections they make—what strikes them; (3) the questions they wish to ask.

First share sessions are quite structured for both the children and me. We need to learn how to go about helping the student who is sharing his writing. My role is to assist the children to focus on helping the author. The best way to do this is to show them how I remember, mention what strikes me, and ask questions. I raise my hand right along with everyone else during the sharing period, which should last no more than fifteen minutes (of course, they will run longer while you and the children are getting used to them). If you feel ready to handle a large group after getting the hang of it with a small session, then proceed according to the same guidelines.

ACTION 9.2:
Broaden the content of the share session.

In Chapter 6 you experimented with "nudge paper." You nudged children into trying new things—experiments in learning for them and for you as a teacher. This experimentation, through your nudges and the children's own self-initiated experiments, are valuable activities to talk about with the entire classroom community. Several times a week, or as a regular part of each share session, I'll ask about new things the children are trying in their writing. Basically, this type of sharing allows everyone to get a sense of the progress their classmates are making and to find out about new ideas.

Once you decide that learning stories, trying new experiments in writing, and taking on self-assigned challenges are important, what children share in this type of session is virtually limitless, since the underlying question is the same: "What's new in our learning?" (Don't forget to include your own journey as a writer in the share session.) Here are some examples (Graves/Sunstein 1992, 89):

- *Did anyone create a new character in their fiction today?* This question deliberately focuses on character formation, the heart of writing good fiction. If someone answers this question positively, the other children may want to ask some follow-up questions:
  - What is the character's name? How did you choose the character?
  - What is going to happen to him/her? How come?
  - How old is he/she?
  - What does he/she look like? Read that part.
  - Read the part where he/she talks.

  Children ask these questions because you have helped them develop fictional characters in a workshop setting (Graves, 1989). You also demonstrate with your own questions how to develop the writer's characters.

- *Did anyone try a new form of punctuation today?* Children should keep track of when they use new forms of punctuation. They can keep track of their first use of the punctuation form on a sheet that records their use of conventions along with the title and page of the piece in which it was used. This helps them keep their own reference book on punctuation. It also helps them notice how professional writers use punctuation. That way, when children share their reading, they can also point out which new conventions they've noticed the author use. (See Figure 9.1.)

- *Did anyone try an experiment—that is, something new for you— today? It may not have worked, but you tried it.* This is a general kind of question to open up the discussion about anything

▲▼ Figure 9.1
Record of Conventions

CONVENTION	DATE	PAGE	PIECE
comma-serial	10/2	1	Dog to the vet
colon	10/3	2	Whales
cap-name	11/6	1	Trip to New York
apostrophe contraction	11/21	3	Space Story

new the children have tried. There is no way to anticipate all the different kinds of new things that might come up.

- *Did anyone try a different form of writing today—a poem, a piece of fiction, or a personal narrative?* I'd suggest the same when children share books. If they try a different kind of book it ought to be shared with the class.

- *Did anyone use some words today that they liked? Maybe it was just the right kind of verb.* You might also say, "Let's read some of your new verbs aloud." This kind of question can lead to a mini-lesson on the importance of precise word use.

- *Did anyone struggle with spelling a tough word?*

- *Did anyone experiment with something that didn't work today? Maybe it was an experiment that didn't quite turn out the way you'd hoped.* This is a good time for children to be interviewed about their experiments—what didn't work, what they learned, and how they might change the experiment to make it work the next time.

ACTION 9.3:

Help children to practice evaluating their own work and the work of professional writers.

Children don't suddenly make good judgments about what strikes them in a piece of writing. The quality of what they observe is the result of sound mini-lessons.

I might take a book like John Gardiner's *Stone Fox* (1980) to read aloud to the children, and introduce them to it before I start:

"We're going to try a new way of listening to pieces this morning. I'll need help from quite a few of you. And this is going to take some good practice in listening. When I read *Stone Fox* I'll need three children to listen for something they just *like* in the way John Gardiner writes the first part of the book.

"Now I'd like three children to listen for places where the author's words create pictures in your minds. Try to remember the actual words the author uses.

"This next one is a little more difficult. Sometimes authors create tension. That is, the author put something in and your stomach says, 'Uh oh, something isn't right here. We've got a problem and I wonder how it will turn out.' I need three people who will listen for that.

"Characters are pretty important in fiction. I need two people to listen for how these characters are introduced. Try to remember how John Gardiner first shows you:

- Grandfather
- Little Willie
- Searchlight the dog
- Doc Smith

"So we have four things you are going to listen for in *Stone Fox*. This means that when I finish reading the first part of the story [about five pages] the three people in each group will put their heads together and talk over what they remember. For example, Alex's group is going to listen for 'tension,' when problems come up in the book. The minute I finish reading these five pages, you'll turn and list those places where there is tension. Each of the other groups will do the same: put their heads together to talk over what they were listening for."

When I finish reading, the book discussion doesn't become a series of committee reports. Rather, it follows from a simple question I ask all the children in the room. "Okay, what did you notice about how John Gardiner wrote this first part? If you find that your group has noticed something, then share it with the class."

With younger children you may need to begin with remembering: "Before I ask you what your group noticed, let's share everything we remember about the story." The list of elements children can learn to listen for in a piece of writing is endless. They can listen for:

- good verbs
- how the author handles how people talk
- how the author helps you to "see" where the story takes place
- how the beginning and end were handled by the author
- how the end was handled in relation to the main plot
- other stories—their own and those in literature—that the piece reminds them of.

Stone Fox is a trade book that helped me introduce children to the various aspects of a piece they can discuss. Of course, my intention is to introduce these same elements into a discussion of the children's own writing. In fact, when children become familiar with these elements, they may tell their audience: "Please listen for any tension you feel in my piece . . . please listen for how I show my main character."

ACTION 9.4:
Keep track of small group, then large group sharing.

A teacher once told me, "When the children read their work to the others I can't tell if they are getting better at sharing. My general impression is that they are improving, but I don't really know." Her comment led me to devise a code system that indicates:

- the frequency of participation by each child
- the nature and approximate quality of each response
- what I attend to as the teacher
- the general quality of responses for a particular author (if an author receives poor responses it is hard for the author to grow).

The codes are organized in two general categories, statements (S) and questions (Q). The second letter registers the general content:

SC or QC: Statement or question about specific content

SL or QL: Statement or question about language

SP or QP: Statement or question about how the author wrote the piece

SR or QR: Statement or question that *relates* content to other work, the author, or the child making the comment (a relational, connecting utterance)

If a statement is particularly apt, I put a plus sign (+) next to the code; if it is irrelevant to the piece or the author I put (IRR).

A Share Session

The share session that follows begins not with receiving the piece Scott has written but with questions and comments. I have recorded the actual coding on the sheet to show how they are used. Figure 9.2 shows how they are placed on a master sheet.

First, Scott reads his piece aloud to the entire class.

THE BAT

by Scott

On Satiday my Dad and I saw a bat in our atic. He must of gotten in thrugh the vent my Dad said. He looked like a fuzy mous. I seen bats on TV but they were all out with wings flyng. This one jes hug around. My Dad said maybe hed leve tonit. Well check.

Ms. Pritchard:	You are in charge, Scott. I see lots of hands.
Scott:	Jason.
Jason:	Did you touch him? [QR: question *relates* to the author]
Scott:	No way.
Spencer:	You chicken or something? *[Is laughing.]* [QR–IRR: question not geared to help author]
Scott:	Nope, my Dad says they can have rabies. You want to get rabies, Spencer? Susan.

Susan: When was "tonight," Scott? I wondered if he was still there or what? [QL, SC+: question about language, a statement about content, + because of specificity]

Scott: Oh right, well he wasn't in exactly the same place but he was on another beam. I guess he's staying around.

▲▼ **Figure 9.2**

child responding → / child sharing ↓	Roger A.	Kirsty A.	Allan B.	Guido B.	Carmella O.	Joe O.	Scott F.	Jennifer G.	Alison J.	Linda L.	Greg L.	Morton M.	Gaila P.	Spencer R.	Susan S.	Sarah S.	Jason T.	Hank W.	Colette Y.	Maria Y.	Zoya Z.
Roger A.																					
Kirsty A.																					
Allan B.																					
Guido B.																					
Carmella O.																					
Joe O.																					
Scott F. 2/18		QA					SC SL						QA IRR	SC+ QL	QA						
Jennifer G.																					
Alison J.																					
Linda L.																					
Greg L.																					
Morton M.																					
Gaila P.																					
Spencer R.																					
Susan S.																					
Sarah S.																					
Jason T.																					
Hank W.																					
Colette Y.																					
Maria Y.																					
Zoya Z.																					

STATEMENTS	QUESTIONS	IRRELEVANT (IRR)
SC Content	QC Content	+Strong, high quality
SL Language	QL Language	- Weak
SI Impression (over all)	QI Impression (intention)	
SP Process	QP Process	
SA Author	QA Author	

Scott:	Allan.
Allan:	Well, what are you going to do if he has rabies? [QR: Question *relating* to author]
Scott:	I don't know.
Scott:	Ms. Pritchard.
Ms. Pritchard:	A good piece, Scott. I had the feel of the bat with the detail you gave us: fuzzy mouse, wings flying. I could see that bat because of your words. [SC, SL: Statement about the content and language]

Questions Teachers Often Ask About Sharing

1. My children seem to fall to the lowest common denominator in the pieces that get shared. One child shared a terribly violent piece and after that I got other violent pieces.

One of the potential dangers of having children share their writing is "group think." There is always a tendency in groups to revert to the mean, to play to the center. This is, of course, one of the potential weaknesses of classroom sharing. Without rich teaching and demonstrations of what constitutes good writing, without an occasional focus on the types of risks children are taking, "group think" can dominate. Two issues are embedded in this question: the first is how to raise the quality of sharing, the second, how to deal with violence in children's fiction:

- **Quality of sharing:** The quality of sharing is governed by the overall mood of expectation in the room. Nudging has much to do with changing what makes children move to the center. I push children to experiment with new genres and try something new in their writing. Above all, I ask children, "What are you working on now to be a better writer?" I can ask this because I am showing them the skills they need in mini-lessons.

  Move away from simply reading children's pieces to consider the risks, the victories, and the breadth of writing. Focus on individual experiments and include your own.

- **Quality of fiction:** Although Chapter 18 deals with this issue in greater depth, a quick look here may help. Children are surrounded by violence in TV, comics, toys, and, for many, in real life. It is only natural that it will invade their writing.

From a technical standpoint, the violence is usually connected with a lack of understanding of character. People kill, are dismembered, or bloodied up in order to have violence. The characters exist to serve violence; the violence does not proceed from any understanding of the character. If someone shoots someone, I immediately ask, "Why did he deserve to die? Tell me about this man who pulled the trigger. Why did he do this? If you are going to write this kind of stuff, you are going to have to deal with "why." Of course, I need to do workshops that help children to acquire the skills to change.

2. What about kids who never share?

Some children do not want to read. They do not like what they write, they see little need to share, and they are concerned about what other children may say. First-grade children are enthusiastic about sharing, but with each succeeding year in school a few more children join the list of nonsharers.

Although I do not require that children share with the entire class, I do expect them to read their work to an audience of their own choosing. "Jennifer, this piece is one of your best. Just the way you describe your kitten helps me to see her. Go get two people in the room you'd like to hear this piece and bring them over for a reading." When it is time for children to share, I point out the details that make the child's piece worthy of sharing. Then I ask them to choose one or two children with whom they'd share it. Many children find it easier to share when they can choose their audience.

The reasons children do not want to share are legion. They may be shy, they may be reluctant to share with certain children, or they simply don't see any purpose in bringing their work before the class. Some children write only for themselves, and in some rare cases, they may be superior writers.

3. There are far more children in my class who want to share with the entire group than we have time for. How do you handle that?

In most classrooms of normal size it is not possible to give everyone a chance to read and get a response from the group every week. Indeed, two weeks rarely allow all the members of a class to share. Two, or possibly three children are the maximum number in a daily session.

There are also other aspects of morning writing and reading that ought to be shared (experiments with genre types, skills, and so on). Thus, if as many as nine children are able to share each week, I feel as though I have done very well.

Sometimes I forget the purpose of sharing and lose my perspective on how to handle the matter with the children.

- Young children literally need to see the effect of their texts on the faces of their classmates.
- Children in the audience need practice in listening and repeating the texts of readers; in this way they gain "reading" experience in maintaining an understanding of the parts and whole of a text.
- Authors need to find out what audiences understand and do not understand in their texts.
- Authors need to experience the joy of joint participation in a well-read text.

I do not find that audiences are much help in assisting an author with revisions. "Maybe you ought to try this . . . or that." Sadly, child authors often get highly conflicting advice that would confuse even a professional author. The actual act of working hard to understand a text is all the help an author really needs.

Of course, there are many other options for audience involvement. When a group has had enough experience with the larger session, set up several smaller groups to increase sharing opportunities. A tasteful display of children's work is another approach to sharing, as is hardcover publication of children's writing. In some instances I also find it helpful for children to go to other classrooms to read their work. They need fresh responses from a new group. Other children enjoy sharing work with a teacher from another year.

4. What about the child who wants to share a fifteen-page piece, all of it, and we don't have the time?

It is a rare instance, indeed, when you have time for fifteen pages. In this case I ask the child to choose a section (two-page maximum) to read for the group's reaction. This requires the author to begin with a brief synopsis leading up to the part he will read. If necessary, he can also share what happens after the selected part.

5. How do you know the best time for a piece to be shared?

I expect children to have reasons for sharing their work. Naturally, I have to take into account the child's ability to express a reason. My records should tell me when the child shared last. The guiding principle is to sense when the child will be best helped by an audience in the development of this particular piece or in the child's overall growth as a writer.

Final Reflection

Writing is a social act. Writers write for audiences. Teachers work to provide a forum for authors to share their work, as well as to help their authors learn how to be good readers and listeners to the texts of others.

There are specific skills that children need to learn in the sharing of writing. Such elements are good leads, strong endings, good use of verbs, authors' approaches, their development of characters, etc. These each require some focus. You may wish to teach them apart from the sharing in mini-lessons or at the actual time of sharing a professional's piece, your own, or one of the children's.

When you help children to share in large group format you also help them to learn the basic elements that will help them share in small groups without the teacher present. You actively participate in group share, along with the children, when you attend to strong language, good listening, and in the sharing of your own writing.

10 EVALUATE YOUR OWN CLASSROOM

I open the printout displaying my students' scores on a standardized test used across the country. I read their reading test scores, and their grade placement scores. I turn another page and review their writing scores on a statewide writing test. I note that in reading they test slightly above grade level. Their writing scores, judged holistically by an outside review team, show that they are slightly above norm. In my teaching I want to improve the quality of both their reading and writing. A normed decimal score and a holistic rating shows me generally if a child is up or down, but it can't help me know how to teach tomorrow morning. In fact, most standardized evaluations are the equivalent of temperature taking: we find out if the patient is sick or well but not what to do next.

I do need to know with some degree of specificity if my children are learning. After a few minutes of working with a child I wonder, "Is he getting this? Will it stick?" On some days I wonder if *anyone* is learning *anything*. I seem merely to be putting my time in. In one sense I do know what's going on. I've been listening to the children for weeks, hearing about their victories, sifting through their writing, and seeing the smiles on their faces when they know it is good. But at the back of my mind I hear a nagging voice, "Yeah, but how do you *really* know if they are getting better?"

Evaluation takes time and we all know that a teacher's time is in short supply. You need to learn how to gather data at those moments which, in the *long run,* will have the most effect on your teaching and children's learning. Several fundamental principles underlie my approach to evaluation:

- We need to understand our schools' basic philosophy and approach to evaluating literacy.
- Our own literacy has an important effect on children's writing. Therefore, we begin our classroom evaluation with a close look at our own writing.
- We need to work to help children become lifetime writers. Therefore, we try to determine which children are headed in that direction.
- Children are important evaluators. Therefore, we need to help them learn how to evaluate (Chapters 13 and 14) and play a role in maintaining daily records.
- It is more important to evaluate some children than others. Therefore, we strategically select some children to examine more closely than others because they give data that help us understand the class and our teaching.

ACTION 10.1:

Review how writing is evaluated in your school.

For this Action you will examine the other writing evaluation systems used in your school system and school building, since you will need to know the evaluative context as you formulate a system for your own classroom. If your students' performance will be judged before you employ your own evaluative designs, you need to understand the local standard of good writing. This does not mean that you will tailor-make your design to fit an existing system, but that you will try to understand the reasoning behind a system's approach and then accommodate it as much as practicable in your own design.

Look for evaluative prototypes in the following places:

- State: Sometimes states design their own or adopt a national assessment, such as the California Test of Basic Skills.

- National: Some school systems contract a private company directly for a commercial evaluation structure, as in the Iowa Test of Basic Skills or the California test mentioned above.
- Local: Some school systems (city or town) produce their own writing prompts or topics for children to write and then meet to score the papers holistically.

I suggest that you check with your school administration and with other teachers to make sure you have considered all aspects of an evaluation system. Indeed, some systems may administer as many as three writing evaluations to the same children. You may discover exams at the building, system, county, state, and, in some cases, national level (such as the National Assessment of Educational Progress).

Various language arts components are used to measure a child's ability to write.

- *Spelling:* note whether children spell a word as dictated by a teacher or if they are merely required to identify correct and incorrect spellings on the standardized test. In one sense, the only true judge of a child's ability to spell is how he spells words when he writes.

- *Language skills:* these test components examine children's understanding of writing conventions, such as punctuation, capitalization, grammar, and so on.

- *Writing test:* children are asked to write on a topic supplied by the examiners: "Write about an interesting personal experience," "Write a letter to a company asking them to send you something you wish to purchase." These papers are collected and usually evaluated holistically by two or three examiners.

- *Portfolio review:* children are asked to assemble a collection of writings during a school year. If these are reviewed by an outside group of evaluators the types of writing are often specified: fiction, friendly letters, business letter, essay. Writing is collected for the portfolio throughout the year and reviewed in the spring. Some approaches ask children to specify the reasons for making their selections.

There are a number of questions you need to be consider in order to understand the implications of the entire evaluation structure for your teaching and your students' learning. Keep these questions in mind as you gather information about evaluation in your school and community. (Figure 10.1 shows an example of how to record your data.)

- *Ask the person you are interviewing (teacher or administrator) to rate the relative importance of the various evaluation components (spelling, conventions, writing sample).* Spelling and conventions exist to enhance the meaning of the written sample, but your interview may reveal that the written sample is valued less than the other components.

- *How does this assessment define writing?* Before you ask this question be sure to write down your own definition of what writing is and what it is for. I refer you to the examples in Chapter 1, which will show you that writing is defined, officially and unofficially, in many ways.

- *What is the purpose of this particular evaluation component?* For example, if the component is spelling or language arts skills, you will want to know how the data will be used. Here are some examples of how data are used:
  - To show how our students are performing in relation to other students in the country.
  - To show our teaching strengths and weaknesses. If the test shows that our children are "down" in capitalization skills, then we need to teach them.
  - To show how a particular child has changed since the last assessment.

- *How will this assessment be used?* How was it used last year? The best definition of "use" is the retrospective one: gather specific examples of how teachers have actually used the data with particular children.

- **Who will use this assessment?** Note the column for audience in Figure 10.1.

▲▼ **Figure 10.1**
Language Arts Component Review

1. COMPONENT	2. TEST	3. AUDIENCE	4. TYPE	5. USE FOR TEACHING
Spelling	Iowa L given 4, 7, 11 grades	P, T, A, B	N choose correct spelling	none
Conventions	Iowa L	cap punctuation language agreement P, T, A, B	Indicate correct usage N	none
writing sample	County R (D) S (D)	T, A	prompt - 50 minutes Holistic scoring	none
portfolio	none			

KEY

R	Regional	C	Child	N	Normed
L	Local	P	Parent		
S	State	T	Teacher		
N	National	A	Administration		
D	Duplicatory	B	School Board		
		CM	Community		

- *What is the child's understanding of what the assessment is and what it is for?* Since this book and succeeding Actions emphasize children's ability to learn how to evaluate their own work, their perceptions of the role of others and their evaluation instruments will be important data.

The questions you have asked look at the content and the health of the evaluation system used in your building and your school system and will be helpful as you devise a complementary system of assessment within your own classroom. Figure 10.1 (reading from left to right) shows that the Iowa test is given for this particular grade level (Grade 4); the data will be shared with parents, teachers, administrators, and the school board (column 3); the type of test is one in which students choose the correct spelling from four choices (column 4), and the "N" indicates that the data are normed. That is, each child's scores will be placed in a percentile with the spelling scores of children across the country. "This child's reading of spelling words is better than sixty percent of the other children taking the same test." Column 5, "Use for Teaching," shows that these data cannot be used for instructional purposes since the child did not actually spell the words.

This type of test tests reading rather than spelling ability. The child does not produce the spelling; rather, she reads until she sees what she recognizes as a correct spelling. Standardized tests become expensive if they include handwritten spelling or writing, since these have to be scored by hand. And even if the word was dictated to the child, it is still outside the context of ongoing writing, which is the truest indicator of spelling ability.

With the exception of the writing prompt, the basic data are all normed ("N"). Figure 10.1 shows that children in the fourth grade are given a writing prompt by both the state and the county. The county prompt, "Write about your favorite animal," allows the children fifty minutes to compose a short written piece, which will be judged on coherence, accurate use of language and conventions, and overall interest to the reader.

The sad thing about most evaluative structures at the local and state level is that their expectations for children are so low. The Actions in the remainder of the chapter are structured to go well beyond any external assessment of what you will expect children to do to improve their abilities as writers. The data you gather will also be useful to those children who most need to be taught how to use it. In addition, the data will help you teach and inform others about your children's progress.

ACTION 10.2:

Review your own personal practices in writing.

The greatest long-term influence on what the children in your classroom do is your own literacy. The reasons for this are complex. First, when you write with the children, your stance toward learning and the world change. As an active observer, you are more confident of your place in the world. Second, as you continue to work at your writing you create your own long-term inservice for learning better ways

Evaluate Your Own Classroom

to write and teach. Third, you give children the clearest demonstration of the power and function of writing.

It is natural for children to wonder, "Why would anyone want to write?" I answer their question by showing them the source of my topics and how I compose by writing short pieces for myself and by generally sharing my writing or portfolio. Children can go a lifetime and rarely see another person write, least of all the educators who teach them.

As I review my own writing practices I take a broad perspective:

- I review the writing I do that helps me to see and understand my world. These may be short pieces (see Chapter 3), letters to others, or even letters to the children.

- I review the writing I show to the children. Some should involve showing the composing as it actually takes place; others can be done at home or at school. If you have tried the Actions in Chapter 3 you are well on your way to enjoying your own literacy. Note how frequently you compose with the children. I find that writing once every week for two to three weeks works best. After this I may write only once every three weeks. Of course, I am writing more frequently on my own without sharing with the children.

- I review all of my writing—notes to the children, letters, memos, materials composed for class, and so on. I find that teachers are often engaged in more writing than they realize.

- I might interview three to four children to record their perceptions of my writing. I simply ask, "What do you remember about what I've written? How did I happen to write it? Why do you think I write?"

ACTION 10.3:
Spot the lifetime writer.

I deliberately take the long-term view in my responses to children and in my approach to evaluation. Basically, I ask myself this question: "What can I do today that will help this child to use writing as a tool for thinking and learning throughout her life?" When I conducted my study for the Ford Foundation a number of years ago, I was struck by how few adult Americans used writing in their everyday lives. If they wrote, they did so nervously and only under duress. Few had witnessed the power of writing as demonstrated by their teachers.

This Action will help you to see which children display the characteristics of the lifelong writer. I am not speaking of the child who will become a professional writer. Rather, I am looking for the child who will use writing as part of his everyday life. I look for the following elements in the children I will call lifelong writers:

- *Initiates writing:* The child chooses to write in order to recount, then understand experience. The child has a sense of "topic" and seeks to tell the story his way.

- *His sense of the power of writing:* The child recognizes what writing can do. She knows that her text can affect what other people will do.

- *His sense of history and of the future:* The child senses where he has been and sees the past as basically healthy and foundational to the future. "See, I used to write this way and on these things, but now I'm going to do this and I'll get better at it."

- *Has a sense of audience:* "I know the kids will like this" or "I wonder if he'll get this."

- *Initiates writing at home and to affect others.* When children write at home, on their own and to affect others, they demonstrate the best of the "lifelong" characteristics.

- *Senses the appropriateness of writing in a variety of genres:* If I have shown children some of the uses of writing in their lives as well as in science, math, and social studies, then I know they will be able to put writing to use. Now I look for signs that they do this on their own.

The children will not necessarily demonstrate all of these characteristics. The most important one, the one that underlies all the others, is "child initiates." When the child initiates writing, she shows an understanding of what writing can do for her as author and for her audience. We stress the importance of the "independent reader" who reads on her own at home. Instinctively we know that children who read at home will become fluent readers. There simply isn't enough time in school for them to get the practice they need in order to read well. The same logic applies to writing. Unless children see that their writing has a purpose, they will not acquire a real sense of themselves and their own ideas.

Take a clipboard and write the children's names next to each of the six characteristics listed above. Consider what you need to do to help children become lifelong writers. Indeed, this entire book is intended to help children become lifetime writers.

ACTION 10.4:

Introduce one aspect of a new system of record keeping that students will maintain themselves.

This Action introduces the first of a number of records you will want the children to keep for themselves. The types of records you will introduce are applicable to all children (including first graders in the second half of the year). I suggest that you begin by working with children's writing folders. A writing folder is a repository for all the writing a child has done to date. All of the children's writing should remain in school in the writing folder (and/or the portfolio, which I will discuss further in Chapter 11). You and the children need to be able to consult the writing as a resource from day to day. If parents wish to view a child's work, it is better that they arrange to see the collected works at one time (see Chapter 21).

When children have four to six pieces of writing in their folders, pull a small group of five or six children together to introduce them to record keeping. Choose children who you feel are ready for record keeping; that is, they are interested in accumulating items in their folders and they don't usually lose the folder contents. I focus on these children because I learn from them the best way to keep records in my classroom. When I introduce record keeping to the next group, I will be more experienced (having learned under optimum conditions).

I suggest that you make a "Record of Writing" by lining off folder covers in the manner indicated in Figure 10.2. If you wish, you can have children mark off their own folder covers using the same data blanks.

When I have gathered the children together, I begin.

▲▼ Figure 10.2
Record of Writing

DATE STARTED	GENRE	PIECE PUBLISH = P	DATE FINISHED OR DROPPED
9/9	Fiction	The avengers	9/14 F
9/17	Fiction	The avengers Return	9/23 F
9/26	Personal Narr.	my Dog	9/28 F
9/29	Letter	Wrote with justin to the Principal	10/3 F

Don: Today we are going to start something that I think you will enjoy. It's a way of keeping track of work in your folder. I'll show you with my own folder first. [See Figure 10.3.]

This helps me keep track of what I'm writing and when I'm writing it. See, right here [*pointing to column*] is where I wrote that piece in class about my dog shedding. And I finished it that same day, so I write the same date and an "F" because I finished it.

See, when I take this out later on, it will be interesting to use. I'd like you to try to put the papers you have in your folder right now in the order you remember writing them. You may not have dates on them so you'll just have to try to remember. Find the first one you wrote and then write it down in the column that says "piece" at the top. Okay, record the first one.

Now that you have those down we'll talk about the column that has "Genre" at the top. Let's look at my folder cover because most of you know the pieces that are here.

Take the first one, "Dog's Shedding." In this one I really wrote a strong opinion piece. I was just fed up with picking up all the hair around the house. My kids were supposed to brush Sadie, but they weren't doing it, or weren't doing a good job. I was sounding off but with facts—all the hair around and the kids not brushing her. Okay, do any of you have an opinion piece, especially one where you are trying to convince someone of something they ought to do? Yes, Mark.

Mark: Well, this piece I did on my trip to New York. I had the opinion that I had a good time and wanted others to know it.

▲▼ Figure 10.3
Teacher's Folder

Date started	genre	Piece	Date Finish or Drop	what I'm working on - my plans	P
9/10	essay	Dogs shedding	9/10 F	wrote in class I wanted my voice to sound "fed up."	
9/14	letter	Letter to my father	9/15 F	I tried hard to be sensitive to my father - to feel like he did	
9/17	hist. fiction	Eben Robie	10/1 F	I focused on character. what was this boy like in Civil War times?	
9/22	pers narrative	the day my car wouldn't Start	9/28	Details I wanted you to see my car and know how I feel	
10/13	poem	First Frost	still going	Details again but have good pictures so you could see that first frost	

Don: Not quite. If you wrote it as a narrative account, like telling the story of going there from beginning to end, it would be a personal narrative. If you chose just certain parts of the trip in order to convince me of how good it was to go to New York and that I ought to go, then you'd have an essay. That's not an easy one to understand but I'll be showing you more about that as the year goes on. This next one is a little easier. Most of you know about the letter. This letter here I wrote to my father. He's been sick and I wanted him to know I cared about him and that I understood about his sickness. Actually, the letter is closest to the essay. That's where essays came from, the letter. I choose certain things to let Dad know that I think and care about him. I want him to end up knowing that. I'll skip down to "The Day My Car Wouldn't Start." That's a personal narrative. It happened to me and I just wanted to tell the story from beginning to end, just like you told the story of leaving New Hampshire and going to New York, Mark.

Perhaps you remember when we were studying the War Between the States that I worked for quite a while on my Eben Robie piece, the boy who lived in Civil War times. This is fiction. I guess that's not too hard to figure out. Has anyone written fiction? You might mark it as fiction at the top of the page and then write that genre in the column on your table here.

Poetry I think you know as well. How many of you have any poetry in your folder? Ah, Karen, I guess you are the only one so far. How many of you have fiction? Just as I thought, every single one of you. Okay, you can go back to your seats and enter in your titles, genres and rough dates. Then we'll meet briefly tomorrow to look over what we've written, discuss it, and especially look at the genres. I know you'll have questions, but we can discuss those tomorrow.

The next day you will bring the group back for a short session in order to examine their progress with this initial attempt at record keeping. When the group returns I'll ask them to do the following: "Now that you've started your records, I'd like you to look them over and say what you notice about yours; I expect that we'll have all kinds of differences. I'll do the same with mine." After hearing their questions, I discuss the final column:

Don: Before I began to write each of the pieces you see listed here, I knew there was something I wanted to try to work on to be a better writer. Look at this first one. I wanted my voice to sound "fed up." Then in the next one, the letter, when I wrote to my father I wanted to be sensitive; I tried to swing around and almost become him so I could feel the way he did. Have any of you tried to do that with your pieces? Janet?

Janet: When my dog died I wanted my piece to feel heavy and sad. I hope it sounded that way.

Don: Yes, you have the idea. Now on the one where my car wouldn't start I worked on details. I didn't want to tell you how I felt; I wanted to show you how I felt and that's a lot harder for me to do. So, when I wrote I tried to give details about how the engine sounded as it groaned and wheezed but wouldn't catch. I looked out the window and showed what I saw wondering—if with the first cool of fall I'd have this problem and if I'd ever get to school. Sometimes I don't know what I'll work on until I'm into a piece and it gets hard and I say to myself, "If only I knew how to describe the sound of a car not starting." What I'd like you to do when you start the next piece is to write something in that final column that you'll work on to improve as a writer. Maybe you already suspect what you'll need to pay attention to in order to make it a good piece. If you haven't done it yet, I'd like you to write down the title and genre of the piece you are working on right now. Okay, let's talk about what you think you'll work on in the piece. Heather.

Heather: Well, I'm writing this fiction and the last time I got stuck and didn't know how to have a good ending. I need to do this.

Don: Yes, that's something to really think about. What do you think you'll need to do to have a better ending?

Heather: I really don't know.

Don: Well, you usually have to go back to the very first page and see what problem you've introduced. I can see that a mini-lesson would be a help to you. There are others who have the same need that you do, Heather. You see, sometimes you know you need to improve on something, like Heather says, but you don't know quite how to go about it. That's fine. Heather is really stretching herself and that tells me too what I need to do with my mini-lessons.

As soon as you finish with this group of students and have sensed what bugs you need to work on, begin with another group. Remember, each time you introduce a record system you should keep the following basic principles:

- Ask children to come to a conference with their folders and take out five to six pieces.
- Take out your own folder with your entries already posted. Show children how you have put your folder together.
- Introduce the new record system. Let children begin to post entries in your presence.
- Next day, answer questions about using the record: what did you discover about yourself as a writer?

ACTION 10.5:

Introduce children to keeping records of their progress with conventions.

Although it is time-consuming to keep introducing record systems to the children, in the long run it will be time efficient. Records help children stay in touch with their progress and help you to be time efficient in sensing overall classroom needs.

You'll want to decide when to introduce the final record-keeping system for the children, "Conventions." If the classroom feels well-organized, then you can proceed with this step earlier; otherwise, wait until the entire class has been introduced to the first step, "Record of Writing" (see Figure 10.2). You may wish to skip ahead and read Chapter 12 before you introduce record-keeping for conventions.

The basic philosophy behind teaching conventions is that children need to be aware of their increasing *use* of conventions, even if their first use is incorrect. Every act on the page is an act of convention (Smith 1982), from putting spaces between words to using periods and commas to spelling words and marking off clusters of ideas into paragraphs. Conventions help the writer understand his own thinking just as they help the reader to understand what the writer is trying to say. Thus, teaching conventions are directed toward accumulating a growing "Record of Conventions" which show the child's increasing skill in using conventions to aid meaning.

Figure 10.4 shows a ten-year-old boy's record of his convention use. Note that this fifth-grader gradually moved to greater accuracy

▲▼ **Figure 10.4**
Record of Conventions—10-year-old

CONVENTION	DATE	PAGE	PIECE	FIRST USE	1/2 TIME ACCURATE	USUALLY ACCURATE
comma serial	11/2	1	Dog to the vet New York		X	11/8
colon	10/30	2	whales New York Space Probe	X	11/6	2/20
cap–name	11/6	1	Trip to New York			X
apostrophe contrac.	11/21	3	space story		X	

in his use of the colon, first in his whale piece, then his New York trip piece, and finally in a science piece on the space probe. Children who keep records like these actually compile their own language arts reference textbook. If a child wishes to get help from other children, he can also consult their lists with their permission. As the year advances, the list grows. Notice that the child records the date when she first uses the convention, uses it again with some degree of accuracy, and then uses it accurately most of the time. It is important to remember that full mastery is rarely achieved. The more difficult the text, the more challenging it is to signal meaning by using conventions.

Figure 10.5 shows a seven-year-old girl's use of conventions.

The teacher points out to this child that she already has an idea of what conventions are because she has put spaces between her words. Indeed, all the second graders put spaces between words. "See, you already know what conventions are," says the teacher. "You helped your reader to see what the words are separately. Of course, there are many more ways to help your readers understand your very important words. We'll spend the year adding to this list when you use each of them for the first time, when you use them with greater accuracy, and when you seem to understand them." This child first used quotation marks in her "Fritzie" piece; her accuracy increased in her "Unicorn" piece.

▲▼ **Figure 10.5**
Record of Conventions—7-year-old

CONVENTION	DATE	PAGE	PIECE	FIRST USE	1/2 TIME ACCURATE	USUALLY ACCURATE
word spaces	9/10	1	Camping			X
name-caps	9/20	1	Fritzie		X	12/8
period	9/20	1	Fritzie		X	
quotation	9/20	1	Fritzie unicorn	X	10/8	

ACTION 10.6:

Consider different ways of using children's records.

Most children enjoy keeping records if the records are used effectively. But some children avoid records, and there are ways to help them. (A subsequent Action will provide some help for you and the children.) The record is a repository of the child's history and can be useful in some of these circumstances:

Child is struggling with a piece of writing in general:

Don: Mark, look over your list here on the folder cover. Find the piece that really worked for you—like when you wrote it, you felt the words were going down quite easily. Tell me about it.

Children who are stuck or find themselves in a down period can be helped by reading pieces aloud from a time when writing was going well. This helps them hear the voice that wrote more easily.

Child repeatedly focuses on one topic:

Don: Mark, what do you see here in your topics? How are they the same and how have they changed?

Mark: Well, I've got four space invader pieces and one about the Bruins I wrote last February.

Don: How have your topics changed? When you wrote the space invader pieces you were working on something as a writer.

Mark: I was trying to make them more exciting.

Don: Okay, how did you work on this last one to make it more exciting?

Mark: I didn't want this one to be boring like the last one.

Don: So, what did you do?

Mark: I figured I needed to do something to like . . . make the reader wonder what would happen next.

Don: And?

Mark: And I got stuck. I don't know how to do this stuff.

Don: That happens to a lot of writers. The key is in your characters. When you write fiction the reader wonders what the character will do next, especially if they really come to know the character. If you do another space piece, come to a workshop on characters before you start.

Children are often stuck on one topic, especially in fiction, when they are trying to vary the action or plot without developing the character. They usually need help with this. See Chapter 18 on teaching fiction or my *Experiment With Fiction* (1989a). The record allows the writer to see patterns.

Work with conventions:

Don: I see that you haven't been adding to your list of conventions, Mark. Do you think you've been trying some and you just haven't listed them? Think back to some of our games (see Convention Game in Chapter 12) or mini-lessons. Were there some you'd like to try and needed more help with them?

A first-grade teacher in Moultonboro, New Hampshire, used children's record keeping in teaching mathematics. The children kept charts on what they were writing and reading and then created number stories from their records. Here are some examples:

Bill, would you take a quick survey to find out how many children have written fiction in the last month?

Karen, will you take this clipboard and check to see how many letters, poetry, and nonfiction have been written in our class in the last month?

Alison, we might do up a collection of pieces about pets; look to see how many we might have from the titles on the covers.

Do a quick hand survey with a small group of children or the entire class. Ask, "How many of you have . . ."

- Used a colon for the first time?
- Tried the serial comma?
- Shown the use of possession with groups?

"Let's share some first-time uses of conventions. Look at your chart, or maybe you've forgotten to put it down. Tell us now and then write it in. When you use one for the first time, please put it in the 'Convention Check' basket." There is a basket where children place papers they wish the teacher to examine their use of conventions.

ACTION 10.7:

Take four folders home each night for a week. Write short, two- to three-sentence letters to students about what you see in their folders and records.

This approach is particularly useful for children who have difficulty keeping records. "I notice" letters call attention to what children are learning and to the patterns you see in their record keeping.

> Dear Sara,
>
> I've enjoyed looking over your folder and I notice that you've had a nice stretch of finishing your work. The piece you worked and worked on, the letter you wrote to the mayor, is really coming along. And that's the first letter you've written. Congratulations.
>
> Mr. G.

ACTION 10.8:

Consider the strategic use of your time in designing your evaluation program.

Some children will require more attention in your evaluation design than others. Consider the approach in Figure 10.6. There are some records that all the children maintain (Level I).

Other records are kept by children who *affect the direction of teaching* in the classroom (Level II). They may be top students, average yet engaging students, or students who cause problems with others. You need to know these children beyond the kind of records they keep in Level I. For each, you will want to conduct the evaluation of potential (see Chapter 8) in order to learn more about their abilities. I will select four, two students who most positively influence other children to learn and two students who most negatively influence other children to learn. I will probably write more letters to these children. My intention is to learn as much as I can about what these children know in order to have them help the direction of learning in the room.

Children at Level III are exceptionally bright and need more challenge, or they are those who get lost more easily in a room designed to foster initiative. It is possible that some of the children in the second group may be in this group as well. I'll select two to four children for this group and do the following:

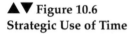
▲▼ Figure 10.6
Strategic Use of Time

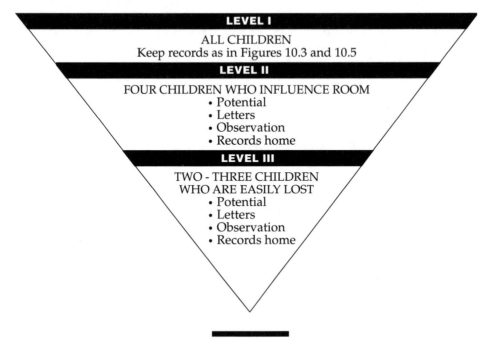

- take their folders or portfolios home more often; write letters to them
- assess their potential (Chapter 8)
- keep close watch on their setting of objectives
- observe and encourage their plans

I may also need to spend more time in helping the "lost" children to have a richer sense of their learning history.

ACTION 10.9:

Consider the children who have problems with evaluation and record keeping.

You probably aren't surprised when I say, "Yes, there are children for whom evaluation, especially record keeping, is a problem." I try to look through the eyes of the child in order to understand why these activities seem to be irrelevant or, perhaps, painful. Children who find record keeping difficult fall into several types:

- The "now" child. Personal history is unimportant to this child. Yesterday is an amorphous haze. Once something is done, it is done. Some of this can be developmental or it can be a personal style.

- The "comparative" child. This child continually compares herself with others. Any chart, folder, or portfolio will only document that she is behind. If her chart or folder is empty, then there is nothing there to compare. No matter what you do, there will be children who create competitive situations.

- The "It's *in my head;* why do I have to put it down here" child. "I know just where I am and what I am going to do. I can tell you anything you want to know." Sometimes children who speak this way can actually tell you what you need to know. They'd rather be doing the actual work than making records on what they've done.

- The "painful history" child. This child has not performed well and finds the work difficult. Records only document how poorly he has done. He worries that other children may see how few pieces he has written or note that many of his selections have not been completed.

The following approaches generally deal successfully with most of these children. It often takes a fair amount of time to overcome some of their very difficult learning and family histories.

- Share your own records in small workshop sessions as demonstrated in the introduction of record keeping.

- Make sure that records are used.

- Write them "I noticed that . . ." letters.

- Carefully build the details of an effective learning history for these children.

- Focus on high yet realistic expectations for these children. When a child has achieved a meaningful goal, there is usually some record counterpart where it can be recorded. Unless you have high expectations, there are no victories to be recorded, especially for children who have difficulty keeping records.

Get into the habit of creating your own records. The records I present in this chapter are only general guidelines to show you what is possible. I've designed these records for me and the children. The more I can involve them in the sense that they are growing as a class, the more they can be engaged in keeping track of how well we are doing.

Some records may be of short duration. I may take just the month of November to note the ways in which children participate in sharing. This record will make me sensitive to their style and frequency of participation. After that, I keep such data in my head. Remember that the record exists to help you teach and the children learn. If record-keeping interferes with children's actual writing and your teaching, you need to reconsider your approach.

Final Reflection

In the United States, we expend more effort checking children's educational progress through external measures than actually teaching them. We send their work out of town for normative assessments but then receive data we cannot use to help the children improve. Worse, the types of standardized assessments given to students rarely resemble the actual writing tasks they practice in the classroom.

Children should be able to write on demand, provided they can draw on the resources that any good writer will use when writing is required. They should be able to gather information, consult sources, and discuss their work with colleagues. Unless we can learn in our assessments whether students can use resources properly and compose over longer periods of time, our data gathering does not replicate actual writing conditions. Unfortunately, most writing assessments expect too little of the writer. An essential skill of effective writers is the ability to read their own work. This chapter brings children into the record-keeping process through careful introductions to a system that will help them develop a sense of their own history as a writer. Writers with little sense of this history find it difficult to keep records or to have realistic plans for improving themselves as writers. Of course, the records are only helpful if the writer is shown how to use them. Assessments ought to help us teach but they should also assist students in setting new learning goals. If children are to use writing as a tool for thinking, learning, and living, they need data that will help them.

We want to have the greatest effect on our children's learning. This means that we must use our time differently than we used to. I have moved from extensive correcting of children's work to showing them how to handle the very problems I might have red-lined in the past. I have also shifted from keeping all the records myself to helping children maintain records that will provide concrete evidence that they are becoming better writers. This takes more time in the short run, but it points the way to greater student involvement.

I save still more time by selecting certain children for in-depth study. They tell me about the status of learning in classroom and about what it is like to feel lost. Another teaching and record-keeping system, the portfolio, needs to be examined. The portfolio system, introduced in Chapter 11, allows children to make selections of their work to exercise their growing ability to examine their writing history and make plans for improving their own writing.

11 EXPERIMENT WITH PORTFOLIOS

The use of portfolios in schools has soared. States, school systems, and cities universally mandate their use. A pool of twenty-one states is considering portfolios as an alternative to standardized testing. Teachers who are uninformed about portfolios are considered out-of-date professionally. Portfolios are now seen as an essential part of the educational landscape. There are just as many approaches to portfolios, however, as there are systems and states in the country.

"What is a portfolio? Start from the beginning, please," is a query I hear frequently in my workshops on portfolios.

A portfolio is the place where a student's selected work is kept. The portfolio container can be a pocket folder, a loose-leaf notebook, or even a special container designed by the student to fit the artifacts he needs to represent himself. One first-grade classroom used empty cereal boxes from the children's favorite breakfast cereal. This chapter, however, will refer only to the writing students may select for their portfolios.

Students usually have two collections: a folder containing all their writing from the beginning of the school year, and a portfolio containing work they have carefully selected from their folder. Students select the work they wish to represent them in their portfolio collection throughout the year. What goes into the portfolio depends to some extent on what you and the students determine its purpose to be.

I invite you to *experiment*. I stress experiment because you need to be prepared to take advantage of what you learn from your students and from the portfolio of your own work you keep for yourself. The use of portfolios in schools is such a new phenomenon that we need to approach them with a degree of openness, trying out new ways to use them. I have changed how I maintain my own portfolio at least six times and how I use them with children probably just as many. Each time I try a better way to make the portfolio help my writing. (For more background on portfolios, see Graves and Sunstein, 1992).

Essentials in the Use of Portfolios

Although we may change our approach to portfolios a number of times, some essentials should always remain part of the process:

- All students keep portfolios.
- Students choose what goes into their portfolio.
- Each time students make a selection, they must justify it.
- Students receive responses to their portfolio collection from the teacher and selected peers.
- Teachers continue to keep their own portfolio and demonstrate how they make judgments about collected work.

The Student Chooses

Students place what they value in their portfolio. For very young first graders, artwork may constitute an essential part of their selections. At first, children do not distinguish between artwork and writing. To a child both are communications; in fact, there is often more information in their very concrete drawings than in their first invented spellings.

Children often do not choose for their portfolios the work we'd like them to include. Indeed, like most writers, the child does not have enough distance from her own writing to recognize its stronger elements. A child may give one reason for making her selection, yet overlook other, stronger components of the piece. You may see growth and change, but the child sees only that he has chosen a topic that no longer interests him. In these instances I do not remain silent; I point out the growth the child has made. The decision for selecting the piece, however, is still the child's. Above all, I want the child to feel a personal investment in the portfolio. (Besides, the child may select at a later time the piece she rejects today.)

The Student Justifies

The child knows that, for each piece she selects, she must say "why" it belongs in her portfolio. For very young children the teacher can record the reason, but by the second half of the first grade most children ought to be able to write one to two sentences. Their reasons may seem quite elementary at first. Wilcox (1993) has observed a rough sequence to the reasons young children give for their selections. Note the following responses to the query, "Why have you chosen this for your portfolio?":

- *"This is a boat."* The child merely names the object. She is unable to go beyond naming it. At the same time, this is probably a piece of high effect and one of her better pieces.

- *"I like the boat."* In this instance the child adds a value, "like," to her response. You might follow with a question, "And what do you like in this piece?" But the child may only be able to respond, "I don't know, I just like it."

- *"I like the boat because I love it."* This statement may not seem to be much of an advance over the last one. Still, she recognizes that choices usually require reasoned evidence, and she introduces the word, *because,* as an important logical construction.

- *"I like the boat because, you see this sail up here? I drawed it good."* For the first time, the child uses evidence from within the piece to support her judgment, although in this case, it is based on the drawing, not the writing. Still, this is progress.

Children use these basic constructions as they grow more sophisticated in providing evidence to support their choices. Gradually, if you read and select from your work and help children to learn to read their own work and experience many audiences, their reasons will become more sophisticated. One of the best ways to chart children's progress as writers is through research that follows the application of values to portfolio selections.

Choosing the Right Type of Portfolio

The most important question you can ask about portfolios is a simple one: "What are they for?" Here are some possibilities:

- for external evaluators, board members, state and national, members of government
- for the teacher and administrators
- for the children
- to compare the work of one child in relation to that of other children in a town, state, or nation
- to aid children on a day-to-day basis in the improvement of their writing ability

Portfolios, if used effectively, can serve many of these audiences. If I concentrate on encouraging students to take responsibility for judging the quality of their work from the outset, it will improve. The portfolio can serve as a medium for teaching and learning as well as for evaluation. The focus on evaluation and the portfolio in this book is the student as an effective reader and evaluator of his own work. External evaluators can be satisfied if the main emphasis is on the student as the improving/learning writer.

I suggest portfolios that contain a number of sections that allow for various types of writer growth. In the past, my notion of portfolios embraced the simple idea that they should only contain a student's *best* work. Student excellence was my objective.

One day I asked a group of teachers who kept portfolios to arrange their work from best to least best and state why they made their selections. Fortunately, Brenda Power, a doctoral student at the time, said, "I don't think this is a good idea because I'd hate to scale my poems from top to bottom. I have different thoughts and feelings that are unique to each poem. I couldn't possibly do that exercise and make those kinds of choices." I was stymied by her response and continued the exercise in bull-headed fashion. But her response continued to fester because I knew she was right. Although excellence is certainly a worthy objective, it is equally important to help students understand a range of values. Therefore, I include a number of sections within the portfolio:

- *Best writing:* choose work you consider to be your best on as many factors as you are able to include in a single piece.

- *Writing in which you learned something new:* this may be work that demonstrates a new skill or a new topic, This may not be "best writing." The emphasis in this category is on learning and experimentation. If I ask a child to show me what experiments she has tried lately, she ought to be able to take me to this section of her portfolio.

- *Literacy that is important to you as a person:* this is a much broader category and may include writing from the child's favorite authors, a letter from a grandmother, a note from a teacher or friend, or a photo or artifact that shows him as person. For many children, this is an important entry point into portfolios.

There will be much overlap between these sections. And of course, it is possible that a selection falls in all three categories, which can become a useful point in a conference or discussion with the children.

ACTION 11.1:

Begin to keep your own portfolio.

The Action in Chapter 10, "Review your own personal practices in writing" is actually a beginning point for your own portfolio. I suggest that you consider the same categories for yourself that you do for the children. I'll show you what I mean with my own portfolio:

- *Best Writing:* Poetry is a very important genre for me. This summer I've worked especially hard on poems. For this reason I'm including:

    "Morning Snow"
    "First Grade Classroom Late Friday in January"
    "Randolph Nelson"
    "Humming Birds"

    I've also written an article for *Primary Voices* (Graves 1993) that I worked on for some time. It finally came out the way I wanted, correcting some faulty notions I had fostered about children's choice of writing topics.

- *Two ten-minute literary occasions:* Neither of these was refined, they were just good ten-minute first drafts, one about a

Teachers Maintain Collections of Their Own Writing

woman in a plumbing supply house, the other about my penchant for predicting arrival times when driving to a destination.

- *A recommendation for a student:* Recommendations take an enormous amount of time. Since they require that I review the person's career and predict something of their future contributions, I struggle, refine, and struggle again to do justice to them in this very important document in their lives.

- *"Writing in which I learned something new":* The four poems I've listed in the first section I'd also list here. I worked very hard to put "things" into my poems. I took this from William Carlos Williams' dictum: "no ideas but in things."

I have placed them in my portfolio, even though they duplicate the first category, because I consciously worked to improve a particular skill.

I'd also include several chapters from this book. In fact, in virtually every chapter I've learned new things. Writing forces me to think beyond my last destination. I keep asking "why" of almost everything I do, and that pushes me into new territories, new topics, and new thinking.

- *Literature that is important to me as a person:* Right now I'm very much caught up in a husband and wife who write: Jane Kenyon and Donald Hall. I'll photocopy the poems I like and the cover of his book, *Life Work* and place them in my portfolio. They both struggle so honestly with life that they breed more honesty in me. To be honest in writing is a constant struggle.

  I also include letters from former students, as well as articles and FAXes from my closest friend, Donald Murray.

  And I keep a nature journal about animals (bears, moose, deer, and so on) and birds in our yard, sunrise, sunset, flowers and vegetables in season, battles with pests, weather. That journal probably represents more of my foibles than anything else.

If you have been writing with your students you will have many short pieces you can choose from to begin your portfolio. You may find that the category *"Literary experiences that are important to me as a person"* is the easiest place to start. Think of items that represent you as a person and put them in your portfolio. Remember, portfolios take many forms; they are designed to fit the uniqueness of the person putting one together. They may be as various as loose-leaf notebooks with large pockets, folders with pockets, or even small boxes.

ACTION 11.2:
Consider different starting points for the children's portfolios.

There are many approaches to introducing portfolios to children. I'll review some of them here so you can choose the one that best fits your circumstances or a combination that you sense will help your children get started. First, consider the ideas you want children to begin to understand as part of the portfolio process:

- Not everything in their collections is valuable in the same way. Items can be important for different reasons. Putting together a portfolio will help them have a sense of these differences.

- They can have a rough standard of excellence to apply to certain items they want to make better.

- Some items have value just because they have learned something in doing them.

- Portfolios are unique to the person; they will include items that are representative of that person in each category.

Children need to understand that a portfolio is a collection and that the contents of a collection can be regarded quite differently. I have a collection of six photos I will use with the children today. I'll show each of them, say a few words about them and encourage the children to ask questions:

1. A bear: This is a color photo of a large, black bear that came into my yard from the woods. He was looking for food.

2. My neighbor's house just after a great storm: I especially like the smooth lines of the snow after it fell. All rough edges are gone and everything is smooth.

3. An icicle with the mountain off in the distance. I like the way the beautiful icicle, though small, stands out against the big mountain off in the distance.

4. My granddaughter at a wedding. I especially like to take pictures of people in my family. I like the way she just looks into the camera.

5. My two-year-old daughter combing my nine-year-old son's hair. I liked the way I caught that one second when he thought she might be hurting him with the comb.

6. A seven-year-old boy looking directly into the camera. The boy has just been swimming and the towel is draped around

his shoulders and covers his whole body. There is something about this boy that shows that he has something on his mind. At this moment I think his thoughts are painful to him. Not everything I catch with my camera is beautiful. But, this photo is important to me because I caught the boy when he was deep in thought, and that's hard to do.

I say, "Okay, you can see these photos. Why don't you first tell me what you see here." (I want the children to talk about the meaning of what they see; what they see may contradict my observations or may affirm them. It is important to go through this process before asking questions.)

Notice that I make brief evaluative statements about each of the photos. I try to vary these statements, as well as what I say about each of them in a personal way. With older students I might include several additional comments in my review of the portfolio:

- what I intend to work on to improve my photography.
- how I view the collection as a whole—trends I see in the overall portfolio. (Notice that I only make statements about each one in isolation, but ultimately, I want to show the children how I regard the entire collection.)

Other Starting Points with Portfolios

There are other people who can help you demonstrate the portfolio idea to children. The art teacher in your building probably has a portfolio, or at least could make one up to show the children. One fifth-grade teacher invited the mother of one of her children to show the class her portfolio on interior decorating. She introduced each of her wares and described how she tried to meet her clients' wide-ranging interests. Through their questions, the children were able to elicit her personal history—how she began to work as a decorator, which elements she valued more than others, and what influenced her selection of materials. You may be fortunate enough to have a local author who can share her writing. If you are uncertain about which authors might live in your area, call the local library or ask the school librarian. When you reach the author, tell her you would like to invite her to share some of her work, to show the class how she regards each piece separately and in relation to the others. If possible, ask the author to tell some öf the process stories that underlie her composing. Then open the session to the children so they can remember, state what they saw, and ask questions.

Children's Collections

Ultimately, I want children to bring in their own collections. A collection can comprise anything a child has put together around a single topic: baseball cards, rocks, plants, dolls, Lego constructions, photos, trucks, stamps, or flies for fishing. If a child has not consciously kept anything, it isn't too difficult to help him select something of interest. The point is that each child has a collection of five or six items he values in some way. He is to think about each one and how he regards it. You will demonstrate by talking about your collection in order to show the children how to handle the "portfolio" interviews. I generally follow this rough order when individual students talk about their portfolios:

- Child comments a little on each piece stating what they value about it.
- Older children may discuss pieces in relation to each other.
- The small group responds by saying what they remember about what the child just shared.
- The small group states what struck them about the collection; then the group responds with questions.

Notice that this order is the same as that for responding to a child's piece of writing. First, the group works hard to remember *what* the author actually said. Second, they comment on the significance of what they remember. Last, they ask questions.

ACTION 11.3:

Make the transition from folders to portfolios.

If your children have kept folders, they will find the transition to portfolios a natural one. Toward the end of September, after a good month of writing, ask the children to take out five or six pieces of writing that interest them. "Maybe you just like it. Maybe it makes you laugh, you learned something by writing it, you worked especially hard on it, or you know it is the best you've done this year. Put them on your desk and read them over once or twice." You will need to gauge how many pieces your children can consider at any one time.

This next Action, from *Portfolio Portraits* (1992), is intended to help children look at their work from many different vantage points before making their actual selections.

ACTION 11.4:
Help students become more acquainted with their range of values.

Every piece has a particular value to it, but these values may be hidden. Our job is to help students become acquainted with their feelings about their work.

Ask the class or a small group of students to take out their writing folders and remove the contents, placing the pieces in an array on the table or desk in front of them. Give them four to six minutes to familiarize themselves with their collection. Young children may work best with no more than six to eight pieces at a time. Then ask the children to take out a pencil and be prepared to write single words at the top of each of their pages. (If they're reluctant to make notes on a finished copy, you can provide them with small pieces of paper about three by five inches, which they can clip to the top edge.) Then, give the group these instructions:

- Pick out a piece that you just like. Your gut feeling is, I just like that one. Maybe you know why, maybe you don't. Label it "like" at the top.

- Pick out one piece where you might have said to yourself "I think I'm getting the hang of this." Label it "Hang of it" at the top.

- Pick out one piece in which something surprised you during the writing—that is, what you had was new information. Before you wrote it, you didn't know this new thing; now you do. Label this one "Surprise" at the top.

At about this point several hands will go up. "I have two words on the same piece. Is that all right?" It certainly is. Some pieces will have as many as three or four labels on them. Students frequently choose those pieces for the portfolio.

Others may say, "I don't have any piece where I was surprised." That's all right, too. They don't have to use that label if nothing seems appropriate.

The directions continue:

- Pick out a piece that, when you were writing it you might have said something like this to yourself: "Oh, I'm the same old writer I've always been." You wanted the words to be better, the piece to be better, but you were aware that the piece resembled your old way of writing. Label this piece "History" at the top.

- Pick out a piece in which you felt you were learning something as a writer. That is, you were aware that some things were happening in your writing that you'd wanted to have there as a writer. Label this piece "Writer" at the top.

- Pick out a piece where you actually learned something about the event or information you were writing about. Maybe you gained an insight into a person, or you put together some facts, or you clarified a relationship. Label this piece "Learn about the subject" at the top.

- Find two places where, if you read the piece aloud to people who had their eyes closed, they would be able to see a picture. Put brackets around those lines and write "See picture" at the top.

- Find a piece whose first line you like. Label this piece "First line" at the top.

- Find a piece you'd just as soon forget you ever wrote. Write "Burn" at the top. Now write for three minutes about why you want to burn it. This writing is just for you; there's no need to share if you don't want to. Or write for three minutes about why you want to keep two pieces.

- Pick out a piece that you just wanted to keep writing even though you'd run out of time. Label it "Keep going" at the top.

- Pick out a piece where you'd like to go back and rework the lines. The piece had promise and you'd like to make the writing more precise. Label this piece "Promise" at the top.

Some of these labels may not be appropriate for very young children. You will sense which ones will apply to your class. Use what you feel is right for your students.

You will find this exercise useful at many different points in the year. As you teach children to read their own work through your writing, folder, and portfolio, their responses to each other, and their reading of trade books, you will add to this short list of ways to evaluate a piece of writing. Unless we show children how to look at their writing and express the values that writers use, the quality of their responses will change very little.

Responses to the Most Common Questions Teachers Ask About Portfolios

Questions about Children

A good share of my children seem to just toss off a quick answer about why they've selected something for their portfolio. What can I do to change this?
There are often several reasons for this problem. The first is that these children lack a language for talking about value and haven't had enough practice in looking at their writing in this way. The second is that they may not have a history of learning about themselves as writers. This means that you have to work hard to help them see what they were able to do in their earlier writing. They need to be able to articulate for themselves what they are able to do. When children are only able to point out their own deficits, then applying values is something to get out of the way as quickly as possible.

Would you describe students for whom portfolios seem to be a tough enterprise?
I think the best way to answer this one is to give some quick thumbnail sketches of the students. Of course, you get glimpses of this type of student in the answer I gave to the last question.

> *Good reader, poor writer:* Some students are better critics than they are writers. For them, their writing is never quite good enough to select for their portfolio. They are often critical of the work of oth-

ers. They are usually articulate and find writing to be a tedious, "useless" exercise. Their work is often unfinished. It takes a bit of work for the teacher to help this student realize that writing takes time. Focusing on the value of writing as communication sometimes helps. That means helping students to see some value, as well as strong points, in what little they have written.

Justification is a useless enterprise: "I already know why this is a good piece. Why do I have to tell you? It's my portfolio isn't it?" Again, this child has not yet seen the value of understanding why he has selected a piece for his portfolio. This child may not be too sure about what he considers good writing. When a child can report progress or understand what they have done well, then the reasons for making a particular selection take on different value. Once again, I need to mention how important it is to help children read their own work and see value in what they have done.

"I just don't like to read and write." This child would rather be doing other things. She has not yet connected another more important world, possibly outside of school, with literacy itself. Our job is to come to know the "other world" of the child in order to show her how reading and writing can help her enjoy her world more fully.

In my district we have to pick the pieces that go in the portfolio, and I have a hunch that isn't helping things all that much, is it?
If the portfolio doesn't belong to the student, you lose your leverage for expecting *more* of that student. Asking the student to justify his selections is meaningless because you are doing the selecting. I cannot stress enough how important it is for students to have practice in justifying why they have selected particular pieces for their portfolios. Admittedly, they don't always select what you would like, but in the long run, consistent practice in applying and expressing their values counts for more than your convenience.

I know of districts that specify precisely what ought to be included in a portfolio: an essay, a short story, a poem, and a personal narrative. I have no problem expecting students to experiment with a wide range of genres in a year's time. But if the uniqueness of students' offerings is blotted out by district-mandated uniformity, then the purpose of the portfolio has been severely compromised.

Questions about Teaching Practice

I'm already snowed under with too much to do. How on earth can I add portfolios to everything else?

You can't. Without question, teachers today are very busy, far busier than when I first began teaching. So much has been added to school curricula during a day already punctuated by constant interruptions. It seems that every time you turn around, there's a new evaluation scheme.

If portfolios are just an "add-on," they are bound to fail. Here are some of the kinds of shifts that need to occur in order to integrate them more smoothly into your classroom practices:

- Shift responsibility to students. Teach students how to read their own work, keep records, and maintain their portfolios in order.

- Stop doing all the record keeping. Move from "corrector" to guide, showing students how to handle the responsibilities you have given them. Not every piece a student writes is reviewed.

- Shift grading responsibilities. The student not only evaluates a piece but puts a grade on it and justifies the grade. Thus, whenever you look at a piece, you already know how the student regards it.

- Push for more uninterrupted time for reading and writing. Teachers who have access to students for only short periods tend to take more responsibility for students' work. It is more difficult to delegate when the student is out the door again so quickly. When students are immersed because time permits it, they use time more efficiently and we can expect more of them.

- If portfolios are used for evaluative purposes then other forms of evaluation have to recede into the background, especially those that are in conflict with portfolios. Something has to go.

What can I do to help parents understand what portfolios are all about?

Above all, involve the students. A number of teachers I know ask the students to come to a parent night with their portfolios about two months into keeping portfolios. The students explain what they've included in their portfolio, why these pieces were selected, and what they hope to do to be a better writer in the future. One first-grade teacher had children and parents meet in groups of three to talk over the portfolios together. In this way, parents learned about other children in the room as well as their own child. They took part in encouraging children to press on with their goals. Thus, each child had three adults and three other children encouraging them in their efforts.

What happens to the portfolio at the end of the year?
I used to suggest that children keep a certain number of pieces for central record keeping. In that way teachers and students could see how the student changed over the years. Now I'm not sure that happens or needs to happen. When students value their portfolios they keep them and bring them to school the following year on the first day of class. But some children need a fresh start. They need the feeling of starting over without impediments from the previous year.

Adults keep portfolios in a wide variety of ways. A good share of my colleagues want a historical sweep to their portfolios. They enjoy looking back over their lives by selecting various artifacts that have carried them ahead. I'm just the opposite. My portfolio reflects selections from over the last six months or so and not much more. I am more interested in the present, and so far, this approach has worked for me. And long live variety.

Won't my portfolio and my writing unduly affect what my students select from their own work?
Yes, at first students may choose topics and approaches related to yours and use the same criteria as they make their selections. They want to try out what you have demonstrated. This, however, is temporary. The more you show them what is unique in their own experience and ideas, the more they will move off on their own.

If you could choose essential elements or approaches that would ensure a strong portfolio program, what would they be?
Well, I begin with myself. I have to renew what it means to keep a portfolio constantly. So, I put in pieces, or artifacts, that I've written in class, letters, all different kinds of things to reflect my literacy. Of course, I'm showing myself even more than the children. I'm going through the process of saying what is important to me. Although I share my portfolio with the children, make no mistake, I'm keeping it

for myself. I need to do that as much as the children do. And I need to write short three- to four-sentence statements about why I've selected the pieces I've put in.

The next point is quite obvious but it is one that we always forget: unless children have blocks of time for reading and writing, they won't write anything significant enough to put in their portfolios. I've seen people try to introduce a portfolio program at schools where the children write for a total of sixty minutes a week. The children write so little, there is nothing to select from. Remember, the portfolio is an abstract of the folder. It contains pieces the children have selected from a larger body of work. The same is true of reading. Unless children read in school they won't read outside of school; they'll have few reflections about their books to consider for their portfolios.

The portfolio must belong *to the child*. Unless we structure the program so the child cares about reading and writing and what is in the portfolio, we can't expect as much. It's as if the child was simply working to please me. I remark, "You say this piece is done and belongs in your portfolio. Okay, what did you set out to do? And how do you think you have done? Show me where in the piece you have accomplished that." Of course, when the portfolio belongs to the children, it will express the very differences you have tried to foster in them. And that is as it should be.

The next point follows on the last one. Unless I show children how to read their own work and the work of other authors critically, the portfolio becomes just another collection of stuff. I must show children (often with my own portfolio and my own writing) how to read their work as writers read. If I fail to do this, I can't expect children to be responsible for the judgments they make about their own writing, or to set plausible goals for themselves.

Portfolios have a forward thrust to them. When children look back through their folders and make a selection, they make a statement about where they see themselves as learners. Portfolios preserve an important history and provide a rich sense of children's present conception of themselves as writers. When the children have the past and present in place in this way, they are ready for a more realistic sense of what they need to learn in order to better writers, readers, and thinkers; and of where they need to go next as learners.

III

TEACH THE FUNDAMENTALS OF WRITING

12 HELP CHILDREN LEARN CONVENTIONS

I'll admit that for much of my life, I've avoided what most educators refer to as "skills." I bear the scars of skills fanatics. In school, much of my writing was red-lined to death. No matter how hard I tried for accuracy, there was always someone who had a bigger book of "don'ts" and "should haves" than I did. Occasionally I'd get a comment or two about the quality of my ideas, but I can't recall a single instance in which a teacher pointed to the damage my poor conventions did to my information.

I have Frank Smith (1982) to thank for my new understanding of skills. He points out that every act of putting marks on a page is an act of convention. As I sit at my computer keyboarding these words, every letter that follows every other letter, the spaces in between groups of letters to indicate words, the capital letter at the beginning of each sentence, the period or stop to end an idea, the spaces between lines, all of these are acts of convention. Like sign posts, they help you, the reader, enter familiar ground so you can concentrate on the information without distraction. After all, that's what conventions are for. To help the thoughts in my head reach the page, I choose words and symbols that allow you to interpret what I mean and what you want to understand.

Of course, conventions help me, the writer, as well. When I use conventions, when I put commas and periods in their rightful places, I express a little more precisely what I mean. In fact, when a writer doesn't understand the meaning of what he writes, trying to use conventions to clarify meaning is a useless endeavor.

If we focus on conventions as aids to understanding what we mean and conveying that to our readers, then we set out on an alternative road to helping our students learn. Conventions now become useful tools. When a child has used a convention accurately, I'll say, "Ah, you know what I understand because you've got that period in just the right place?" Or, "I see you've got that capital on the city. How did you know how to do that?" Often children don't know, but I want to sow the seeds of understanding, the seed that makes the child ask, "How do I know how to do these things? What are these things for anyway?"

In the last few years I've begun to understand that the English language is marked off with commas and periods, semicolons and quotation marks, so both the reader and the writer can understand the meaning of the text. My perspective has changed. If I take the view that conventions are there to help me, and that each one offers an opportunity to better understand what I am trying to say, then I want them in my repertoire of tools for writing.

My approach to working with children has also changed. "Look what this can do for you," I say. "Maybe you want the writing to slow down or you want it to set off certain parts; then put in the commas." Or "You know how you like people to speak on your page. Well, here is a way to let yourself and other people know they are actually talking. Here are the quotation marks to signal that actual speech is taking place."

Children are already spotting conventions in the trade books they read. I want them to acquire a sense of the power of these tools gradually, from the time they first tentatively use a convention to the time when they can use it correctly and confidently. My basic approach I use is simple. I point out to them the conventions they are already using. Indeed, I ask them to apply a concept (pausing, stopping and so on) and then note every single convention they've actually used or suspect that they've used. Once they understand what conventions can do, I want them to aspire to add more to their repertoire. Underlying all of this work is the simple question, "All right, how does this help you to understand the writing?"

ACTION 12.1:

Conduct a small mini-lesson to show five children the conventions they already know or apply.

The purpose of the mini-lesson is to help children understand the meaning of conventions and begin a list of the ones they are already using. I usually conduct this mini-lesson with an entire class; then I'll move to work with a small group of children who I suspect have difficulty understanding the concept of conventions. For this mini-lesson, choose five children of mixed abilities and observe their understanding of conventions and how they have used them in their own work. The following transcript is an example of the kind of dialogue I have with the children:

> *Don:*   This morning we are going to talk about conventions. I have a
> page of my writing here to show you what I mean. I'd like you to

Teach Through Mini-Lessons

take out a page of writing. You are already using conventions, so we'll take a look at what some of these are. Some are simple and obvious, others are more complex.

All right, everything I do when I write is an act of convention. That is, things are done in a certain way, so the reader and I can understand what I'm trying to say. *[I'm holding my page up so the children can see now.]* One of the simplest conventions is how my letters and words go from left to right across the page. When I get to the right side of the paper and I still want to continue, I move to the left side of the next line below. In some languages, the letters or symbols start in the lower right hand side of the page and go straight up. That's a start; what are some other conventions that we use almost every time we write?

Child: How about I put spaces between my words?

Don: Sure, let's have another.

Child: Well, the words should really be spelled just one way. I don't always do that though.

Don: Right, sometimes I know a word isn't right and it really bothers me. I know what the word is when I write it, but someone else might not know. There are other marks I'll put in that are conventions like these. I know some of you are using them. See this capital at the beginning of this sentence? That shows where the sentence starts. Okay, I see lots of hands now.

Child: Then you put a period at the end. I've got one here but I don't know if it is right or not.

Don: Why do we need that convention?

Child: You have to separate things or it would all run together.

Don: *That's* right. The period is a stop mark. It means *Stop,* this is the end of this idea. Nancie Atwell, a teacher in Maine, told me about this next one. She read from another teacher, Alan Farrant in a magazine *[Teacher,* March 1977] something about the history of the period. Did you know that mark has been used for 2000 years, since the early Greeks? Instead of a dot they used a circle like this: "o." It meant the author had gone all around the subject and it was time to stop. But people got tired of making circles so they ended up just making dots. Have any of you used this? *[Many hands are up.]*

Let's have a few more now that you seem to have the idea. Quickly, and show in your piece where you've used it. If you can, say why you think it is needed.

Child: Got an apostrophe. Shows this belongs to someone—to John.

Child: Got a comma. I don't know why I've used it but I think it belongs here.

Child: Got someone talking and you use quotation marks.

Don: I think you have the idea. I want you to make a list of any conventions you think you've used on your page. List them on a sheet, put an asterisk * like this where you've used them, and attach it to the top of the page. If there are some you'd like to use and haven't, draw a line under your list and put them there below the line. When you finish, put the sheets in the "Completed Work" basket. If you want help from a friend, who will look your page over and see if there are any conventions you've used that you have forgotten, you can do that. We'll be spending this year adding to your list of conventions so that you and your readers can better understand what you are writing.

I'll be doing additional mini-lessons to help you learn new ones.

And, we'll also be looking in the books we read to see if we can spot what the authors are using when they write.

This Action overlaps with Action 10.4 on record keeping. When I review the children's papers I'll be looking for several things:

- their understanding of the concept of conventions
- the range of conventions they are using
- conventions they are using but overlooked
- the accuracy of their conventions

Take the Meaning Road

Yesterday I looked over the transcript of an address I gave at a conference here in New Hampshire. I prepare for an address by going over outline after outline, scrolling images in my mind's eye, even memorizing certain lines I want to deliver with precision. I deliver most of the address, however, without a prepared text. I do this to be able to concentrate on the audience; I feel it helps the audience to understand my ideas better, at least that is my rationalization. The transcript, however, is tough medicine. All the meaning markers I add with my voice (stress, pause, and intonation), hands, eye contact, and posture are lost to me when I read the transcript. People speak of writing as talk written down. My transcript is rude truth that it isn't.

Writers need a thorough knowledge of conventions. They need to put markers in to help the text flow like speech, so that readers feel that the writer is present and talking directly to them as they read. When the writer provides a clear text whose words are well chosen, whose meaning is precise, and whose use of conventions is consistent, the reader can focus on interpreting the meaning of the text.

Conventions aid meaning. Try reading the transcript of a conversation between two people without any conventions to guide you:

> I think you ought to lose some weight. No, I shouldn't. The trouble with you is you think losing weight is some kind of badge of salvation. Be thin and go to heaven. But you'll be subject to more physical ailments if you don't lose weight. It will be a strain on your heart. But you'll die ten years later than I will and your life will be so boring, all that tasteless, inane stuff going between your teeth will make those extra years as dull as cardboard. But that isn't the choice; dull living and dull food. I have exciting tastes. Prove it.

It is difficult to know who is speaking and when. To solve this problem, writers use new paragraphs every time there is a change in speakers:

> I think you ought to lose some weight.
>
> No, I shouldn't. The trouble with you is you think losing weight is some kind of badge of salvation. Be thin and go to heaven.
>
> But you'll be subject to more physical ailments if you don't lose weight. It will be a strain on your heart.
>
> But you'll die ten years later than I will and your life will be so boring, all that tasteless, inane stuff going between your teeth will make those extra years as dull as cardboard.
>
> But that isn't the choice; dull living and dull food. I have exciting tastes.
>
> Prove it.

The meaning is certainly enhanced once you can distinguish one speaker from another. The paragraph, used well, does more to help the meaning of the text for me, the writer and you, the reader, than quotation marks. Naturally, I'd like to know more about the people speaking; I'll learn more if I identify the speakers with details and use punctuation to separate the details from the actual words they speak. These additions are in italics:

> *Svelte Eve finally addressed her roommate, Sharon.* "I think you ought to lose some weight."
>
> *Sharon abruptly looked up from her reading.* "No, I shouldn't. The trouble with you is you think losing weight is some kind of badge of salvation. Be thin and go to heaven."

The determined lines on Eve's face shifted to concern. "But you'll be subject to more physical ailments if you don't lose weight. It will be a strain on your heart."

"You'll die ten years later than I will," *Sharon interrupted*, "and your life will be so boring, all that tasteless, inane stuff going between your teeth will make those extra years as dull as cardboard."

"But that isn't the choice," *Eve sighed*, "dull living and dull food. I have exciting tastes."

"Prove it," *said Sharon, slamming the book closed.*

As I look over the text I notice I have a comma separating roommate and Sharon. The name and the identity are helped by the comma. I have a person and who the person is. The comma clarifies the classification. The quotation marks are especially helpful when I want to separate the actions and the descriptors from the actual words in the conversation. Some might argue, "Well, why do you need quotation marks at the end of one person's speech when you shift to a new paragraph for the next person? You'd know the person had finished speaking." Good point. In fact the writer William Carlos Williams doesn't use quotation marks in his collection of short stories, *Farmers' Daughters*. My only response is, "When in doubt, ask the reader." Meaning and conventions are connected. Help yourself and the children in your classroom to begin to question how the meaning of a text is enhanced by the use of conventions. Sometimes you may have no clear answers, but you might find it interesting to speculate.

ACTION 12.2:
Use mini-lessons and keep track of them in a notebook.

Conventions are as much for us as for the children, especially if we try to understand their connection with communication. Pushing our understanding of how they work to enhance a text will clarify our writing. Lucy Calkins, Nancie Atwell, and Mary Ellen Giacobbe have come up with a number of formats to help children to include convention that lasts approximately ten minutes and occurs during most writing sessions. In each case teachers show how convention clarifies meaning.

Buy a notebook. Make it a supple, three-hole looseleaf type in which you can keep track of your mini-lessons with the entire class or with small groups. You can insert the material you use for demonstrations or the dated, written plans in your notebook. You can also record the names of the children who attended the small group mini-lessons.

Since you put time into planning the mini-lessons you ought to keep a record of them. Sometimes you can use them again; at least keep a detailed enough account to help you when you teach the convention at another time. Think of ways of classifying your mini-lessons for easy retrieval. I frequently make acetates to teach a skill on the overhead projector. (You can keep the acetate until you use it again.)

The notebook can also be a useful reference source for children to use. Although I like children to keep their own records of skills in their writing folders, the notebook can be used as another source for refreshing their memories about lessons they have had in the past.

Mini-lessons are short because they are usually about *one* convention. Children keep lists of conventions that are part of their repertoire; they also make plans about which conventions they wish to learn. I try to survey folders for the conventions children wish to learn and to note when I review their work which ones they need to work on.

ACTION 12.3:
Set the tone for conventions.

The first mini-lesson can be a demonstration with the entire class using the overhead projector. This session is similar to other demonstrations in which you compose with the children or talk aloud about the decisions you make during the composing process. In this Action emphasize the relationship between the meaning of the text and the conventions you use. The tone should be one of discovery, as I tried to demonstrate in the sequence about working with dialogue. *The conventions are there to serve us; they are tools to help us and the readers who will read our text understand what we are trying to say.* If the tone of the mini-lesson is one of preoccupation with accurate use of the convention in a first draft, it will not serve its purpose. The following text should demonstrate what I mean; one part is the written text, the other, my conversation with the class about the use of conventions in the written text.

First the written text:

Squirrels make me itch. Know why? Have you ever watched them? Take a good look and you'll see their tail, nose, legs, even their fur, all on the jump. That's when they're supposedly sitting still. When they move they scoot, jump, and leap. I have the feeling that something is chasing them, even though I don't see anything. When something is chasing them, that's when I really jump inside. They have a kind of crazy zigzag across the yard, a leap for a tree, and then a zoom up to a lower branch. It is like one of those police car chases I see on TV, cutting this way and that down alleys, around corners, stopping dead and then starting up again.

And my commentary, "Just this morning I looked out my window and watched a red squirrel under my bird feeder. Have you ever watched one? Try it. You'll see all parts of the squirrel moving at one time. To get the meaning I want, I'll show all the parts that are moving at one time. See, that will get the itch effect I want. *[I might ask the class what they've seen moving when a squirrel sits. If they have a list I'll use it.]*

"Then there's this sentence:

Take a good look and you'll see their tail, nose, legs, even their fur, all on the jump.

I wanted a list all in one sentence because that's the picture I want, a lot of things happening at one time. But I'm going to put these commas in there to make that sentence twitch a little; the commas will separate all those twitching things so we can keep them straight. Now let's read it with the commas in and see if you can feel the squirrel doing all those things at one time.

"I've also tried to capture the squirrel's rapid motion through another kind of phrase listing separated by commas.

"Notice:

- zigzag across the yard
- leap for a tree
- zoom up to a lower branch

or showing they are like police cars:

- cutting this way and that down alleys
- around corners
- stopping dead
- then starting up again

Can anyone think of an animal or something that has a lot of things happening at one time? Make a list and experiment with a sentence." (The serial comma could just as well be used in a list of things I possess or a series of places I've visited.)

The children may wish to take a piece of scrap paper and experiment while we are working. In fact, I find it useful for children to have scrap paper handy so they can doodle or practice conventional tools during the mini-lesson. The serial comma example about the squirrel didn't occur to me until I had written it. I simply asked, "What's going on here? How is this punctuation helping what I'd like to happen?" Start talking aloud or questioning your own punctuation and you'll discover a vast array of tools out there that can clarify what you are trying to say.

Examples of Other Conventions

The actual number of conventions and tools that might be useful in a mini-lesson is infinite. The ones that follow demonstrate a repertoire of tools that enhance meaning.

The Colon

The colon, like the comma, the period, and the semicolon, is a punctuation mark intended to stop the reader or to separate ideas into component parts. A few years ago I noticed that a young first grader had used a colon in her writing. She wrote, "There are many kinds of whales: humpback whales, blue whales, and sperm whales." I had never seen a first grader use a colon and wondered what she understood about its meaning. I pointed to the colon and asked, "What's that? What do you call it?"

"You know!" she responded indignantly. Her look said, another foolish question by a researcher. Sensing that she might not know the name, yet noting the accuracy of its placement, I then asked, "What's it for?"

"Oh, that means more to come," she mumbled diffidently, an answer that could have come from any textbook on punctuation. The colon, like the comma in a series, allows us to list information in a short space. Both the writer and the reader can benefit when a lot of information is available in a compact form.

Let me mention a quick example. When I go skiing I often forget things. If I get to where I'm going to ski and find that I have left something behind, I get very angry with myself. I should always check to be sure that I have these items: gloves, ski poles, skis, small pack, extra wax, hat, boots, and extra shirt. If I group all those items together after the colon, maybe it will help me remember everything next time.

The Period

The period is one of the most difficult forms of punctuation for children to add to their repertoire of conventions. They often have trouble understanding when one idea ends and the next one begins. Yet any number of textbooks and curriculum guides, in an attempt to be systematic, state that the period is the form of punctuation you should teach first. First graders, who usually compose one sentence to go with a picture they have drawn, seem to pick up the notion of a sentence naturally. But the minute they join two ideas end to end on the same page, periods go out the window. It is not unusual to find high school and college students who are still puzzling over how to mark off their ideas.

The sentence is a meaning unit containing the doer (subject) and the action (verb): "He crossed the room. He ran. She sews." These are the simple ones. When we have a more complex idea to express, things become more difficult: "I'd like to go downtown to pick up a book so that when the snow comes tonight I won't be stuck tomorrow for something to do." I could write, "I'd like to go downtown," and put the period after "downtown." That would be a sentence. What's left ("to pick up a book so that when the snow comes tonight I won't be stuck tomorrow for something to do") isn't a sentence, and that can be the hard part for children to understand.

That's where demonstrations come in, to show what goes together and how. As we look at the remaining half of the sentence above, I'll probably ask the class, "Anything missing here? Anything you want to know?" Some children, because they already know the first part of the sentence, find it difficult to understand that adding a period to the second part does not make it a sentence. It needs a verb to be a sentence. Again, of all the forms of punctuation, the period places the highest demands on both writer and reader. Young writers—and their teachers—need more patience in learning how to use the period as a sentence marker than they do in acquiring just about any other tool in the writer's repertoire.

The Comma

The wonderful part about commas and the other forms of punctuation that slow down ideas is the way they mark off the pictures in the mind, like frames in a film. Commas keep one meaning unit from interfering with the next. They help us to clarify imagery and maintain the logic of our thoughts in a good argument. They provide separate rooms in the house of meaning. Their position, laid end to end on a line, keeps things in just the right order so readers will not be too confused by a change in decor from one room to the next. Yet there are times (a moment of anguish or surprise, for example) when I want a grating change of scene—from the quiet of the drawing room to the bustle of the kitchen—and the comma, put in just the right place, helps me to signal readers that I am shifting their attention.

Commas keep things straight. They keep subordinate ideas in their places so that we can understand the main ideas they support. Ideas sometimes have "interrupters" that serve as asides to the reader. Here's an example:

> When Yassir Arafat, a leader of the Palestinians, extended his hand to Yitzhak Rabin, leader of the Israelis, I was filled with joy.

In this instance, I felt the need to explain who Arafat and Rabin are. There are many more reasons for using commas than I have mentioned here. I have simply tried to show how they function to order information so the reader can follow our line of thought.

ACTION 12.4:
Help children speculate about conventions.

Learning is embedded in the ability to hypothesize. Children need to practice predicting where conventions need to be placed in a text. In your mini-lesson on the overhead projector or the chalkboard, ask children to speculate with you about where certain conventions are needed. (The acetate you prepare for the overhead can become a permanent record of the lesson. It can also be copied and immediately mounted on the bulletin board as a reference for you and the children.) Ask them why they think the meaning of the text will be enhanced by their judgments.

In my demonstration I compose but leave out the conventions, and stop after I've written enough text to ask for comments:

> By the end of the baseball season there are so many players with injuries I hardly know who is in the lineup there is a mixture of players from the minor leagues and second rate players who have been on the bench all season I suppose they have to get a good look at the players of the future but I have a hard time getting interested in end of the year games my team the red sox seem to be in this position every September

Commentary follows:

Don: Yes?

Child: I think you should put something after lineup.

Don: Why would you put something there?

Child: I don't know. It just seems right, that's all.

Don: Sometimes wanting to put something in a place is just a hunch and that's where good experiments start. Anyone like to help out?

Child: I think it should go there because you started talking about something new like players from the minor leagues and second-rate players.

Don: Okay. So I started something new. How is the period going to help you, the reader?

Hypotheses begin as hunches—here, the gut feeling that something belongs without knowing why or whether it should be a period, a comma, or a question mark. But it begins with the idea that *something* ought to go there. Next comes the notion of how the convention helps the writer or reader, which helps children determine the appropriate mark.

This approach is designed to help children start thinking about *listening to their texts* so that they can assess which conventions they need and where. By being generally aware as they work through a draft, children learn how to be more precise during their final edit.

ACTION 12.5:

Share conventions.

This Action is a mini-lesson in which children share information about the different conventions they are using in their writing. As in other sharing sessions, we gather around, look over our writing, and talk about different conventions. This discussion can also be a five-minute segment of a regular sharing time. As the teacher, I also share my own writing. There are several ways I can do this:

1. Mention a convention, read a section of my writing in which the convention is used, and tell how the convention acts as an aid to meaning.
2. Mention a convention I have used but not why I used it. Ask the children for their thoughts about it.
3. Find the same convention as #1 in a trade book and state how the convention clarified the writer's meaning.
4. Point out marks and other conventions the children do not understand. "What's that? I've never seen it before. What's it for?"

Keep records of who participates. Put a list of conventions and who knows how to use each one on the bulletin board (or keep it in a bound folder). In this way children know which of their classmates to consult if they wish to find out about a particular convention. They should also have access to photocopies of past mini-lessons. These can be kept in a folder with a table of contents in the front so children can locate specific conventions more easily.

ACTION 12.6:

Introduce the convention game to the children.

About four years ago I developed a game that helped children become acquainted with conventions. I wanted them to learn conventions through their own writing as well as through the authors they were reading. What surprised me was how quickly children began to experiment with the conventions they had encountered in the game.

First, I grouped children in teams of three persons. (I like the groups to be as heterogenous as possible. This allows children to learn from each other within the context of the game.) Then I talk with the children both before and during the game:

Don: We are going to start a new game today; I call it the Convention Game. You'll be working in teams. You'll need to bring your writing folder and the book you are reading in order to play. So, move your desks or chairs together. You'll need to be close to each other in order to talk quickly.

[Now I'll make the teams of three people each and make them quickly. I deliberately structure the teams for their heterogeneity. I do this rapidly to avoid any impression of obvious deliberation about who should work together.]

This is the way the game is played. I will put a sentence up on the board that shows a particular convention and I'll underline it. That's the one I want you to find in your folder or book. Now I'll write this sentence:

There are many kinds of whales: blue whales, humpback whales, sperm whales, and right whales.

Notice that I've underlined this mark here, the colon. As soon as I underline the mark, your team can go to work. First, look in your writing folder, and if you can't find it there look in your books.

The minute one team member finds it he says, "I've got one." Immediately, the other team members turn and give it a look. Your next job is to talk over these important questions: "How does this convention help the meaning of the sentence? How does this help readers?" Take this group of boys here: Robbie, Mark, and Daryl. Maybe Robbie finds it in his book, but Daryl is able to come up with how it best helps the meaning of the sentence. Daryl's job is to teach the others. When *everyone* in the group thinks they know how it helps the meaning, all three put their hands up. Unless I see three hands I won't count that team as ready. *[This is often one of the points of adjustment in the game. Children are so used to individual knowing that the child who finds it and knows its use raises his hand ignoring the partners. Or two in the group will get it and not teach the third member who is having a hard time understanding what the other two have said. In this instance I say, "I see two hands up but by the look on Robbie's face he wants you two to do a better job of teaching him."]*

When I have three groups of three with their hands raised I stop this part of the game and call on a member of the team who got this convention first. "All right Robbie, what's the convention and how does it help us to understand this sentence better?" I can call on any member of a group to answer; I don't need to know who found the convention or who first understood its meaning.

All right, here's the first one for a trial run.

I can't decide whether I like pizza with pepperoni, mushrooms, or sausage.

Notice where I've underlined. Now see if you can find a structure like that.

All right we now have three groups with three hands up. I'll call on you, Janet, from your team. What is the convention and how does it help the meaning?

Janet: Well, it separates the different pizzas. It organizes the sentence better.

Don: Good thinking. *[I then call on a member of each of the other two groups before putting another example on the board.]*

If you find that you have the convention I've put on the board in your writing and it isn't on your list of conventions you have used, make a note of that and put it in the completed work basket over here and I'll check it out.

Don: Okay, from now on the credit is going to go this way. If your team finds the convention in your writing it counts for two points and in the book you are reading, one point.

I play the game for ten or fifteen minutes every eight to ten school days. The game heightens children's awareness of conventions. They often find conventions in their trade books, but they don't know what they are or how they help meaning. This is a good point of departure for teaching. You may find it helpful to take sentences from children's own writing to use in the Convention Game. The game moves more quickly if you have the sentences with underlined conventions written out on an acetate before the game begins.

ACTION 12.7:
Ask different children to interview.

Children should be more aware of which conventions are being used in the classroom—and by whom. Each week, one or two children could move around the room with their folders interviewing other children to see if they have experimented with any new conventions.

ACTION 12.8:
Use trade books to demonstrate conventions.

Trade books are an excellent resource for finding and discussing conventions. In this mini-lesson, I want children to notice how professional writers use conventions to enhance the meaning of their texts. I take a paragraph and make a copy of it on an acetate for the overhead projector. Then I ask the children to examine the paragraph for these elements:

- kinds of punctuation marks
- use of nouns and verbs, pronouns in relation to nouns, adverbs in relation to verbs
- how each convention clarifies the writer's meaning
- what might be misunderstood if the convention were not present
- how a convention may have been deliberately broken and how this did or didn't help (as in sentence fragment)
- the use of language, particularly strong verbs

This particular mini-lesson with trade books could also be used as backup for other lessons about conventions.

ACTION 12.9:
Work on scheduling mini-lessons.

First, consult the children. If they know you expect them to have plans for their writing, they will be more aware of which conventions they need to learn and which approaches to writing will help them. Refer back to Action 12.3 in this chapter ("Set the tone for conventions"), since children will be continually exposed to new tools they can use in their writing.

Mini-lessons are closely connected with Actions. Although the Actions in this chapter have been largely connected with conventions relating to punctuation, they can apply to just about any tool a writer uses. Here is a partial list:

leads
organization

ending
character development
revising
endings
choosing a topic
dialogue
proofing
issues of plausibility
use of verbs
use of adverbs
use of nouns
use of adjectives
sentence combining
planning fiction
use of capitals
letter writing
possessives
storytelling
poetry
argument

After consulting with the children on Friday, I take their folders home over the weekend and look through them for examples of conventions that are teachable and within what Vygotsky (1962) calls the child's "zone of proximal development." Some of the children will have needs that are broadly based, and a demonstration for the entire class will be fruitful. Others will benefit from mini-lessons with clusters of five to eight children.

As I schedule the mini-lessons for the week, I combine children's requests with my observations from the folders. On Monday, I post the schedule on the board. It lists the type of mini-lesson and the day of the demonstration. The mini-lesson in the small-group format is both voluntary and required. In this way, although some children are expected to attend, those who may have a current need for the convention can select it.

In the course of a month, I usually schedule a minimum of sixteen to twenty mini-lessons. Because a running record of each mini-lesson is posted on the board and a copy of the acetate is available in a folder, children can refer back to a particular mini-lesson when they need to. Some mini-lessons may be repeated in a month's time; others will recur about every three months.

In my mini-lesson notebook I keep a record of which children have attended the smaller sessions and which have demonstrated an ability to handle the convention under discussion. At the same time, I recognize that, although proficiency in a tool can be demonstrated, mastery of the tool is another story. When the topic is difficult and the need for information extensive, conventions suffer. And when an idea is not clear to the writer, the writer's language will often become confused, full of convoluted sentences and poor punctuation.

In a well-structured classroom, where children are expected to take responsibility for their learning and writing tools are constantly demonstrated, children will be able to help each other. I frequently refer children with problems to others in the room for help. Most of the time they already know who can help them.

ACTION 12.10:
Help children conduct mini-lessons.

Children should be able to assist in mini-lesson demonstrations. Select a child to work with you as you prepare the lesson. Then, as you go through the steps involved in teaching a mini-lesson, the child will become more proficient in offering advice to classmates through the informal classroom network. The basic steps I point out include the following:

1. Select one tool for demonstration.
2. Define what the tool is for and how it enhances the meaning of the text.
3. Show what you mean by composing and example or by selecting a sample passage from an earlier piece.
4. Involve the other children in the demonstration; let them apply the tool.

The child I select to teach the mini-lesson may have already demonstrated a knowledge of the tool or may be ready to learn it. Teaching the tool may lead to acquiring it.

Final Reflection

Conventions belong to all of us. In acquiring them we gain the power to say new things, extend our meaning, and discover new relationships between ideas. For too long teachers and editors have stood guard over conventions, as if they were esoteric knowledge available only to the few. Seldom did children see their teachers demonstrate how they used conventions where they belong—in writing—or ponder how to use a convention to say something more clearly or more effectively. Conventions are tools we, as teachers, want to give away. The more we give them away through mini-lesson demonstrations, the more children will regard them as a vital part of their writer's repertoire.

13 HELP CHILDREN TO READ THEIR OWN WORK

I remember passing papers in to Miss Thompson in seventh grade. (We never failed to call her *Miss* Thompson in those days.) I tried to write to turn her head and get kind words at the top of my paper. When I wrote I wondered if she'd like my writing. She wanted coherence, a word I stumbled to speak, much less comprehend, when she said, "Now I want a good coherent paper." She kept using the word, occasionally reading a paper that she considered had met this standard. I was fortunate. Miss Thompson usually liked my writing, but I had no idea whether I was being "coherent." Even when she commended me for coherence, I didn't know what I'd done other than to "luck out" on another assignment.

Coherence is important in a piece of writing, but the term is highly abstract unless teachers actually show children what they mean. Until Miss Thompson could show me what her word meant, I didn't know how to read my own piece to see if it was coherent.

I use this illustration to point out how important it is to show children how to read their own work. Children spend 95 percent of their time alone with their papers before we ever see them. Why not help them to improve as their own first readers?

I find that in my own work, except for a chapter in *Portfolio Portraits* (1992), I have done little to help teachers show children how to read their own writing. I have spoken of the importance of details but beyond that simple item I haven't really shown teachers or children how to begin to become more effective readers of their work.

In Chapters 3 and 4 I speak of the importance of "reading the world," the first and most important kind of reading. What I mean is that children—and writers of any age—need to be constantly mining the world around them for ideas and answers to their questions. You have experienced several Actions in which you have shown children how you read the world in order to write about it. I'll begin with the same mini-lesson on reading the world but show how I go on to read an actual text.

ACTION 13.1:

Conduct a short mini-lesson as a review of reading the world.

I'll start by showing my reading the world. Then I'll move on to additional mini-lessons on how to review a text in relation to my first reading.

Don: Let's see, I need to go back to yesterday morning when I went to the Registry of Motor Vehicles. You see I'd lost my driver's license while hiking last Saturday. I put the license in my pocket and somehow it had fallen out. That wasn't a very smart thing to do but I didn't want to drive around without it.

Have you ever lost anything and felt kind of funny when you did?

Yes?

Child: I lost my lunch money.

Don: How did it feel?

Child: Well, I hoped somebody would give me a piece of their lunch. I didn't really want to tell the teacher 'cuz she might tell my mother.

Don: Yes?

Child: I keep losing my gloves and hat. I go to school and it is cold and then I take them off when it warms up and I forget what I've done with them.

Don: How did you feel?

Child: Stupid. I just wish I'd stop doing that. My mom is really on me. When I remember it's too late to do anything about it.

Don: Then you know how I must have felt going into the registry. I felt like I was back in school forgetting my lunch money or something. Some things like that make you go back to feeling like a kid. Do you suddenly feel a lot younger than you are when you lose something? Yes?

Child: My mom says I ought to be an example to my younger brother. I hate that. Then I feel like I'm in first grade even though I'm in fifth.

Don: Like I said, I felt like a kid again. I went into the registry feeling embarrassed because I had lost my license. I stood in line waiting for someone to wait on me. I even hoped I'd be the only one when I got to the window so no one else would hear me speaking. When I got there the woman asked me to fill out a form, and I had to do that and then wait in line again. When she spoke, her tone implied, "Don't you know that's what you have to do first?" When I finally got to the window, she simply said, "That will be ten dollars. Take this stamped sheet to that line over there; they'll give you an eye test and then take your picture." When I got to the other line, the man asked me for two kinds of identification. I knew I'd need that ahead of time. He looked at my passport shot, looked at me again, and then took my picture. I suppose the driver's license is really important as far as establishing who you really are.

I'm going to stop here. What I'm curious about before I write is why I feel strange going in having lost something. People aren't supposed to lose things; I've known that since I was a kid like you, but it happens. So why should I feel strange? That's what I want to write about. It happens to people who are careful all the time. As a matter of fact, that was the first time I'd ever lost my driver's license.

When I write, I'm going to show myself first in that room at the Motor Vehicle place. I'll write very rapidly, changing nothing about the room and myself in it. So, I'll write it right here on the overhead for ten minutes. Here goes:

I stood in the waiting room of the Motor Vehicle Registration office. A woman in a line on my left said, "But I've already sent this in and nothing happened. Have you lost it?" She was really pushing herself to the person behind the counter.

I was in my line with two people in front of me because I'd lost my license while hiking in the woods. I'd been careless because I'd taken the license out of my wallet to travel lightly. I can still hear my mother's voice while I'm standing there, "Donald, you are a dreamer. Why don't you try living on this earth for a while?" I felt like answering her out loud. "Well, this is the first time I've ever lost my license."

Now I feel strange because I don't know the procedure for dealing with a lost license. I leave needing to return and start the same line all over

again. I'm in a foreign country where there are new laws and I don't
know the local customs. I fill out the form. There's always a form for
something like losing. Maybe filling out a form is my worst punishment.

Anyway I go back in line. I'm hoping that no one will be behind me when
the state woman speaks to me. She simply says in a routine, monotonous,
dull voice, "That will be ten dollars please." I'm so happy to pay just ten
dollars with no comment from the woman like, "You mean you lost it?
That's a very serious matter!"

"Take this paper and stand in line over there where it says License," *she*
says with a wave of her hand.

Within minutes I'm looking through a camera and asked to read line five.
I had no idea that my eyes needed to be checked again after only two
months when I got my lost license.

"Please give me some identification. You need two kinds," the woman
asks curtly.

Okay, that's the end of ten minutes. I want to show you how I'll
read this to help you to learn to read your writing.

I've written the above text on my computer, without editing, in ten
minutes. In the classroom, I'll write it on an acetate and then put the
plastic on the overhead projector for the children to read. I use different colored pens to mark off the various elements I'll want to focus on
for the mini-lesson.

ACTION 13.2:

Conduct a mini-lesson in which you show children how you decide the one
thing your piece is about.

Now I'll take the piece I've just composed and say to the children,
"What I've written can only be about one thing. I want to write in one
sentence what that one thing is." I do it on the spot:

Okay, I know the piece is about me. I'll start there. Also, I know I felt
embarrassed about losing my license. Let's see. I think it is more than that.
Maybe it's this. This is about how strange and embarrassed I felt as an
adult at the Motor Vehicle Registry. See, I think it wasn't just because I'd
lost my license. I was just plain lost in the new place. What do you think?

After I've struggled a bit, I ask the children what they think my piece
is about. Usually, if I don't have it on the overhead or the chalkboard,

I have to read it aloud again. I find that children and other adults are often better at seeing the one thing the piece is about than I am. What I think the piece is about based on my musings:

> *This piece is about how I went from feeling lost after losing my license to feeling strange at the Motor Vehicle Registry.*

If the children are older I'll ask one partner to choose a short piece, read to the other child, and then ask the other child to state in one line what the piece is about. You can vary it by having the writer speak first with help from the other person.

Depending on the age of your children, I suggest that you break the reading of your piece into a series of mini-lessons. One option is to cover all the mini-lessons in one session to help children get an overview of reading their work. I'd try this approach with older children. For younger children, however (say primary level), I'd introduce them to reading their work in my demonstrations by choosing one element for each session.

Writers struggle as they write to come to terms with the one thing, the one element, that governs the piece. Thus, when I confer with a first grader, I ask, "What's your piece about, Margaret?" At first, Margaret is unable to abstract the main idea and she tries to tell me the whole piece from start to finish. "No, I don't need to hear it all, Margaret," I respond, "just say quickly, just like that, what it's about." Usually children can say it quickly and more naturally select out the main action. Because focusing on one main idea is so important, children can practice it at many different points:

- When a child reads to a group, she says, "This is what my piece or book is about."

- After a child has shared her writing, the teacher may ask the group, "What is Margaret's piece about?" Then after the group responds, she turns to Margaret and asks, "What do you think about what we said?"

- During conferences with the teacher, the teacher asks, "What's this about, Margaret?" When I conduct conferences with children I expect them to state first what their piece is about without my asking.

- A child is reading a book, poem, or short selection, "What's your reading about, Mark?" the teacher asks.

Deciding what your piece is about is the most basic step in learning to read your own work. All further reading flows from this first decision. Sometimes I'll ask children, "When you first wrote this, what did you *want* your piece to be about? [this often hearkens back to their first reading of the world]. Okay, now how do you think that has changed or not changed?"

I cannot emphasize enough the difficulties associated with this important step. Some children select a topic that is emotionally laden or one that results in complicated forays into information they are only beginning to understand. For this reason, they may not know for some time what their piece is about. They may shift back and forth between one main idea and another, trying all the while to find a focus. Children need to know that this is a natural part of the writing process, especially when they take on challenging assignments. I find it helpful to confer with children in order to discuss their options. When the child remains confused I may ask, "And Angela, what do you *wish* this piece was about?" Sometimes the child is trying to write about an underlying wish. Sometimes.

ACTION 13.3:
Conduct a mini-lesson on how to show the subject of a piece in the text.

I hope that somewhere in my writing I have highlighted my main idea so the reader can see what my central concern is. This is a difficult concept to teach, yet it is one that writers try to practice with regularity. I'll turn back to the text and try to find such a place; if I don't find one I'll probably revise it to add:

> I stood in the waiting room of the Motor Vehicle Registration Office. A woman in a line on my left said, "But I've already sent this in and nothing happened. Have you lost it?"

I'm afraid this is the closest I've come. I tried to describe myself looking at others in the waiting room, but it doesn't do much to help a reader see that I'm setting the scene for what the piece is about. I'm not going to punish myself for not getting that in on a first draft; the important thing is to determine what the reader needs to know and then rewrite. I'll do that now to try to show more clearly what I'm writing about:

> I walked into the room wondering where I belonged. Three lines of people stood obediently in front of three women working behind a counter. In front of the women and above the counter were bars like you'd see in front of tellers at the bank. On the side of the room and on the walls posters declared new regulations about number plates and licenses. A small table on the side was filled with forms for various requests and requirements. The place smelled clean, clean with the same substance our school custodian used when he swept the floors. At the first barred window a woman with papers in her hand leaned into a conversation with the clerk behind the counter. "But I've already sent this in and nothing happened. Have you lost it?"

That was a quick attempt to describe the room, to let the reader see what my eye took in as I tried to understand what I was to do. I wanted the reader to feel my own sense of strangeness. Although this passage needs much more work, I feel better knowing I'm on the right track. It's as if I needed a camera to see how to proceed.

ACTION 13.4:

Look for a line that tells what the piece is about.

The "telling line" is much easier to identify, since it states what the piece is about quite simply and directly. Not all pieces have telling lines, but I will look to see if my piece has one. In most of my writing, however, I want to "show" rather than "tell." When I look at the last passage, I find the line immediately: "I walked into the room wondering where I belonged." I've realized that telling lines often come at the very beginning or the very end of a paragraph.

For this Action, have your students try to find a "telling line" in their writing. If they don't find one, they can try writing one, even though the line may not belong in the piece. They will find that the telling line is quite similar to the line they wrote stating what the piece is about.

ACTION 13.5:

Examine the nouns in your "showing" section.

"No ideas but in things," advises the poet William Carlos Williams. "What things are in the room that you can see?" I'll ask the children after I have read my revision to them a second time. They come up with the following:

lines
people
women
counter
bars
walls
posters
table
forms
papers

Other important nouns name things that are not actual objects in the room, as in the case of a smell (substance on the floor). I might also have put in a line about sound: the buzz of computers, the telephones, and low speaking voices. All of these contribute to "showing," but they are subservient to what the piece is about: a sense of strangeness and mild tension or fear because I've lost my license. Good nouns are often hard to find in young writers' pieces. They write with a good narrative sense but include very little that sets the tone or conveys the meaning of the action.

ACTION 13.6:

Conduct a mini-lesson on rereading a piece to see what verbs the writer has used.

Remember that the mini-lessons I list here as Actions can be spread out over a series of days, unless you wish to give students a quick overview of what is involved in rereading an early draft of a piece of writing all at once. Each of these elements requires a lot of work—indeed, a lifetime of work.

Writers write with strong verbs and nouns. By "strong" I mean vivid, well-chosen words that capture the movement of the action. I turn to the first draft of my text and glance at some of the verbs:

stood
sent
happened
have lost
was pushing
was
lost
hiking
had been
had taken
travel
can hear

I'm not too pleased with what I see. Verbs in a first draft usually need help and certainly my verbs are no exception. Until a writer discovers a subject and decides what interests him, the nouns will often be thin and colorless and the verbs lifeless and imprecise. Until I discover what my subject is and have some conviction about it, how can I have verbs that will walk across the page with force and energy? Actually, it would be better if I went to the verbs in my rewrite, where I have tried to show more clearly what I mean:

walked
wondering
stood
working
were
would see
declared
was filled
smelled
used
swept
leaned

I feel better about these verbs, and they are probably worth working on a second time. Rewriting will be a better use of my time at this point. I'll make a new list of the old verbs and the new verbs I'd consider:

- *Walked.* Actually *surveyed* would be more accurate. I want the reader to sense how I checked the room out before I did any walking. Working on verbs helps to line up the essential action of the piece.

- *Wondering.* I'll stay with this one.

- *Stood.* I'll stay with this one.

- *Working.* This is too general. My question is, "What were they actually doing while they were working. That needs a new line like: Three women shuffled and stamped papers, punched keys, and leaned into state business through barred windows over the counter. That's a little too much but I like the shift to these new verbs: *shuffled, stamped, punched,* and *leaned.* They also create a sense of activity in the room.

- *Were.* I've probably eliminated this one with the new sentence for "working."

- *Would see.* Eliminated with new sentence.

- *Declared.* I'll stay with this one.

This will give you some idea of how I work with verbs and nouns. Try this mini-lesson with students and enlist their help in choosing better words. It takes a great deal of work before children are ready to fine-tune their language. If children are still struggling with narrative sequence, with what the piece is about, they are too preoccupied to work on language. Still, there are students who ought to consider language at this point and learn how their choices can enhance a text. I conduct mini-lessons with those I feel are ready for this next step. Above all, I try to be sensitive to the ways professional writers use language in the books the children are reading and point them out. Consider including a session that looks at both the books the children are reading and their own pieces.

ACTION 13.7:
Find one or two lines you just like and try to say why you like them.

Up to this point the mini-lessons have been quite analytical. Shift gears now and simply say to the children, "I know you've done all kinds of rereading of your pieces but I'd like you to read them one more time. When you read, look for lines you just plain like. Maybe you know why, maybe you don't. At the very least you know you like some more than others."

Ask the children to read those lines aloud. If they can say why they like them—or even if they are unable—ask the class to comment on why they are struck by the lines. I'll take a look now at my "showing" passage and see if such a line catches my eye.

Way back in my first draft I wrote, "I'm in a foreign country where there are new laws and I don't know the local customs." I like it so much I know I'll use it in the final draft. In fact, it is a better telling line than the one I've already chosen for telling. Looking for good lines, especially in a first draft, is also important because the spontaneity and freedom of a first draft may have resulted in good lines that should not be easily rejected.

ACTION 13.8:
Reread the sentence that tells what the piece is about and then find the one or two sentences that have the least to do with the main purpose.

This Action requires more skill. Learning to delete or even to perceive that some information, words, or sentences are not needed is difficult. It takes a mature writer to realize that some of the information they've included is unnecessary. For the longest time writers, young and old, carry the mistaken belief that a piece is good if it is long. Although this mini-lesson will be far above the heads of most of your young and inexperienced writers, I want them to know that this important step exists. Of course, children can tell other writers what they need least better than the writer herself.

As a topic advances and the purpose becomes more clear, the writer should at least be able to say which information is less important after deciding what is most important. For many this is an important first step in considering what information can be deleted or moved somewhere else.

Consider this experiment with a strong writer. Ask her to read her piece to the class or a small group. The task for the group will be to first receive the piece, then state in one line what they think it is about. When the group has finished ask the author to state (in one line) what she thinks the piece is about or what she *wishes* the piece would be about.

Reading Writing Across Genres

This chapter has focused on helping children read their own writing while emphasizing those skills that will be applicable to many kinds of writing. Basically, the rereading I've described is directly applicable to narrative, the essay, even to poetry.

I think it's important to review some of the common elements I consider when rereading work in almost any genre:

- The piece can only be about one thing.

- The writing is highly personal. The piece reflects the writer's view of the world in relation to the views held by others.

- Good writing shows the subject under discussion to both the author and reader. Good showing is good teaching. Precise nouns and verbs teach. Good showing and teaching are usually more persuasive than telling.

- The author is usually on the side of the reader and invites the reader to join her in an expedition on learning.

Children are also inspired by the writers they read. I find it useful to explore how professional writers write in the genres the children are working in. You may wish to look ahead at Chapters 18 to 20 to review reading specific to these genres. Another resource your students may enjoy is *First Words* (1993), edited by Paul Mandelbaum. This book includes the early writing (when they were in school) of such authors as Amy Tan, Pat Conroy, Michael Crichton, Susan Minot, Gore Vidal, and Stephen King.

Final Reflection

Children are seldom shown how to read their work using actual texts. Rather, they are cajoled into "writing better" without knowing how good writing unfolds or how a writer thinks. Worse, they aren't made aware of strong writing within their own text. Even in my poorest piece I need to know the best section, the strongest line, or the best use of language.

Children are our most important evaluators. If they are allowed to choose their topics, write about what they know, and share their passions with us, we must show them how to reread their work. Having a topic but not the skills to read your own work produces an enormous vacuum. Indeed, choice without help is an invitation to anarchy. In my own work, I have been negligent in showing children how to gain some manner of meaningful independence in their writing. When a child can say with some degree of specificity, "This is good because . . ." then we know that child is becoming a better reader and a more independent writer.

14 HELP CHILDREN TO REVISE THEIR WORK

"How do I get children to revise? They don't want to go back and look over their work; once a piece is done, it's done." These are some of the most common words I hear from teachers in a workshop. I feel I'm to blame for their predicament. But first, a little history.

When we began our work on children's writing in 1978, we were surprised to find that children were revising their writing. Some of their changes were simple and spontaneous, but others, under teacher direction, were complex. Yet everyone had assumed that children weren't supposed to be able to revise; our data surprised the field. Suddenly, large numbers of teachers wanted their children to revise. Children's revision would be a signal of their success.

Through articles, books, and videotapes, we encouraged teachers to help their children revise. In my first book, *Writing: Teachers and Children at Work,* I wrote many pages extolling the virtues of revision. Yes, I said, children can revise. Indeed, there are many situations in which children can review their work and make changes in their texts. Although data in our early work shed some light on the conditions for sound revision, much more research was required in order to know how best to help both teachers and children.

To revise is to "resee," to look at a work, a page, or a text again. It requires reflection and some sense of other possible options. If the writer's rereading is sophisticated enough to recognize a gap between his intentions and what he sees on the page, he will want to rework his text. To some degree, a child's decision to revise on her own is developmental. It depends on the child's ability to read the world and express her perceptions and understanding in her writing. Even more, it depends on the teacher's demonstration for her students of her own reflective stance so that they will look at the world in a new way.

Indirect Elements That Encourage Revision

Children don't suddenly begin to revise during writing time. They need guidance. "Let's take another look at that," the teacher says. "What did you have in mind? What might be a better way to say that?" She asks questions like this because she genuinely wishes to find out what the children think.

If classrooms are constantly busy, if the teacher changes plans and activities every twenty minutes, children will hardly learn to reflect on their writing. Instead, their general unstated question will be, "Well, what does she want?" But in trying to meet another person's expectations, children learn to reflect on that person's thinking rather than their own. The teacher who wishes the child to rethink his work wants above all for the child to begin to trust his own thinking and to see himself as someone who can solve problems on his own.

Time
Teachers need time to rethink the way they use time if they wish to have a reflective writing classroom. This means that children need to write at least *four* days out of five. When there are several daylong spaces between one class and the next, children lose touch with their thinking. This is especially true for very young children, but clearly, it affects older children as well. When children miss a day of writing, they spend the next writing day reorienting themselves to the text and their original intentions. They sometimes lose interest and wish to start a new piece, since they find it easier to start a new piece than to revisit an old one that has grown stale with time. If you wish to take a more comprehensive look at rethinking your use of time, see Graves (1991, 11–33).

Revisit Your Writing

Following the dictum "Reflect on your writing and revise it" doesn't guarantee a magical cure. As historians of their learning, we need to help children to know how they think and become acquainted with the kinds of thinking that work for them. We say, "Please take out four pieces of writing so we can get a feel for how things are going with you. All right, let's see what's going on here."

ACTION 14.1:

Interview a child in order to help her have a sense of her own recent writing history.

Ask the child to reread four pieces she has recently written and then explore the following questions in an interview. Your objective is to help children understand what is working for them in terms of their intentions for the piece.

- *Which one of these pieces do you feel best about? All right, what is it about?* (Listen carefully to the voice of the author. At what points do you hear emotion, something the child likes or delights in?) *Confirm for the child what you've noticed:* "Just as you spoke I noticed that when you told about the way the snake wound his way up the tree, your voice went up with excitement." Obviously, some children give more clues in the way they read and speak than others. Some speak in a monotone and display little emotion. With these children, look to see what delights you, what interests you in what they have done.

- Show me some parts in it that you like. Read aloud a sentence that you like and tell me about it.

- *Tell me about one of these pieces that may not have turned out as you'd hoped.* Include these elements in chatting about the piece.
  - how they happened to choose to write about the topic
  - the spot where it started to go sour
  - what they think they need to do to straighten it out

- who they thought might read the piece while they were writing (writers often choose an audience during writing and then grow disillusioned when they decide their intended audience won't like the piece)

I like to help children see what is going right in their work and what may not have gone as well. If a child chooses a piece of writing she has abandoned, it is possible to clarify how she regards work like this. To understand a child's learning history, it is important to see what works and what doesn't.

Listen to Your Writing

Children who are able to listen to themselves more often become effective, reflective learners. Thus, the listening conditions in the class-room are important. This means that children must first be able to listen to each other. In our research we have found that children first externalize their listening ability—that is, they concentrate on what others say before going "underground" to listen to themselves.

I want to distinguish between the egocentric learner, who can only hear her own voice, and thus disregards her audience, and the reflective learner, who can listen to the voices of others and keep them in mind when listening to her own. The reflective learner is able to shift back and forth between one point of view and another while still retaining his own. In this regard, teachers are often the ones who first show children how to focus on what others are saying: "Let me see if I have this right. What you said was that the snake sort of rose up on its tail, then started winding through the branches. Pretty soon it got higher and you could hardly tell the snake from the branches. Is that what you said? Did I get that right?"

When children share their work with each other in class, we ask them to listen carefully. They work hard to remember what the writer has read aloud. Once the writer is satisfied that they have heard her piece, the children may ask questions. If you wish to work on listening more systematically, see Graves (1990, 83–105).

Classroom Arrangement

Finally, the classroom is set up to enable children to help each other, so that when they need readers or listeners they can easily consult with each other. A child says, "Listen to this; tell me what you think of it." In this way they gradually gain sophistication in helping each other to look at their writing from different points of view.

Direct Elements That Encourage Revision

The elements I've mentioned thus far indirectly influence children's revision. They are related to the conditions a teacher sets up for the writing program in her classroom. There are more direct influences, however, that help children to revise. Some the teacher can control; others are due to the child's development as a writer.

I find that children who have a sense of their options from the time they consider a topic to the time they complete a piece of writing are ready to revise. These children also demonstrate these behaviors in other subjects and in their general functioning in the classroom throughout the day.

Geoff

Geoff is in second grade and enjoys writing. He particularly enjoys fiction and composes pieces about interplanetary wars in which "good guys beat bad guys," a classic theme used by many early elementary school boys. When Geoff decides to write, he does not entertain other topic options; he knows he will write about space. Many of his friends compose pieces in the same genre. Each space piece will have some small twist that distinguishes its plot from the other pieces he has written: a new weapon, a different space ship, another planet. The characters seldom have names and exist simply to carry out a predesigned plot. Drawings dominate the text and usually require far more detail and time than the writing. The words are usually tacked on at the end. Get close to Geoff in the midst of composing and you will hear sounds of warfare as he draws. (The sounds, the drawing, and the look on his face are the same when he plays with his planes, guns, and trucks.) When Geoff draws or writes he does not go back to change things unless he needs another explosion to emphasize the war. And when he completes a piece, he quickly puts it in his folder and begins another.

If I ask Geoff what he will write or draw next, he can usually explain both his next piece and the one to follow. He knows where each piece is going and displays little sense of alternatives: the events are set, and the crayon or pen merely record his preexisting notions of what is to occur. Last year, when Geoff was in first grade, he may have known the next thing he would write about, but little after that. Geoff draws and writes, makes few changes in his work, and has practically no sense of any other options. His behaviors are very similar to those he demonstrates in play; indeed, the drawing and writing are play. He composes only in drive; reverse (and revision) does not exist.

Stacy

Stacy, a third-grader, displays the sense of option that Geoff may demonstrate some day. Today she ponders what she will write about. Will it be a piece about her kitten or a new episode about the baby-sitters club? She'd like to write about her new kitten, but two other girls want her to continue with another episode. All three girls are reading the *Baby Sitters Club* series and writing their own versions. "I'm going to do my kitten today," she tells her friends. "Maybe I can do a "Sitter" piece another day."

Stacy sits tapping the top of the table with a pencil. She wonders about how to begin her kitten piece. "I think I'll start with how she plays with my toes in the morning," she says quietly to herself. Stacy composes the first few sentences quite rapidly:

> I wake up in the morning and the first thing I feel is my kitten biting my toes. She is a cute little thing. So I kick my foot and she bounces after it.

She pauses for a moment, rereads what she has composed, and says, "Hmmm, what's next?"

"What did you have in mind?" I ask Stacy.

"Well, I'm not sure if I'll do the part about how she keeps on playing when I try to put my socks on or if I'll show her asleep. See, what really happens is she cuddles up against me and then as soon as I wake up and move my foot she goes after it. This isn't really what happens. I probably ought to start with that first, then put this part on."

Stacy is struggling with the meaning of natural order. As she explains what she'll write next, she also realizes that even her first part isn't the way she wants it. She fully recognizes that problems present options: "Do I go back and start again or move ahead to how the kitten plays with my toes when I put my socks on?" Stacy writes more rapidly than Geoff; changing or rewriting doesn't present the motor problems for her that it might for Geoff. Nevertheless, there are issues beyond handling a pencil that would stymie Geoff. His fiction doesn't create *intelligent unrest* in a text; the words are secondary to the drawing. But Stacy ponders, writes, and rereads. Each of these acts is evidence of reflection and offers a stronger probability that she will revise at a later time.

ACTION 14.2:

Interview children to see if they have a sense of their options.

Choose three or four different children to interview. You will want to find out how different children manifest their sense that they have options. Here are some examples at various points in the writing process:

- *Is just beginning:* "I see you have just started a new piece, Derek. Tell me what will happen next." I listen carefully. "Well, I think it's going to be about my hike, but I may write more about my friend." With very young children the answers are usually direct and simple. "It's about my hike. We're going to get lost."

- *Is in the middle of composing:* "I see that you are well along in this piece, Derek. What's going to happen next?" "I don't really know. I'm stuck."

- *Is faced with a problem:* "What do you do when you are stuck? Tell me some things you can do to get out of this fix." "I could talk to a friend, or I could do some more drawing."

- *Has completed the piece:* "Now that you have finished, what do you plan on doing with it?" "I'd like to read it during share time. And I want to show it to my mother."

Of course, there are many other places in the process where a child might entertain a sense of various possibilities. Although these are more mechanical aspects of writing, I am still interested in the child's sense of option:

- how to go about spelling a word
- where to place conventions
- whether to publish or share a piece
- (looking back) what topics were considered at the time of first writing
- who can be helpful on particular problems
- where to get tools that can be helpful in composing: pencils, crayons, stapler, staple removers, paper

The notion of revision in its broadest sense is connected to a way of thinking about problem solving. When children know what options they can exercise when they run into writing problems, they are developing good habits for learning. Where children explore their options is closely connected to the types of experiences they have had with composing. "What do good writers need to be able to do in order to write well?" When you ask this question, you may find that children focus on their struggle of the moment, whether mechanics (spelling, letter formation), topic, or content.

Much depends on the richness of the child's learning history. When children become aware of how they have composed and solved problems in the past, they are more able to approach new problems in the future. Just involving children in this Action contributes to their sense of their history as a learner. Of course, I try to play the role of learning historian: "Ah, I see that you have several ways to solve that, Derek. You could go to a friend, or you could do some drawing."

A Rough Developmental Sequence to Children's Revision

Since our initial research into children's composing, we've discovered a rough developmental sequence to how children begin to show changes in their work. (Teachers in these classrooms usually demonstrate revision with their own work and create a climate for rethinking completed writing.)

- *Add on at the end:* When children first recognize that they have additional information they want in their text, they add it to the end. They are often unaware that they can insert the new information into the text in its natural order.

232

- *Discover temporal understanding:* When I listen to a child speak about his piece in a conference, I may be able to identify the importance of a particular item or event because of the emotion in the child's voice. I then say something like this: "Karen, when you were speaking about the sleepover at Carol's, you seemed especially interested in her computer. Did I get that right? All right, when did that occur? Oh, just after you got there. Would you please read your piece over? I'm curious. If you were to put that in your piece, put your finger on the place where it actually happened. Find where it would go in your piece." In my first contact with a child about revision I am only interested in whether the child knows where the new information goes. I do not ask the child to deal with a large amount of information. It is enough to start with just a small chunk.

- *Make a first insertion:* Once I notice that a child understands where the information can be inserted, I'll ask her to write out the sentence(s) on a separate piece of paper. She can then star (*) the place where the sentence would be inserted. Until the draft reaches final form, the paper with the star on it can be attached to the page. There is no need to copy the piece over at this point; indeed, the piece may not reach final form. Still, the child will end up knowing how to insert important material. Children will be adding information, filling out their pieces for a long time before moving to the next level of learning how to focus.

- *Find the main idea:* Think back to "The Wedding" in Chapter 5, where the child wrote the longest selection of all. This piece, as I mentioned there, is commonly referred to as "the bed to bed" type—the child gets out of bed, goes to the wedding, comes home to eat supper, and goes to bed at the end of the day. The actual wedding, the subject of the selection, is embedded somewhere in the middle of the piece.

  Children are able to cite the main idea of their piece long before they are able to apply the concept of focusing on the one thing it may be about. I ask the child, "This is about the wedding, right? If this is about the wedding, why do I need to have all this material about leaving the house?"

"Because you wouldn't know how I got there," the child responds. Until I can heighten the importance of the wedding, the child will have a hard time deleting extraneous material.

- *Regard information as flexible:* For the longest time children (and even some adults) write with the notion that words are "right" the first time they go down on the page. For them, it is enough of a miracle to write down a recognizable word on the page in which the letters are formed correctly and spelled fully. They make some changes, but these are the erasable type (they make a few short rubs and the job is done). The first indication that the child sees the words as temporary or flexible is when she lines out rather than rubs out. The lining out says, "I shall return to this matter later on. I sense something needs work but I don't want to lose the flow of ideas." I try to demonstrate the temporary nature of words when I write with the children.

Mechanical Revisions

The revisions I have mentioned to this point deal with adding, changing, and shifting information. The more common type of revision is the mechanical change, or "repair." These revisions are more like manicures in which the idea unit is at the word or line level. The child rereads and makes a few changes in misspelled words or adds needed capitalization or punctuation. Clean, correct copy is certainly desirable but it doesn't necessarily involve the student in a struggle to tell the truth about her subject. I am suspicious about programs that emphasize correctness above the struggle to say something truthful.

ACTION 14.3:
Confer with several children to find out about their readiness for revision.

Choose children whose ability differs widely. Then follow these procedures as best you can:

- Chat with a child about his piece. "What's this about? Tell me some more about it."
- Listen carefully for something the child mentions that may not be in the piece.
- Respond by saying, "Did I get this right, that you said this?" If it seems right, say, "Just the way you said it, it seemed important to you."
- Say, "You don't have to write this but would you show me where this would go in your piece? Read it over and put your finger on the place."
- Follow up on adding information. If the child indicates an appropriate location, ask, "How did you know to put this here?" Then ask, "How would you go about putting this in without having to copy the whole piece over?"
- Ask, "Do you think you are ready to put this material in? Would you be able to do it on your own?" If the child wishes to put it in but doesn't know how, show her how to write it on a separate piece of paper, star (*) it, and insert it later on.

Experiment further through both observation and your questions to find out more about your children's readiness to revise.

When Revision Is and Isn't Appropriate

Most of what children write shouldn't be revised. If children are writing extensively each day and throughout the day, most of their writing is only first draft material. They should be writing in such quantity that you can't possibly respond to a good share of it. On the other hand, amid such volume they ought to be selecting some that are important enough to them to take to final copy.

I seldom encourage very young children (kindergarten, first grade) to revise. I want them to write extensively and to experience the flow of writing. They may occasionally add information and work to improve certain skills, but they ought to concentrate on only one skill at a time when they write.

Children, however, do get a response to their writing even though they may not revise. After going over what I understand in a piece, I shift to the problems: "I'm having trouble understanding what is happening here. Will you please explain what is going on?" Very young children handle revisions by learning in one piece what to apply in the next rather than going back and changing the first.

When Revision Is Difficult

There are many reasons why revision is difficult for some children. It depends on the circumstances and the child involved. Here are some signs to watch for:

- *Lack of knowledge about the subject:* If children are uninformed about their topic and unable to discuss content, they need to remedy the situation by finding out about their topic before they can consider revision.

- *Lack of understanding about the uniqueness of writing:* Writing is intended to transcend the writer in space and time. Unless children realize they may refer to this piece at another place and time, or understand that they will not be present when another person reads it, revision will not make much sense. Young children often believe they will be available to supply the extra information their readers may need. If your students have this problem, set up projects that involve writing letters or sending a written piece to another class. (See Graves 1991, Chapter 4.)

- *Lack of audience sense:* "Why do I have to do anything with this? I know what it means." In this instance the writer doesn't necessarily care if the audience understands; she is merely writing for herself. Or the situation could be one in which the author is sure readers will understand what he means. It takes a great deal of practice before the writer can shift her point of view and play the part of reader of her own text. This is one reason why teachers have children share their own writing with a variety of audiences and act as audience for others. The teacher deliberately has children shift back and forth between the two roles of writer and reader.

- *Motor problems:* Some children, particularly boys, do not wish to rework a piece because the task is long and tedious. If this is a problem, I try to reduce the amount of writing that needs to be inserted. Using the computer is a great help to children with this problem. I find, however, that when children are genuinely interested in what they are writing (and write daily) problems in fine motor control are greatly reduced.

- *Lack of time to write:* When days pass (even only two or three) between one writing session and another, children lose interest in a piece. Picking up the lost trail of an old idea can be a frustrating experience.

- *Writes too much:* How easy it is for children to lose control of a piece when it gets too long. This is particularly true in fiction writing. Some children, particularly girls, get caught up in a plot, lose sight of their characters, and simply don't know what to do to help themselves. They wish to abandon the piece and start another. Workshops on character early in the process can help them gain control of their writing.

- *Is unfamiliar with the genre:* When children are not used to writing reports, poetry, or fiction, they do not know how to reread their work and revision is difficult for them. Workshops on these specific genres can begin to remedy this problem.

If you find that a child is confronting any combination of the above problems, revision may not be appropriate at this moment. What is paramount are the child's interest in and information about the topic.

You may notice that for very young children, particularly those in kindergarten and the first three grades, writing is play. It involves reenacting events gone by, or reliving favorite television programs, or telling stories about specific toys they use in play. You hear sound effects and discover them lost in the act of writing. For young children, play usually involves transformation: "Now this truck here will be an army truck; we'll call it an army truck." "Play writing" is preparation for revision. It allows children freedom to explore, to practice sound/symbol correspondences, and to experiment with words. Of course, we hope this *sense* of play will last a lifetime and encourage flexibility in thinking as in writing. This sense of possibility results from the teacher's demonstrations and workshops as well as children's growing sense of what an audience needs.

ACTION 14.4:

Reread the section on the difficulties children have in revising and look through your class roster. List the names of children in your class that have trouble revising. Choose two and plan what you need to do to show them how to make revision part of their writing repertoire.

Abandoning a Piece of Writing

There are times when children ought to abandon pieces they've started. Our research shows that children are quite articulate when they explain why they want to abandon a piece. For most of my teaching life I've insisted that children finish each piece, because I worried that abandoning one would trigger a mass of uncompleted writing. But obviously, any writer will sometimes choose poor topics, especially very young writers. For this reason, teachers need to demonstrate in their own writing when they've made a poor choice, explain why, and then put the piece in their folder as a learning experience. I also tell students that it might not have been the right time for me to write that particular piece. When children feel they have made a poor topic choice, they can ask for a conference or chat with another child, to whom they explain why continuing would not be beneficial.

ACTION 14.5:

Look through children's folders until you find some incomplete pieces and ask the children why they have not worked on these pieces recently.

At this point it is hard to know whether a child has simply lost interest in a piece or has actually abandoned it. When you carry out this Action it will be important to maintain an inquiring, nonjudgmental tone. You want children to feel free to talk about their pieces with objectivity, even those that no longer interest them.

Final Reflection

We want to help children learn how to reread or "resee" their work. Above all, we want them to have a growing sense of the options available to them during composing. We need to show them, through our own writing, just what kinds of options are open to them as writers. What we demonstrate is not so much how to revise as a certain stance toward the world, a sense of our intentions, and how we listen to ourselves when we write.

Only a small percentage of what children write will end up on the revision table. Most of it is simply flow—getting ideas down and learning how to keep in touch with their own thinking. Very young children usually apply their notion of revision only when they start a new piece. If a child finds a better way to begin or end a piece, for example, it will be easier to try out in the new piece than in the one at hand. None of these approaches works, however, unless children write every day.

We need to be more acquainted with the conditions that foster sound revision. At the head of the list is the child's real knowledge of the topic. How hard it is to revise when the content is unfamiliar. A sense of audience is another major factor that contributes to effective revision. Until children can begin to step outside themselves, take other points of view, and become effective first readers of their texts, they will find revision irrelevant.

Most of the focus in revision concerns the addition and deletion of information. In most traditional writing instruction, teachers have focused only on mechanics, the conventions of the craft, at the expense of what the writer is trying to communicate. They have required young writers to tinker with minor details in lieu of breathing new life into the piece. Make no mistake, conventions are important, and if they are poorly applied, both writer and reader are ill served. But if teachers focused first on the children's intentions, then these young writers would connect more easily with themselves and be energized to continue writing.

15 HOW TO KEEP HANDWRITING IN PERSPECTIVE

"Handwriting is for writing. Children win prizes for fine script, parents and teachers nod approval for a crisp, well-crafted page, a good impression is made on the job application blank . . . all important elements, but they pale next to the *substance* they carry. The contents of international agreements to free hostages, the Declaration of Independence, a love note, a personal diary, all take precedence over the script. Handwriting is the vehicle carrying information on its way to a destination. If it is illegible the journey may not be completed. Handwriting, like skin, shows the outside of the person. But beneath the skin beats the living organism, the life's blood, the ideas, the information" (Graves 1983).

I wrote the preceding paragraph in the early days of writing process research, and my basic philosophy has not changed. Although meaning is still my central focus, I have seen it emphasized to the exclusion of good handwriting. Just because meaning is more important does not mean that handwriting should be neglected altogether, which is all too often the case. In a time of ever-decreasing amounts of teaching time, handwriting has been too quickly relegated to the shelf. Yet I believe it is possible, through sound observation and intervention in context, to give adequate attention to handwriting. When children first put pencil to paper, they begin the journey from the highly self-conscious act of shaping letters to the point when writing words and sentences becomes automatic. Once the mechanics of writing are under control, children can devote their attention to information, to the sentence under construction, to the verbal details of their letter, poem, or story.

How children form their letters and use space on the page show us the course and progress of their development. In this chapter I will focus on the nature of this journey and the problems children need to solve to add clear handwriting to their repertoire of skills.

Children develop their handwriting through movement in relation to the page. Their hand moves across the paper from left to right making letters, one after the other. This hands-on action is called *praxis*. How they learn is shown in the pressure they apply in forming the letters (light versus heavy) and in the way the letters occupy space.

Toni, a child in first grade, has just written the word *super* on her paper (see Figure 15.1). Note the differences in the size of the letters and in the pressure she puts on the strokes that go away from the body. The word overflows the spatial confines of the lines. Toni is interested in getting the word down, in "doing" writing, as opposed to the exacting function of filling a space. Her writing also indicates that she applies more pressure when her hand moves away from her body. These two aspects of her writing tell her developmental story.

Pressure

Toni, like any other writer, controls the pressure of her pencil on the page through the dismission of larger muscles and the facilitation of smaller muscles. Small muscles have a better chance to work when the following occurs:

1. *Placement of the work:* The paper needs to be slightly to the right of midline and turned at a forty-five-degree angle. In this way it is possible to maintain small-muscle control from the top of the page to the bottom. Otherwise, as the writer's hand moves down the page and gets closer to the body, the large muscles come into play. You can try this out for yourself:

▲▼ **Figure 15.1**

A n D
I
KISS
h M
I Love soPPtowh

_____

    a. Place the paper directly in front of you with your mid-line bisecting the center of the paper. Now move your arm down the left side, one inch in from the edge of the paper. Do you feel the pull of muscles in the upper arm and the right side of the torso?

    b. Try the same exercise but this time move the paper slightly to the right and turn it at a forty-five-degree angle. The same on the left for those who are left-handed.

2. *Arm and wrist placement on the table:* When the wrist and arm are not in motion but rest on the table, the action of the larger muscles is diminished and the fingers can come into play. This also reduces the motion of the torso, again helping the fingers.

3. *Pencil grip:* If the hand holds the pencil at an angle to the paper, its full downward thrust is reduced, and it meets the paper with the right pressure. The grip is aided by the coordinated action of thumb, index, and middle fingers. (It is not unusual to find very young children gripping a pencil or pen like an ice pick or writing with a stirring motion.)

Control

The writer discovers the space on the page by writing. Fine control of pencil motion is dependent on the development of the small muscles and the growing precision of eye and hand working together. The eye coordinates with the hand to achieve the right pressure. Like gunners shooting at a moving target, children undershoot and then overshoot the lines. They jump into work energetically, writing in bold strokes. It is natural enough that children use larger script, since they usually equate size with quality.

There are two basic motions in working with letters in manuscript, the circle and straight line. The circle is the more sophisticated of the two in terms of small muscle rotation, the straight line more susceptible to the problems of dismissing force.

ACTION 15.1:

Observe three children during composing.

Make up a small chart with three sectors, one for work placement, one for arm and wrist placement, and one for pencil grip (see Figure 15.2).

▲▼ **Figure 15.2**

John's Handwriting Observation

WORK PLACEMENT	ARM and WRIST PLACEMENT	PENCIL GRIP	CONTROL
straight on	arm raised off of table thus bringing in large muscles	alright but when his arm is raised his grip is too tight	alright at first but fatigue or whatever(?) causes arm to raise

Leslie's Handwriting Observation

WORK PLACEMENT	ARM and WRIST PLACEMENT	PENCIL GRIP	CONTROL
slightly turned	flat, thus allowing small muscle involvement	light	good control with small muscles doing most of the work

If I am looking for a setup that will lead to the best handwriting, I'll see the following:

Work placement: The paper will be slightly turned away from the writer, about 25 to 30 degrees. As the child writes down the page, his arm is comfortable to the last lines (see Figure 15.3).

Arm and wrist placement: The arm should again rest at an angle to the paper and be placed flat on the table. This position allows the small muscles in the finger and wrist to come into play. For some children, particularly boys, it takes quite a while to dismiss large muscles, thus allowing their fingers to work.

Pencil grip: The pencil or pen is held lightly yet with enough of a grip to allow control. A pencil held high off the paper produces great pressure, and functions more like an ice pick.

Control: When the previous three steps are followed, there is a fluidity to the writing.

In John's case (see Figure 15.2) we note that the paper placement, along with the lift of his arm, brings in his large muscles. In no time he becomes fatigued by the physical process of writing. Leslie is just the opposite. She is comfortable and fluid in her composing.

▲▼ **Figure 15.3**
Work Placement

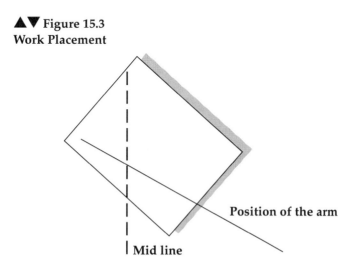

Position of the arm

Mid line

Examine the data in the separate columns and note how each element contributes to the ease or difficulty in composing. I suggest that you choose three children, one representing those who struggle, one those who write with ease, and one those who demonstrate good handwriting. Of course, you may find that in spite of the apparent lack of effective hand placement a child still writes quite legibly. Some children develop their own effective but highly idiosyncratic approaches to holding a pencil or placing the paper. If children's approaches are already working quite well, I do not seek to change them.

ACTION 15.2:
Work with a child who needs help with handwriting.

Choose one of the children whose handwriting you have observed. First, ask the child to examine her work and find the words or phrases she feels represents her best handwriting. Then ask them to find a section in which they have not written as well. Ask, "What is good about this one and not so good about this one?" The purpose of this Action is to find out the criteria they use to determine good and poor handwriting. Remember, children can often show you good handwriting yet not know *why* it is good. You can help the child find the language to express her evaluation.

Your next move is to help the child with her handwriting. Show the child how to work with straight lines and circles on lined paper. If the lines are too controlling, use unlined paper or, better still, a slate with chalk. The broad point of the chalk makes it much easier for the child to control. I observe the child as she makes circles and lines, noting the fundamental problems that may be contributing to her poor letter formation. When the child begins to sense the fundamentals that underlie basic handwriting and show some measure of control, I ask her to write a sentence from her text on another sheet of paper and "make it the very best that you can."

All too often, children with major handwriting problems are asked to spend inordinate amounts of time recopying their work. Unfortunately, they quickly learn to narrow their thinking and write as little as possible. I prefer to start by making sections of text better, then gradually increase the amount.

Phase Overview

There are five general phases that are discernible in children's handwriting development. They overlap and perhaps ought to be thought of as general guidelines for viewing the development of the young writer. Much more research on these stages, and on handwriting in general, is needed to look at the effects of acquiring handwriting skills in the midst of the composing process. Handwriting has not been viewed enough as a tool of composition.

All five of these phases of development can come in the first year of a child's schooling. This depends, of course, on how much opportunity children have to write, and what kind of help the teacher gives them.

Get-It-Down Phase

Children are relentless in their pursuit of writing when they first come to school. Children persist in putting letters, numbers, and drawings on the paper like waves rolling to the shore. For Mary and Dana, the push to express in writing is the same as that of playing with blocks or with dolls or with trucks in a sandbox. They simply express. They observe some conventions with letters following letters and words following words. But at first, just putting the words on paper is enough for them. And they do it in undulating fashion across the page—Toni's words rise and fall as her voice does.

Within a few weeks, most of the children have grasped the idea of composing from left to right, but their concern is just that—*generally* from left to right but with little consideration for spacing.

First Aesthetics

From the beginning, children show their concern for aesthetics when they reshape a letter or word. They gauge word placement as they check the length of the page in relation to their message. In particular, many show it with a curious "cleaning" of their pages. Just before they start to write on a clean sheet of paper—a paper without smudge or lettering—they brush it from top to bottom. There is a sense of wanting the page to be clean and fresh for the writing. This same behavior has been observed in older writers—all the way from grade school children up through professionals. If they change a letter or word, they devote a lot of time to erasing the black or smudge away. They want it to look "clean."

When children first make "errors" they want to banish them forever. The eraser is their strongest ally. How to control an eraser is another story. It is an even more sophisticated action than controlling the point of a pen. There is greater resistance between eraser and paper, demanding an even lighter touch and therefore more precise use of small muscles. Often, the child wants to eradicate the error so strongly that he attacks the paper, rubbing hard with the eraser. The effort is so great that the child often rubs through the paper and rips it. It is also not unusual for the child to have to deal with two or three errors on the same blackened spot. Frustration at correcting the "burned out" paper is clearly reflected on the face of the child. More durable writing surfaces need to be considered for beginning writers who wish to erase and rewrite as they compose.

Growing Age of Convention

Toward the end of the first grade many children want their writing to appear conventional. (Depending on the background of the child, his experience in writing at home, and his general aesthetic orientation, this phase could come much earlier.) They are fussy about spacing between words, about margins, and about writing above and below the line. This age of convention affects not just handwriting but spelling and punctuation as well. There is less of the relentless urge to write and more looking over, the beginning of introspection, the critical eye that slows down production. Children hear and feel the critiques of other children and of the teacher. Before this, the child had such an egocentric urge that he just ignored his audience or suggestions from others. He didn't look back at a piece. The *doing* was everything.

Now all this begins to change. The child starts to look back and look back critically. Content now takes a backseat because he wants to do things the right way. Output decreases as well.

Breaking Conventions

This phase is almost completely dependent on the teacher's approach to the craft of teaching. About the time the child has gained early mastery of handwriting and spelling conventions, problems of information arise. In a conference it becomes clear to both child and teacher that important information belongs in the text. This raises problems for the child. If more information is to go into the text, how is this accomplished once the text is already written? Problems of space and aesthetics arise. Note how Mary Ellen Giacobbe deals with both problems in this conference with Chris, a first grader:

Ms. G: I see that you were able to put in the word "may" to show that "Brontosauruses may travel in families." *[Chris had been able to sandwich in the small word without erasing.]* But you didn't say why they travel in families.

Chris: They travel in families to protect the young.

Ms. G: Do you think that is important information?

Chris: Yes, but there isn't any place to put it. *[His writing goes from left to right over to the right hand margin at the bottom of the paper. Above the writing is a picture of a brontosaurus.]*

Ms. G: Look the paper over and show me where you could write it in.

Chris: There isn't any. *[voice rising]*

Ms. G: Look the entire paper over and put your hand on any space where there isn't writing or drawing. *[There is space above the drawing.]*

Chris: Well, I could put it up here *[motions to the top of the paper]* but it would look stupid. The other part is down here.

Ms. G: How could you show they were connected?

Chris: I could put an arrow down here pointing to the part that's at the top.

Ms. G: Good, but you'll need to connect the arrow with the top. This is what writers do when they are getting their books ready for the publisher.

Chris knew that additional information would create a mess. His usual approach was to erase words in order to put in new ones. Now his teacher has shown him how to control new information when there is a problem of space. She has also shown him for the first time that the draft is temporary, that rewriting is necessary. Young writers need to learn a whole repertoire for "messing up" their paper to deal with new information, reorganization, and adjustments. This also adds to the importance of crafting the letters in the final draft. If children have control of the process and know their information is good, the quality of their handwriting usually improves.

When they understand the draft concept, older children like eight-year-old Andrea show it in their handwriting. Andrea, like writers of almost any age or range of experience hoped her first draft would be her last. About the sixth word into this selection, her handwriting shows that she decided another draft would follow (see Figure 15.4).

Later Aesthetics

It is a significant moment when a child decides to line out instead of erasing an error. This immediately signals that the paper is only a draft, that the text can be reworked and further copies made that will be much more pleasing. It shows that the child perceives a progression from rough to smooth. There are only a few children who are able to compose a first draft with all the information needed.

Children who have reworked material through several drafts, who have taken greater pride in their information, do transfer this into

▲▼ **Figure 15.4**

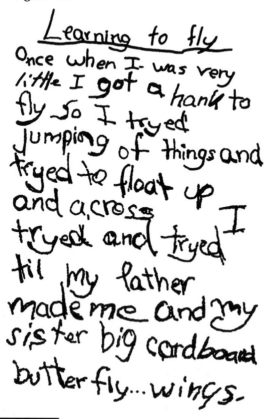

more pleasing final copy. Teaching children italic writing, making final copy with special paper or writing instruments, is especially helpful to those who have recrafted their work and now feel positive about its content.

Professional writers are often portrayed as slipshod about the appearance of their writing. But the literature is replete with the fetishes of writers who must have certain pens and certain kinds of paper or they simply can't compose. There is a time for all writers when crisp copy, free from scratch outs, revisions, and notes, is necessary. After revising a paper four or five times, including the notes, I find that I have to sit and keyboard until there are no errors. There are some pages, especially leads (the openings to pieces), that have given me great difficulty, that I can't wait to retype without error just to look at them and say, "There, that's that; the copy at least looks and *feels* good."

Time and Topic

Time and topic still have as much to do with a child's handwriting development as any issues mentioned thus far. If children have enough writing time and are in control of their topics, their handwriting improves. Children ages six through nine ought to have a *minimum* of twenty minutes a day for writing about topics of their choice. When children have a well-chosen topic, their urge to express so dominates the activity that they lose track of the conscious aspect of handwriting to focus more on the message. Thus, they become more relaxed in dealing with the mechanical aspects of handwriting and concentrate on being "lost" in the message.

Writing Speed

Speed is closely connected with practice. If the familiar motor pathways are not built up through regular writing about topics the writer knows, then slowness can hamper the expression of content. The writing goes down on the page so slowly that the writer pokes along word-by-word on the page. That is, each word takes so long to write down that the next word, or even the rest of the sentence, cannot be contemplated at the same time as the one under construction. This hampers thinking. The writer does not have the same access to experience as the person who can write quickly. In short, speed begets access and a more complete view of the entire piece under construction. This leads to a different kind of cohesion in the text than in a piece composed at the word level.

Children who first write often compose at a rate as slow as 1.5 words per minute. Adults who wish to experience the impact of such a rate can try writing a six-word sentence in nine minutes. Since it is difficult to take that long, they will need someone to call out the time to them to make sure they take the full nine minutes. After composing at this rate, they will be aware of the issues slow speed raises: What was the overall impact of slow speed on information? How well could the writer retain the overall picture of what she wanted to say? What would her composing mean if she were writing about something she knew nothing about? Once again, for children who write slowly it is *all the more important* that they choose subjects for which they have an experiential, chronological base, since slow speed hampers access to information as well as the sense of where the word or sentence under construction fits in with the overall idea of the paper.

ACTION 15.3:
Gather basic data on handwriting speed.

I suggest that you choose two of the children you observed in Action 15.1, but you will now observe their handwriting speed in three different situations (see Figure 15.5).

Column 2, Self-selected Topics, refers to topics the child has freely chosen and ordinarily writes about each day during writing time. Column 3 refers generally to a worksheet the child may have to fill in or on which he is to write prescribed answers. Column 4, Computer, is

▲▼ Figure 15.5

STUDENT	SELF-SELECTED TOPIC	ANSWERING QUESTIONS	COMPUTER
Leslie	7.0 mpm	5.0	4.6
John	5.2	3.0	4.9

an option. You may find it interesting to compare the student's composing speed on a computer versus that with a pencil or pen.

Data are gathered in the following manner: First, I do not want the child to be in a position of writing as fast as she can. Thus, I try to gather the data informally and note when the child starts and stops. You will need a stop watch or a watch with a second hand (or a digital watch that displays seconds). Take three readings for each of the three headings. If a child is composing on a self-selected topic, I will time the word flow for a minimum of twenty seconds before I try to record the child's speed in composing. I use the same measure for the other two columns, Assigned Writing and Computer—how many words does the child write in twenty seconds. If the child stops in the middle of a timing period before twenty seconds has been reached, I wait until she resumes writing again. Then I begin the timing again. When she has composed for twenty straight seconds I will have completed the session.

Writing speed has much to do with the quality of the piece. Good writers in the nine- to ten-year-old bracket write from eight to nineteen words per minute when composing. I do not have data on older children. I would never give young writers a speed check, but for some children who struggle, I may do informal time checks to see if speed is a factor. The check is made only during a start and stop interval. This is a handwriting speed check, not a composing speed check, although the latter may be useful for other reasons. In this instance, the check is merely to see if the child's motor rate is slow enough to influence the content or accessibility to it.

But now the disclaimer. For writers who have a strong urge to compose, a message that must be written, the intensity of the message and the persistence of the writer push aside the issue of handwriting speed. The writing will get down on the paper *regardless of the factors* that might slow it down.

Appearance as an Issue

If handwriting is divorced from content, two kinds of problems result: One group of writers feel that their information must be good because the handwriting is clear. Another group dismisses their experiences and their views about issues as unimportant because their handwriting has been deemed unacceptable.

Many writers, particularly males, have heard for years that their writing is messy. Sadly, they equate messiness with lack of knowledge. If the writing is not pleasing to the eye it must not be pleasing to the mind. They accept too quickly the low state of being without worthwhile information. Mina Shaughnessy (1977), in her work with young college students entering the New York system under open admissions, found that the barrier of poor handwriting was one of her most formidable obstacle in helping young writers. As she observed:

> Thus, it is not unusual to find among freshman essays a handwriting that belies the maturity of the student, reminding the reader instead of the labored cursive style of children. Often, but not always, the content that is carried in such writing is short and bare, reinforcing the impression of the reader that the writer is "slow" or intellectually immature. Yet the same student might be a spirited, cogent talker in class. His problem is that he has no access to his thoughts or personal style through the medium of writing and must appear, whenever he writes, as a child. (15)

Make no mistake, if handwriting has a poor appearance, the writer is judged poorly by our culture. This won't end tomorrow. Surface features will always attract far more attention than underlying structures. For a person who has poor handwriting, the road ahead is difficult. In spite of the high quality of his ideas and information, the writer will bear a lifelong burden. But such a fate is unnecessary. For teachers who practice writing as a craft, following the writer's intention within the topic choice, and for those who know how writers develop their skill in handwriting, both the objectives of good writing and a pleasing script are attainable. Handwriting can be taught within the act of composing itself. When the handwriting flows, the writer has better access to his own thoughts and information. This is why writers want to write. This is why handwriting is for writing.

Today, the teaching of handwriting is in flux. Most of children's writing still involves the use of pencil or pen. Nevertheless, more and more children have access to computers and are learning to keyboard effectively. Time for teaching is scarce and many teachers are using the time normally spent on handwriting to help children learn to use a keyboard. In some instances schools provide computer labs, and the children hone their keyboarding skills there.

16 SPELL TO COMMUNICATE

"I wish teachers wouldn't tell children not to worry about their spelling." The speaker is Mary Ellen Giacobbe, the teacher on the cover of *Writing: Teachers and Children at Work*. She had an enormous influence on my early work and continues to do so as she works in classrooms across the country observing teachers and children and helping them write. According to Mary Ellen, "What they should say is, 'When you write, try your best. Spelling words as best you can is helping your readers.'"

Spelling does matter. It matters far more than we in the profession realize. Spelling, probably more than any other aspect in the school curriculum, is used to mark social status. Words used to have a variety of spellings until Noah Webster regularized them in the mid-nineteenth century. Indeed, spelling and handwriting marked the educated person. "He can spell and has a good hand" was a high compliment. The American public still sees good spelling just behind reading and mathematics in importance. In the eyes of many, spelling is even more important than what it's for: writing.

Spelling matters for another reason. Children who initially write down words using inventions or temporary spellings are establishing their learning habits and attitudes toward words and writing. As arbitrary as spelling may appear specific things should be taught and certain attitudes established. It is not enough for the writer to know what the text says. As Mary Ellen Giacobbe points out, the reader needs to know as well. Writing is communication. Although this chapter demonstrates specific strategies to help children learn to spell, you need to become acquainted with other materials. I strongly recommend Sandra Wilde's *You Kan Red This!* (1991), a book on spelling and punctuation for whole language classrooms, K–6. It gives an excellent review of the research as well as specific approaches to help children spell, all in a context that celebrates language and learning.

In spite of our research I'll admit that when one of my daughter's papers contain misspellings, I itch. I want the unsightliness removed from view. In my knee-jerk response, I overlook the message. I am much more objective about the misspellings of others . . . but, within the family? What will other people think?

Experienced administrators and teachers know that they need good data on spelling progress. In the political climate of education, negative spelling scores can make parents and school board members forget other successes in the school curriculum. Of course, there is no correlation between spelling ability and intelligence (otherwise, we might lose a third of the people in law, teaching, and the medical professions). I am fond of quoting Harold Rosen: "Any idiot can tell a genius how to spell a word." At the same time, spelling is a necessary social skill.

Young children, however, don't suddenly write effectively any more than they begin to speak perfectly. When our first child pointed a crooked finger at a bird and spoke her first word, "bir," we nearly wept with joy. We raced inside to tell my mother, her grandmother and namesake, Marion, what her namesake had done. We didn't pull our ten-month-old aside and say, "After us, Marion, let's say all of it and get that final 'd'." It was enough of a miracle to hear her first word. Naturally, as she grew older her vocabulary expanded, but if Marion had continued to drop the final consonant in later years we probably would have worked with her on it.

Emergent Spelling and Writing

Much of this chapter will focus on helping very young children, five- and six-year-olds particularly, begin to write. Although I will focus on how to help children with inventive spelling, or a first approximation of writing, we must never lose our focus on what writing is for—

communication. Just yesterday I was in Louise Wrobleski's combination kindergarten and first-grade classroom in Madison, New Hampshire. Louise had penned a one-sentence statement to a child, an observation about something the child had done successfully. The child, in turn, sent a one-sentence note back to her. Louise continually introduces many reasons for writing: keeping weather records, sending Christmas letters, reporting the morning news, writing stories, writing about personal experience, writing in relation to drawing, and so on. The children's own published books will be shared and circulated within the class.

The Actions in this chapter are designed to aid you in becoming systematically involved in young children's writing and spelling. All these Actions are intended to move children toward conventional spelling.

For Primary Teachers

ACTION 16.1:

Observe a child who is using inventive spelling.

When I refer to "inventive spelling," a term first used by Carol Chomsky (1971), I mean the spellings children formulate before they know the full conventional spelling of a word. Children usually approximate the full spelling by writing the word down according to the way it sounds. Many researchers have shown how these spellings evolve from consonants to final spelling. Inventive spelling allows children to begin to make meaning before they know how to actually spell a word. If children had to wait for full spellings from the teacher, the teacher would have to don track shoes and sprint around the room accommodating every child.

Here is a quick snapshot of how the spelling of several words evolved for two children (Graves 1983):

TONI		SARAH	
10/17	D - and	11/3	AVVETAG
	D		- everything
10/23	ND	11/6	AVVETAG
10/25	AD	1/31	EVERYTHING

11/10	ND		11/20	FLLAOWZ - flowers
	LA			FLLAWRZ
	ANE			FLLAWR - flower
11/16	AND		1/11	FLAWRS
11/18	ND		6/1	FLOWERS
11/28	AND			
12/1	AND		11/6	SLLE - silly
12/8	AND		11/15	SALLE
			11/17	SALEE
11/10	LC - like		12/7	SALEE
	LAT - liked		1/3	SILLEY
12/8	LOCT - liked		3/15	SILLY
12/19	L - like			SILLY WILLY
4/10	LICT - liked		3/26	SILLY
	LIC - like			
5/14	LIKE			
5/21	LIKE			

For this Action you will want to move in close to a child composing using inventive spelling. Nearly all first-grade children need to use some version of sounding out. For about ten minutes, record on paper how two children actually do this. Figure 16.1 shows a short version of how one child composed a message. Notice that there are three sections, one for what she says, another for sounds, and a final one for what the child writes.

Reading from left to right we see that the child first announces orally what the message will be: "We were at Mom's work." She then begins to sound "wu" to get the first sound in "we" and writes a capital "W." For "were" she needs to make the "R" sound repeatedly before hearing it well enough to put down an "R." "AT" is another story. She merely says the word and then writes it with no sounding out. Apparently "AT" is a sight word.

As you can see, a detailed record of a child's composing with inventive spelling gives a clear picture of just what strategies she may use in composing as well as in sounding out and spelling. Sometimes children consult with other children to ask for help. You'd record that information under still another heading. I might add another section below "Writing line" to record the use of any resources. (Note that I have written "Jennifer, how do you spell 'were'?" next to an asterisk.

▲▼ Figure 16.1
Recording a Writing Episode

WORDS SPOKEN LINE	"We were at mom's work" "We" "Were" "at"
SOUNDING LINE	Wuh Wuh err err err
WRITING LINE	WE W R AT
RESOURCE USE	* Jennifer, how do you spell "were"?

If the child had said those words, I would have recorded them there.) I strongly suggest that you listen to two very different children in order to observe two different composing strategies. Line some paper off with the four categories as in Figure 16.1 and enjoy listening to the fascinating world of children's composing.

ACTION 16.2:

Help one child or several to sound out slowly. Place their finger on a letter they have written down and listen to the remainder of the word.

When children first spell words they often merely write the first consonant. For them that stands for the entire word. Unfortunately, when they try to read the word at a later time, there are too few cues for them to know what they have written. For some children this is upsetting, and it remains so until they get some help.

For this Action you will help one child (or several) to learn how to say a word slowly enough to hear the various sounds within it. The children may not know the symbols that go with the sounds they hear. That's another kind of mini-lesson, one you will do shortly. This mini-lesson with three children might look like this:

Don: We are going to practice saying a word slowly. That will help us to hear some of the sounds in the word. Mark, will you give us a word you've used that you'd like us to say slowly? [*Mark may not know yet how to choose a word. The concept of separating out a word from the spoken text is yet another concept. You will notice that children run their words together without spaces between.*]

Mark: Dog.

Jason: That's easy, d-o-g.

Don: Good, Jason, you already know that word. Right now we are just going to practice saying the word slowly together to see what we can hear in it. Listen to the way I say it slowly. DOOOOOOG. [*When I say it slowly I can sustain the vowel but not the consonants. Nevertheless, I show how to make the initial and final consonants distinctive in the way I carefully enunciate them. Many children stumble on sounds because they simply don't enunciate the word clearly enough.*] Let's have another word from someone. Jennifer.

Jennifer: House. I'm going to my Nana's *house.*

Don: All right, say it with me. H, sustain H sound, OUUUUUU, S S S S, sustain S sound. Now someone choose a word and show us how you'd say it slowly. [*I work today noting who can sustain sound with me. When they are able to do so, I move to others, taking a word and showing them that they know how to do it. Notice in this mini-lesson we aren't writing yet. That will come next.*]

Some children will need many repetitions of this last mini-lesson. Other children may find it too easy. If so, move right on to the next mini-lesson.

Now have the children try to *write* the words they are saying slowly.

Don: Now that you have a pretty good idea about saying words slowly, we are going to try to write some and I'll need your help. I'll choose the first word, *recess.* Let's say it slowly together: RRRR EEEEE CCCC EEEEEESSSS. Tell me the first sound.

Danny: R, that's easy.

Don: Notice what I do. [*I will write on experience chart paper so that everyone can see. I sound RRRRRR and write R.*] Notice how I've written the R. I'm going to put my finger on it so I can remember I've said that part and say *the rest* slowly again. EEEEE. What do I write?

Child: E.

Don: Good. Write it on your paper and put your finger on it, say the rest and see what you get.

Child: I don't know how to write SSSSS.

Don: Look at this chart here and see if you can find a picture that makes that sound.

Child: Snake, S. (*I am using the Picture/Letter chart that represents each sound pictorially. This is a valuable resource for children who don't know the letters that go with the sounds they hear.*)

I will spend the next ten minutes observing which children need more time with this mini-lesson. As in the first, some children will need many repetitions before they pick up the strategy.

Use of the Picture/Letter chart is another mini-lesson in its own right. A Picture/Letter chart helps children who may know a sound but not the letter that goes with it. For example, a child may wish to write *ball*. He is able to make the "b" sound but does not know how to write it. He looks at the chart and finds a picture of a bear. Beneath the picture is the letter "b" in both upper and lower case. He then writes the "b" on his paper as the first sound in *ball*. There are many commercial programs and charts with sound and picture combinations, as well as alphabet books to help you and the children. It is also not difficult to compose one of your own or enlist the help of the children. The chart should be large enough for all children to see at a glance.

I bring together a small cluster of children to conduct the mini-lesson. We will play a game by helping each other to sound out slowly, place our finger on the letters we're written, and use the Picture/Letter chart. I find that some children need to have a copy of the chart with them as they compose. That means you'll need to reduce the chart on a copier and make about fifteen copies for each class of twenty-five. The children who need one can keep it right inside their writing folder.

One caution: Although most children benefit from sounding out, you will need to be sensitive to the strategies children are actually using when they compose. If some children are having obvious difficulty with the process, you'll need to double back and observe them compose (see Figure 16.1). There are many strategies children use that work for them but are not described here. When in doubt, observe.

High Frequency Words

There are certain common words children need to know how to read and spell. Marie Clay (1993) points out that these are anchor words that help children in beginning to read. The eleven words starred below have been identified by Richard Lederer (1991) as constituting 25 percent of all words used in spoken language. The words in the first two columns are Marie Clay's. Obviously, all of them are important words to learn and have handy for children when they write:

*I	look	here
*is	this	up
am	*a	go
come	*in	*it
see	*to	*you
*the	like	*of
we	me	*that
at	my	
on	*and	

These are not the easiest words for children to learn, even though most of them are short. Most do not lend themselves to imagery and therefore they need to be taught in the context of reading or writing.

Another group of words make up the next half of all words written in texts. The first twenty-five (Fry, Fountoukidis, and Polk 1985) are similar to those listed by Marie Clay. Certainly it is important that children be able to spell them (see Figure 16.2).

Spelling Tests and Personal Word Lists

There should be a definite time, especially toward the middle of the first-grade year, when you make it a point to call attention to certain words the children will learn to spell. Beginning with the first day of class in September, Pat McLure, a first-grade teacher in Lee, New Hampshire, focuses on one word a day; heightens the imagery surrounding the word; shows its use in a sentence; and has the children learn the word and write it down. She does this at a morning meeting when children are gathered together on the rug. Further, she expects each child to come with a word of his own to spell. The class often

▲▼ **Fig. 16.2**
The Instant Words* First Hundred

These are the most common words in English, ranked in frequency order. The first 25 make up about a third of all printed material. The first 100 make up about half of all written material. Is it any wonder that all students must learn to recognize these words instantly and to spell them correctly also?

Words 1–25	Words 26–50	Words 51–75	Words 76–100
the	or	will	number
of	one	up	no
and	had	other	way
a	by	about	could
to	word	out	people
in	but	many	my
is	not	then	than
you	what	them	first
that	all	these	water
it	were	so	been
he	we	some	call
was	when	her	who
for	your	would	oil
on	can	make	now
are	said	like	find
as	there	him	long
with	use	into	down
his	an	time	day
they	each	has	did
I	which	look	get
at	she	two	come
be	do	more	made
this	how	write	may
have	their	go	part
from	if	see	over

Common suffixes: -s, -ing, -ed

*For additional instant words, see *Spelling Book* by Edward Fly, Laguna Beach Educational Books, 245 Grandview, Laguna Beach CA 92651 (1992)

The NEW Reading Teacher's Book of Lists, ©1985 Prentice Hall, Inc. Englewood Cliffs, NJ 07632. By E. Fry, D. Fountoukidis, and J. Polk.

discusses where various children found their words. This helps children to learn from each other, as well as to learn whom to consult when each is working alone. Pat may also use the session to teach conventions. For example, a child may come up with a proper name requiring capitalization. She discusses the convention and how the children can use it in their writing.

Each child needs to compile a list of words she uses frequently. The list can be kept in her writing folder with enough room allowed to add new words as necessary. Some teachers encourage certain children who need more help by making a photocopy of a drawing, then writing down the words that go with the objects in the drawing. This creates a small "pictionary" for children who may not have enough sound/letter knowledge to remember particular words. It is especially helpful with children who are learning English for the first time. The pictionary approach provides the child with a fund of nouns, but because early drawings contain little motion, it is more difficult to provide precise verbs in this way.

Some teachers have found it helpful to expect children to learn to write specific words on a weekly basis. Depending on the age of the children, there may be three to four words every week. The word is given in a sentence, one that the class has already discussed earlier in the week. After you have asked the children to write the words expected of everyone, ask them to write the two words they have chosen from their own lists: "Now write your two words."

The traditional weeklong learning of spelling lists commonly found in published spelling books with Monday to Friday skills exercises has a bleak history. Cohen's data (Graves 1977) shows that calling attention to word parts, phonetic respellings, dictionary skills, and so on actually caused regressions in children's spelling ability. Cohen's research showed quite clearly that using words in the children's own writing was the strongest contributor to spelling power.

Emergent Writers

Although some children seem to acquire full spellings from Easy-to-Read books, a strong visual memory, and an immediate knowledge of sounds and symbols, most first graders require mini-lessons that cover the variety of skill components emergent writers naturally need.

Without question, children possess a natural urge to write, but many of them need specific help—from learning how to sustain sound to learning certain sound/symbol combinations, how to separate words with spaces, how to use Picture/Letter charts, how to spell frequently occurring words and compiling personal word lists. For some children these mini-lessons need to be repeated again and again while the teacher carefully observes how they use the available resources to help them write.

Help the Older Writer to Spell

Just as we have seen with the young writer, if the older writer cares about the piece, you are in the best position to help her with her spelling. Students who don't care about their writing or have no idea of what writing can do are the most difficult to help. Even top teachers work hard to find out how a student's energy can be channeled into something they care about. When the writer's voice is in the piece and the teacher has brought a class to be a good audience, then the author cares more about being respectful of those who will read his work.

Virtually all my efforts here are directed toward helping students care about their work. When you get to know your students through the three-column exercise, show them how to read the world and their texts, integrate reading and writing, introduce portfolios, and encourage students to realize their potential, you are contributing to that important goal.

Computers can help. Only 46 percent of words in the English language can be spelled the way they sound; the remaining 54 percent draw on the writer's visual memory of what the words look like. But poor handwriting produces visual images of words that are inconsistent and unstable. A word processed text offers clearer evidence of a misspelling. "It doesn't look right," the writer looking at the screen might say to himself.

Computers are still new enough to connote a certain kind of sophistication. Using this technology, which simplifies the practical side of writing, also offers multiple opportunities to change the spelling of a word until it is correct.

ACTION 16.3:
Help the poor speller.

In this Action you will work with a youngster who has apparent difficulty with his or her spelling. In choosing a youngster to interview, look for one who is articulate yet has difficulty with spelling when he writes (misspelling as much as 15 to 20 percent of his words).

First, you want to get some fix on what writing means to him. Try these questions:

- I'd like you to take out your folder. Let's look over your last five papers here. What can you tell me about these pieces? (*Listen for interest, positive or negative.*)
- What do writers need to know how to do in order to write well? (*Quite often a child will mention the areas he struggles with as essential to becoming a good writer.*)
- Who do you like to read your work? (*How much of an audience sense does he have?*)
- What do you want to work on next to be a better writer? (*The child may have already answered this indirectly in his response to what writers need to know.*)

When the child has finished answering these questions summarize what he has said about writing and what he needs to learn next. If he hasn't mentioned spelling, you'll need to say that some of the words in his writing confuse you because of their spelling. Show him a piece you find unclear and talk about what he wants to say. Above all, affirm the child's meaning, but show him that he needs help with his spelling and that you intend to give it.

Take another written selection, one the child seems to care more about, and ask him to start at the end and read backward toward the beginning. (It is easier to locate misspelled words this way because the reader is less likely to be lulled by the meaning and skip over words.) As he reads he is to circle words he thinks may be misspelled or that look strange to him.

Your first step in working with this type of child is to help him gain confidence in at least recognizing misspellings. Poor spellers find it unsettling to read their writing for misspellings because they know it is a fruitless exercise, especially for children who really struggle. Even if they find a misspelled word, for them consulting a dictionary is equally tedious and difficult. The result is that poor spellers often avoid rereading their writing and therefore never gain a margin of power in at least recognizing their errors.

The poor speller will often circle words that are spelled correctly and miss some that are incorrect, but she will also get some right. Help her see that she can spell correctly. Ask, "Why do you think you got this one here but missed this one over here?" You may see a pattern to the errors. Some of the more frequently misspelled words can be added to the child's list of words to learn. Each time this struggling writer completes a piece, have them reread it from the end and circle words that may be misspelled. The next four to five papers will chart her improvement in discovering which words may be misspelled.

ACTION 16.4:
Construct a spelling program.

Spelling programs for older students contain many of the same elements you would include for emergent spellers, but working with older students who have spelling problems is more difficult. As students grow older they tend to label themselves—with a little help from their teachers—as good or poor spellers. The self-diagnosed poor speller is the most challenging. Sadly, unless readers respond to the importance of his content, he tends to say, "I can't write. What I say is boring." In reality, the poor speller is confusing ideas and intelligence with the ability to spell. Your program will need to try to accommodate this student.

Continue to Work with Lists

Weekly spelling tests can be effective if students are adding to the lists of words they need to learn because they are useful to them in writing. The weekly tests will include:

- high frequency words (see Fry, Fountoukidis, and Polk, 1985) for additional groups of words beyond the first hundred.
- two to three personal "bugaboo" words that the student has selected because he continues to misspell them.
- two or three words the student wants to use in writing.

At least four to six of the words on the test have been selected by the student (these make up about 25 percent of the total words on the test). I dictate the first fourteen words in sentences from the high frequency list and then say, "Now write your two bugaboo words and then the new words you wish to use in your writing." This approach to spelling works if students have the three lists, high frequency words, bugaboo words, and personal words, in their writing folders.

First Drafts

I don't expect first drafts to have full spellings. I want the writer to concentrate on the flow of her ideas and not be preoccupied with accuracy at this early stage. On the other hand, I should see a *growing improvement* over time in first draft spelling and convention use. More and more conventions should become automatic. Thus, if I do not see an improvement I need to speak with the student to help her focus more on what she is learning.

The Weekly Paper

Each week students should hand in at least one page of writing in which they've pushed themselves to the limit in using conventions correctly. This page is labeled "Weekly Paper" at the top, and is distinguished from other completed writing I am to read. It can come from a much longer piece or be written just for the occasion. I want students to be highly conscious of conventions in at least one page of their writing in order to help them focus on their growing ability to handle this important area. If they are using new conventions for the first time (see Chapter 12) and are able to use them effectively, these may be added to their list of conventions they know how to use. For students who have difficulty with spelling I expect to see fewer errors and more recognition of incorrectly spelled words.

Include the Use of Computers and Publication

I've already mentioned the contribution of computers to spelling. Computers are also helpful in publishing student work. When children compose or copy work on a computer disk, they merely push *print* and the text is ready-made for publication. For children who face the tedium of recopying work for publication, computers allow for easy rewrites and edits.

If you have little access to computers, there are other ways to highlight student work. Use bulletin boards, stapled or loose collections, or wallpaper-covered cardboard covers to "publish" student writing. Above all, arrange for student writing to be circulated in the class and throughout the school. Again, knowing that someone else is going to read a selection focuses students' attention on conventions in a more realistic way. "John, you've got to look that over again. This is a good piece but this spelling is going to detract from its quality."

Answers to Common Questions Teachers Ask About Spelling

1. What about spelling books?

Cohen's study (1968) shows quite clearly that the chief contribution of spelling books is their word lists. It demonstrates even more conclusively that the majority of word skill exercises offered in the typical Monday through Friday A-Z exercises do not contribute to children's spelling success.

Lists such as the compilation of high frequency words by Fry and colleagues (1985) are useful. Certain words appear again and again in texts and need to be learned.

2. I have some spellers who won't go ahead unless I give them the full spelling of a word. How do I help those students?

This predicament is a common one with very young children. I often find that children who are highly anxious about the spelling of a word are quite intelligent yet fear making mistakes. They know that words are spelled only one way and want their work to be accurate. Their parents are often well educated and keep a watchful eye for errors in all of the child's work, not just in spelling.

First, it is virtually impossible in any classroom to spell every word children need, and I think children can understand this predicament. Second, some children need to have something to do to deal with the "hard part" of the word they are trying to write. Usually, children who are concerned about full spellings are able to get most of the word. Ask them to write as much of the word as they can and to leave a space or put in a dash for the parts they can't get. I will make a point of giving this child more help for words he wants to learn. For example, I'll say, "You do the best you can with the spelling and then put stars (*) next to the four words you want me to spell for you." Above all, I want children to practice inventing spelling, but I do respect their wish that I help them spell for full spellings.

3. What does reading have to do with spelling?

Reading provides both an image and a clear visual memory of what a word looks like. Such words as *elephant* or *baseball* are easy to spell because they evoke so much emotion and imagery. Other words—like *that, those, this, which,* and *when*—are difficult to spell because their job is to point to or connect the words that carry the imagery. Some good readers have a way of noticing details that help them to remember. At the same time, some very good readers do not take in the visual features of a word and continue to have a difficult time with spelling.

4. How do I interpret inventive spelling to parents?

Show parents how their children develop as spellers. Earlier in this chapter we saw how Toni's and Sarah's spelling evolved from their early inventions to conventional spellings. Parents worry that their children will stick with these approximate spellings. They need to see their children's development. One teacher took two writing folders from one year, photocopied them (with the child's and the parents' permission), and used them the following year to show parents how children change over an entire year. It is very difficult to explain inventive spelling to parents without actual papers that show how children develop as writers. Parents find it difficult to accept an idea in theory, but they are receptive to practical evidence that their children are learning and growing.

Explain your program. Review the mini-lessons in this chapter that help children become better spellers. Show parents which skills are embedded in each lesson and how they nudge children from early invention toward full spellings. Sometimes parents can only see a misspelled word. They do not see the progress toward correct spelling. I use children's writing to show them that change.

17 ANSWERS TO FREQUENT QUESTIONS TEACHERS ASK ABOUT TEACHING WRITING

I have divided the questions into two sections, those that focus on children and those that focus on teaching practices. Of course, my response to each question will require discussion about both children and teachers.

Questions about Children

1. What do I do when some of the children just don't finish their work, time after time?

Short-term solutions

First, let's look at short-term solutions. You need to confer with the child about the last incomplete piece. It is hard to conduct a conference in which the child may know you are exasperated because he has failed to complete his work. I take a deep breath and try to relax. Begin the conference by just dealing with the last piece rather than saying, "You've got six pieces that just haven't been completed, Mark. How come?"

I place the most recent incomplete selection face down on the table and say, "Mark, tell me what this was about." I want to focus on the content and move back over the history of the piece. I may say, "Mark, when you began this piece you had something you hoped would happen here. You had something in mind when you chose this topic. Tell me about that." Sometimes I am able to get some sense of the child's vision. Quite probably, the vision of the possible just didn't match what was happening on the page. There are several other reasons why a topic reaches a dead end in an incomplete paper.

- The child chose the topic because of a friend's advice: "Hey, let's write about wars."

- The child knows little about the subject. She simply doesn't have enough detail to achieve satisfaction with the text.

- The child allows little lead time before she starts composing. She doesn't know how to find good topics. Thus, because she doesn't know the source, she generally starts thinking about topics as she is composing. Writers who think about topics well in advance of the actual composing are much more likely to complete their work.

Sometimes I sense that the writer is blocked by what will happen when the piece is completed. It is more difficult to help children to talk about this aspect of the problem. My first question may be: "Mark, who did you think would read this when you finished?" Children respond in a number of ways:

- "I don't know. I didn't have anyone in mind." For some children there isn't any audience. They are just writing for themselves. Indeed, in their mind no one would be interested in the work.

- "I'll probably have to share this if I finish." In this instance completing work is followed by the penalty of having to share work with others. In this situation I allow the child to choose the one or two children he thinks would be interested in his work. The notion of sharing with an entire class is anathema to some children. This child solves the sharing problem by not completing his work.

- "My father will read this." Some children are blocked by very critical parents.

- "I just got interested in something else." Like skipping stones, some children keep finding very interesting things to write about in the next, the next, the next. They enjoy the beginning and all the possibilities in exploration. For them the work is completed emotionally in these first explorations. This is particularly true for children who enjoy drawing, yet find composing the written text very difficult.

Sometimes children need to complain. If I sense a complaint underlying the child's continual abandonment of pieces I'll say, "It must be upsetting to keep running into walls or to keep abandoning your pieces. Complain a little. How does that feel? List your complaints to me about that last piece." Some children's complaints are eloquent and informative. Indeed, when I listen to these complaints I can see that these children have substantive reasons for not finishing. Help is needed.

Longer-term solutions

For some children there are more fundamental and deep-seated issues at stake that require me to look carefully at some of my basic teaching strategies. Mary Ellen Giacobbe says, "Focus on the writer and the writing will come." This means that I have to focus on what a child can do, set out to find out information with which the child is acquainted and share these details with the child: "I know that you know these things." Although the child may demonstrate her knowledge of conventions, I need to focus on her information base and the processes she is able to carry out. "I didn't know that you knew so much about Rollerblading. And you have the details of what you wear for protection: helmet, elbow and knee guards, and even gloves."

Fundamental to any writer is a strong notion of what writing can do to satisfy self-interest. For too many, writing is something to avoid. They see little connection between their writing and their "becoming" as persons. Writing, in fact, is a barrier to becoming. Yet writing allows us to transcend ourselves in space and time. I write to influence myself and those around me. For some children, however, there are no others. There is nothing they want to understand about themselves much less to do it through writing. Writing will only document what they can't do. "I know I know nothing about history and writing will only *prove* that I know nothing about it."

2. What do I do when the child only wants to write about one topic?
I don't usually conclude that a child focuses on only one topic unless he or she has maintained that choice through four or five pieces in a six- to seven-week period (assuming that children are writing a minimum of at least four days each week). First, let's look at some of the reasons children focus on one topic and one topic only:

- Some children become identified with one topic. A boy writes about trucks and the class assigns certain prestige to his choice. To change the topic is to change his place in the class. This is a kind of typecasting.
- Another group of children use the topic focus as a means to improve. Each piece adds something new to their repertoire.
- Let's face it, other children simply enjoy writing about the same topic. It's like playing with the same truck or listening to the same piece of music again and again.

First, we have to see if writing about one topic is a problem. I call the topic a problem if the child isn't growing as a writer. My first urge as a teacher is to ask the child to branch out and try new things. (Besides, I may simply be sick of the child's choice.)

I ask the child to put the four or five pieces on this topic in order from first to last. Then I ask, "How do you see that you've changed as a writer from this first piece to this last one?" or "What were you trying that was new for you in each of these?" Of course, the child may not know. The child may have tried new things yet may be unaware of them. I need to read the pieces myself to try to discover how the child may be changing. *I* may be sick of the topic but, in fact, *the child may be improving.*

On the other hand, the child may not be improving. The topic may serve as a trap for a kind of nonthinking, rote action. "This is what I do when I write; I just choose this topic." When I sense that this kind of problem exists, I say directly to the child, "You keep on writing about the same topic. I'm curious about why you do that. Tell me about it."

I need to review my demonstrations to see if I am providing adequate entry points to writing in my "reading of the world." Am I composing in a variety of genres so that children can discover new options? Children are often prisoners of last night's TV plot or Saturday morning television. Unless I help them see what the professional writers of their trade books are doing, I may be surrendering the class to the television set.

One of the possibilities at share time is to have children explain where they find their topics. Other children may be better sources than my own demonstrations.

I may give the child a nudge. "All right, it's time to change and write about something new. I'd like you to write down two or three other topic choices. You may want to discuss your choices or get advice from someone else. Then I want you to decide which one you'll choose."

Sometimes I have to face the fact that I'm the only one who is bothered by the child's topic choice. It seems insipid to me or it is filled with too much violence. Violence in children's writing provokes the greatest reaction. But I have to be careful. Children live in a video world that caters to their fascination and their fears about violence. Violence is especially prevalent in children's attempts to write fiction. The fiction is often poorly done. There is little reason for the violence. "Why did the bad guy shoot the good guy?" I ask the child. "He's just mad, that's all," the child replies. Above all, I need to work with the child on writing fiction (see Chapter 18). Usually, when children have to think about motives and plausibility, they portray violence in a different way.

3. What do I do with the child who has good ideas but writes sloppily, spells poorly, and uses few conventions?

Children who hand in papers like this may not know that their ideas are good, just as they also may be oblivious to the fact that they are self-absorbed and unaware of the needs of their readers. They simply want to write for themselves, to play with their text and not to publish. Of course, they may also lack skill and need particular help through mini-lessons.

Above all, focus on the child's ideas. Let the child know that his content is good; and here I am quite specific: "Alex, I see that you have all the details about how a fullback maintains his position in a soccer game. That's good information. But, you need help to shape this material so someone else will understand what you know. What place do you think you need to start?" The point is to begin. When a child has problems in three major areas, handwriting, spelling and conventions, I don't work on all three at once.

Some children don't care about the burdens they place on those who read their writing: "I know what it says and I write for me," is their unspoken answer. We can't make a child care about conventions. On the other hand, I take every opportunity to move children's work out of the classroom and into the school, to be read by other children. In talking with these young writers, I focus on what the child knows, all the while pointing out that other people need to be able to read his text.

Handwriting and spelling are linked. Research shows us that when children write with an unpredictable scrawl, they get a poor visual image of the word, which hinders them when they spell. Thus, if Alex can work on a computer or typewriter, the machine text not only adds prestige to his work, it enhances the spelling as well. The machine text signals a more adult way of sharing a text. In the mid-1930s Donald Durrell of Boston University did a study for the Royal Typewriter Company. It showed that using a typewriter greatly enhanced children's spelling. I suspect that the same factors are operative when children use computers.

List building helps children learn conventions. I begin by letting the child know which conventions she uses accurately and then work to expand the list (see Chapter 12). Starting with the area the child has chosen for improvement (children *do know* where they need to improve) I expect her to decide where there are misspelled words or where punctuation is needed. If the area she has chosen is spelling, she circles words she thinks may be misspelled. Remember through all this work with the child to maintain your focus on the content. People write to convey important information.

4. What do I do when I have children who come from another culture and language and yet need to write in English?

Above all, make sure the non-English-speaking child does not become isolated from the rest of the class or the school. If a child is disoriented within the school or confused about the ongoing work of the classroom, writing will be even more difficult. Designate particular children to sit next to him and interpret overall classroom work and school life for him. Where possible arrange to have children ride on the bus or walk with them to school. If you are in an area with high concentrations of non-English-speaking children, ask those who are more advanced in their transitions to help.

Use pictionaries. Ask the children to make drawings to accompany their work, then photocopy the drawings and write in words to go with key items represented in the drawings. In this way it is easy to build a vocabulary of nouns. (Verbs are another story.)

It may be necessary to let children write in their first language when they come to class. Indeed, I need to see how fluent they are in the first language to get a sense of what sort of transition they will make. Children who write extensively in a first language have a much easier time.

Children who are new to a culture and a language are often quite homesick for the country they have left behind. Here, it is helpful if these children write letters to relatives and friends. Further, since many of them have already done some work in English, I ask them to write in both their native language and in English.

Don't underestimate the power of music and dance. Both are unique in their power to make children feel at home and to introduce them to the new culture. Children acquire language much more quickly from songs. They absorb the lyrics in a short time, and move on to use the words when they write.

Children who do not read and write in their own language are more difficult to help, especially if they are older, say beyond the age of eight. Chapter 16, "Spell to Communicate," will be of special help to these children.

You can also write letters to the children using language you know they can handle. Comment on their skills and classroom involvement. Allow them to consult with a friend in reading the letter and in writing one back to you.

Photographs help. Take photographs that record children's involvements in various classroom projects, on the playground, or in sports. Some photocopy machines do an excellent job of reproducing photos, allowing you to put together a kind of photo pictionary for them to use in their writing.

5. My children simply don't like to revise. What do I do?

First, look at the age of the children. Primary-grade children, especially those in first grade, need not consider revision at all. They usually display new skills in the next piece they write, rather than go back over something they've already written. They may add information to the end, but they do not usually go into a text to revise. You may, however, have a few more advanced children who are capable of handling some preliminary work on revision.

On the chalkboard or the overhead projector, I demonstrate how I handle changes in my text. At points where they want more information, I show them how I put it in. Today many primary classrooms have computers, which makes revising much easier.

Revision often involves clearing up minor errors in spelling, grammar, and punctuation. If a piece is going to be published, displayed, or sent out of the room to other audiences, I insist that children focus on *one or two* areas that are within their grasp and concentrate on them in their final copy. I want the children to see how these changes enhance the meaning of the piece. Above all, I want these revisions to become part of their growing repertoire in the use of conventions.

For young children, but especially for older children, revision that deals with content reflects the fact that the writer knows more about the subject than is evident on paper. Revision makes little sense to a child who knows little about her topic. If children are asked to revise pieces when they know little about the subject, they have little personal investment in their writing. Obviously, our task as teachers is to show children how to choose well and continue to help them know what they know.

Revision also makes little sense for children who have not yet grasped what writing can do. These children are often in transition from speaking to writing. Indeed, early in their primary years, their text is filled with interjections, blacked out words, and words that are two lines high, all evidence that the child is trying to put speech on the page, to make the text sound like speech. Children at this point in their development are often puzzled if asked to revise a text they treat more as a "spoken" document than a written one.

The ideal conditions for revision include the following:

- The child cares about the piece.

- The child knows the subject well.
- The final text will exist independent of the author: it will be posted on a bulletin board, published, or leave the classroom for other audiences.
- The child understands what writing can do.
- The child has a sense of the audience who will read the piece.

Although not all of these conditions are present when a child revises, the list serves to remind you of the areas that you need to attend to over a long period of time if revision is to achieve an important place in children's development.

My entire response to the revision question is based on one very important assumption: that children are writing every day in a variety of genres and the teacher writes with them. Children revise best when they can choose, from a wide variety of writing, the piece they wish to move ahead. Sadly, too many children are forced to revise when they have written only one piece and write only one day a week.

Questions About Teaching

1. How do I find time to teach writing?

Finding time to teach writing usually means saying "yes" to new things and "no" to some practices you've followed in the past. "That was easily said," you retort, and you are right in your judgment. Without question, teaching time today is continually eroded by annual additions to the school curriculum. The day is punctuated by one interruption after another. It seems that school administrations respond to a crisis with yet another quick-fix solution. Even at school, children experience a fractured world that seems to reenact the jumpy rhythms of the TV hour, with its short bursts of programming, followed by advertisements.

Such a busy zigzag world requires more reflection, not less. The faster the world spins, the more we need to slow down. Thus, writing and all other expressive forms that seek to see, understand, and express become still more important. As long as I can appreciate what writing can do and its role in the lives of my students, I will struggle to find time for it. This is yet another reason to add to the list of why we need to write.

Where then do I find the time? First, I combine the teaching of reading and writing. One process is the flip side of the other. I teach writers to read as writers read, and readers to note how writers write. I bring out the children's writing and reading at the same time and look at each in similar ways. You will find the *Reading/Writing Teacher's Companion* series helpful if you need more information, especially Chapter 2 in *Build a Literate Classroom* (1991), "Rethink Learning and the Use of Time."

An underlying concern about fitting writing into the curriculum is the gut question, "How on earth can I respond to all the writing the children are doing? I'm up to the gills now. Adding that on is more than I can take." You are right again; you can't *add on* more work. As I've already mentioned, you need to begin to say "no" to some things and "yes" to others. Teaching children how to take more responsibility for their own work is a long-term commitment. Working on reading and writing simultaneously allows a higher quality of response. When I expect a child to speak first in conference regarding: (1) telling me the one thing the piece is about; (2) where he is in draft; and (3) what he will do next or what he will need help on, I have provided a frame for the child to be self-oriented and self-directed.

As for responding to children's work, I don't need to respond to each piece a child writes. Indeed, if children are writing every day, the way they should be, it is virtually impossible to respond to all their writing. Nor does the child need a response to each piece. Every four days or so I expect children to put a self-chosen piece in my "Read" basket. I want the child to tell me what I ought to look for when I read; children above grade three should *write out* how they want me to read their work. Of course, this works only if I am also demonstrating how to read our own writing in mini-lessons. If some children need me to read more frequently, I may say, "I'd like you to put this in my 'Read' basket this morning so I can see how things are going," as I move around the room.

2. Finding time for my own writing is even more difficult than finding time to teach writing. How do I find that time and is it really that important?

It is hard to find time for something new. Obviously, something has to be put aside. And it takes time simply to learn how to find the time.

Let me explain with an example. I've been a runner now for about thirty years. But the running is an up and down proposition. There is always some part of the year when I'm woefully out of condition. I want to start running again, but I just never get the right urge to do it. I'm too tired or mentally I'm not ready for the agony I know I'll feel in my first run. I have to lower my expectations: showing up is good enough. The second day is a little harder; I have some pain from the first day. The third day is still more difficult—more pain. By the fourth day I'm delighted that I'm still there and now the aches are going away. This example breaks down here, however, because I know from experience that after four days I'll feel better. Best of all, along with getting in shape, I find I'm learning the most important aspect of all: how to find the time to run. (As I write I'm in the best shape I've been in for at least fifteen years, and I see time to run everywhere.)

How does this apply to your writing? Commit yourself to ten days of writing for ten minutes. Write at a time when your biological clock will work for you—in the morning if you are a morning person, and in the evening if you are an evening person. Or write along with the children in class. Buy a small spiralbound notebook and examine your day for things you wonder about. When you write, lower your standards: "show up," get the words down, write rapidly, and change nothing. Lest I sound like a used car salesman, I would add that at the end of ten days you'll see all kinds of moments to do your writing.

3. How can I be sure the children are really becoming better writers? In short, what's the best way to evaluate?

Once again, it is through our own writing, our own commitment to becoming better writers, that we see from the inside what good writing is. Practice reading your own work using the elements writers use to read writing:

- Write in one sentence what one of your pieces is about. Help children to read for the "one thing" their piece is about. When you help children to do this, you will see how their work is becoming more focused.
- Look for "showing" in their work, where they help you to see what a piece is about.
- Look for "telling."

- See which children are choosing their topics more effectively; that is, they know more about their subject. Even more, they *care* about it.
- Look for more precision in the use of nouns and verbs.
- Listen and record how children speak about their work. Are they becoming more specific? Listen when children share and respond to each other, and in your conferences with them.
- Observe children's growing lists of conventions they use in their work.

4. How much does reading help writing or writing help reading?

It is difficult to know how much one actually helps the other. It is rare that a good writer doesn't read and absorb how a piece is put together by another writer. But there is no guarantee that good readers will write. I suspect this may have to do with the emphasis placed on reading in school curricula to the exclusion of writing. Writing is a demanding part of the curriculum for both teachers and students.

There is no reason, however, why one process cannot help the other, provided adequate time is given to each during the school day. At the same time, we need to demonstrate how we read in the writing process and "compose" in the reading process. (The entire *Reading/ Writing Teacher's Companion* series is devoted to the relationship of one to the other.)

Writing is the making of reading. If we know how to construct reading through writing, we will better understand how to take reading apart. This means that young writers are aware of how writers compose because teachers have shown them using their own composing. Teachers show how they read and reread a text during the writing as well as afterward. Further, when we expect children to evaluate their work as writers would, composing a critique and attaching it to what they pass in, we will more effectively combine the two processes.

It is helpful if students read in the same genre in which they write in order to learn from other writers. Of course, we need to show students *how* to read these texts. Try to combine the reading/writing time into one block. Above all, do not separate the processes and assign separate teachers to each, as often happens in middle and junior high schools. The processes have too much in common to waste time in this way.

5. Our local and state systems for evaluating writing simply don't resemble process approaches to teaching writing. How do I deal with the testing problem?

Above all, don't change how you teach from day to day. At the same time, I find it helpful to talk the entire process through with the students. I want them to understand just how different the process is and give them hints for dealing with testing. Unfortunately, too many states still test using the one line prompt, which allows children little chance to use the full range of the thinking process. Students do not have a chance to gather information, organize it, try a series of drafts in order to clarify a subject, or discuss their composing with other writers. In short, there is little "construct validity" to the operation, little resemblance between the writing students ought to be doing in class on a day-to-day basis and how they are expected to perform in the assessment.

If your students are used to composing short opinion pieces following discussions in content areas, they ought to be able to do well on such assessments. From time to time children should write on demand:

- *Following a classroom discussion:* "We've just had a long discussion about how we might rearrange the room. There are several sides. Now I want you to state your position in one or two sentences and then give some reasons to support your ideas. You'll have fifteen minutes. Begin." *In this instance children have a fund of information from the oral discussion. I expect them to take a position and write it down. Sometimes I may vary the assignment by asking them to state both sides of an argument and then take a position. Such writing can apply to science, social studies, and so on.*

- *Letters:* Sometimes there are issues that need to be addressed through letters to people outside the classroom. I may direct one or two children to compose such a letter.

- *About learning:* "I'd like you to write the next two things you think you need to learn to be a better writer. Discuss how you think you will go about that learning." *Since I am constantly asking children to state their next learning objective, as well as how they will reach the objective, I will also ask them to do this in writing.*

Sometimes children don't know how to handle the unfamiliar prompt and then develop a piece. But their greatest problem in working with a prompt is its decontextualized nature. Their own writing is very much embedded in the context of the classroom—as it should be. I try to help children deal with the context of a test and to develop a few strategies for the prompts. You might take several of the prompts from previous years and show children how you would work with them.

IV

BROADEN THE CHILDREN'S REPERTOIRE FOR WRITING

18 HELP CHILDREN READ AND WRITE FICTION

Children want to read and write fiction. Of all the genres, fiction is usually their favorite. In recent years more and more schools have moved from basal texts to trade books, from readers designed to teach reading to books by professional authors written just to be read. Children want to be immersed in the fiction of these great storytellers. At the same time, a good share of them wish to write fiction themselves. They wish to create characters in situations of their own design. In many classrooms the child who has moved from writing her own personal narrative to composing an imaginary tale has become a "real" author.

When children choose to write fiction they take on a difficult assignment. Of all the genres, I think fiction is the most demanding. This does not mean that children should be held back from writing fiction. Rather, it means that we need to do much more to help them than we may have realized in the past.

Most of the fiction that children write reflects their impression of what fiction is like. They want their stories to be exciting. Thus, their focus is on high-speed events reminiscent of Saturday morning cartoons. Older children choose bizarre and violent plots from evening television shows that involve high-speed automobile chases, space shootings, or war with modern weapons. Sometimes children put in so much violence that teachers simply outlaw fiction writing. One teacher in our research told the children, "No fiction until after Christmas; I simply can't stand it!"

I was so troubled by children's fiction that I decided to study it (Graves 1989a). I didn't know where to start and turned to Donald Murray's (1990b) collection of quotations to see what writers, from the early Greeks until modern times, have said about writing. I focused on fiction and found their vote nearly unanimous: character is all. The study of fiction—whether in reading or in writing—requires us to focus on children's use and understanding of character in the books they read and the stories they write.

Figure 18.1 (Graves 1989a) illustrates the results of my study of children's use of character in their writing.

First, a review of the columns: Generic characters are those children already know, like Snoopy, Garfield, Teenage Mutant Ninja Turtles, 007, or unicorns and Care Bears. Children may see them on television or sitting on the shelves of a toy store. Children also use the names of their friends in their stories or, writing in the first person, appear themselves. Finally, they actually create new characters that have first and last names. When children begin to give their characters names they have never heard before, it marks the beginning of a more three-dimensional treatment of their characters. In my study, no new

▲▼Figure 18.1
Children's Use and Revelation of Characters in Their Fiction

Grade	Generic	Friends	First Person	Created Names	Dialogue	External Description	Internal Reflection
1	★★	★★	★				
2	★★★	★★★	★★★	★	★★		
3	★★	★★★	★	★★	★★	★	
4	★	★★	★★	★★★	★★★	★	
5		★★	★★	★★★	★★★	★★★	★★★
6		★★★	★★★	★★★	★★★	★★	★★

★   Minimal use
★★   Moderate use
★★★ Extensive use

characters with first and last names appeared in first-grade writing and I found them only occasionally in second-grade writing.

I want to call attention to the final column, "Internal Reflection." What this means is that the main character reflects on the conse-quences of his actions or the actions of other characters in the story, "Oh, I see why he did that. His brother must have made him do it." In this kind of story we begin to understand why people do things. There is motive, there are consequences to human action. For a long time the characters in children's stories exist merely to serve the plot: "We are going to have these people go to the moon, then they will meet space invaders who will take over their ship. In the end the invaders will be burned to a crisp with lasers." What happens in the story has little to do with the nature of the characters.

At the same time, fiction offers children one of the best opportuni-ties to begin to understand other people, themselves, and the human condition. When children receive help in writing fiction in mini-lessons and teacher demonstrations, they learn how to create charac-ters and struggle with the ambiguous problems of their everyday lives. Unfortunately, at about the time children can deal with the seri-ous demands of fiction in middle school and junior high, schools switch to essay writing and responding to literature as the main writ-ing diet. The amount of time available for writing drops off in the upper grades, and this may account for the small amount of fiction children are allowed to write.

ACTION 18.1:
Examine how your children use and understand characters in fiction.

This Action has three parts, which together will allow you to see how well children understand the central concepts of fiction. For the first part, read two pieces of fiction several children have written and then look to see how well you can understand the characters' actions through their earlier behavior or background details.

Interview the children whose work you have just read. Ask them these simple questions: "Why did your character just do that? Why did he go to the moon? Tell me what the space invaders had in mind when they took over the earth. There must have been something that happened before that made them do this." In most instances, children have not thought about these matters before. What I am interested in, however, is whether they can come up with reasons on the spot, whether they can create a context that will explain the actions of their characters. Remember to allow the child enough time to think about all of this, which will require good waiting time on your part.

Finally, ask one of these same children to read a short selection from a fiction book, preferably, the one the child is already reading. (I like to have children do some reading in the same genre in which they are composing.) Once again, explore with the child the reasons for the characters' actions as evidenced or implied in the text. I work back and forth between what the authors are doing in the books children are reading and their own compositions. I do not do this with the notion that children will do exactly what the author is doing but that they will appreciate what goes into a work of fiction.

John Gardiner says, "Every line of fiction is a promise of something that you will have to deal with later on in the work" (Gardiner 1985). If you say in the first paragraph that the boy's brother was very sick, you will have to deal with that sickness later on. If you say your character is evil, that character will have to do something evil and you will need to have some understanding of his behavior. Of course, unless teachers show children how to deal with these matters, they will remain prisoners of video plots that seldom give attention to motivation and ignore the consequences of a character's actions.

Remember that in all three parts of this Action you are trying to get a sense of the child's knowledge of character and of the reasons for the characters' actions. The child may not have written about these directly; it is enough that the child can orally explain why things are happening.

In this chapter, the basic approach will be to experiment, creating characters, learning how to develop them, and finally, writing a short piece of fiction. When you demonstrate the Actions with the children, in most instances you will want them to learn more about fiction. They won't necessarily carry out the Action on their own. With some older students, however, you may wish to have them also carry out the Action on their own in class. You will need to exercise your best judgment about their readiness to do the assignment.

ACTION 18.2:
Read the world for characters.

In this Action you'll be involved in a familiar practice, reading the world (see Chapter 3). In this instance, however, you'll be reading the world for characters, learning how to develop them, and writing a short piece of fiction. I'll do the Action first in order to show you what I mean.

I'm writing this chapter on Christmas day. I'll look back at yesterday, the day before Christmas, for potential characters I could use in a short piece of fiction. I'll be looking at other people as well as myself. Here is a first draft. I write as I think aloud about characters:

- I'll start my reading at about noon yesterday. Of course, since it is the day before Christmas we are working hard to be ready for our guests, two of our daughters and their families. My wife, Betty, has a good list of things for me to do: make two beds, get trash to the dump, vacuum upstairs and down. She's busy making cranberry bread while I do the other chores. As I make one bed and put in the hospital corners I recall my mother teaching me how to make beds for the boarders that lived in our home. Mother was a nurse, as is my wife, and making those corners bring back memories. *The character I feel within me is a boy who is trying to help his mother as part of the war effort. Suddenly my mother is a woman who is raising a boy alone and he is trying to help her make ends meet by doing his part in cleaning the rooms where the boarders stay.*

- I work hard, occasionally glancing at the clock and trying to estimate when the company will arrive. Our granddaughter, Margaret, races inside followed by their dog and Corie, our daughter Laura's dog. It strikes me that the dogs are as excited by our excitement as the children. Dogs catch moods quickly. *I see a child here who can't wait to tell a story to grandmother. She's been rehearsing a bit of news all the way in the car. The child is very close to grandmother and has come on a long journey.*

- Everyone is in the house now making comments about the tree. "Where did you get it? We have more presents to put under it." Greg, our grandson, enters with a Christmas present he has already opened at home. He wants to show me the mechanism, the speeds, switches, and controls. I am baffled by the toys children have today. *Suddenly I'm an old man who can't keep up with the world, with toys, with the electronic items in his life. He's an old man visiting his daughter; he is eighty years old and wants to make some coffee and lunch, and he is trying to figure out the electronic devices in the kitchen. It is all very baffling to him. He longs for the simple kitchen of the old days.*

- Christmas is a homecoming, a homecoming for our daughters and the grandchildren. It is different for the sons-in-law. We live in a new house, one that is only four years old. I wonder if one of our "children" is yearning for the old house we lived in for twenty years. But we have kept the same Christmas rituals in each place and I think the rituals make the holidays. *Ah, I sense a character coming here. There is a character who lives for ritual, invariant ritual of food, sleep, presents, singing. This year she is in a shaky marriage and she is counting on the rituals of home to secure a strong base for knowing that all is well in the family around her.*

That's a quick fifteen-minute look at yesterday and the events of yesterday. Remember, I am looking for characters I can draw from my own makeup and experience and from that of the people I meet. I'll look at the four episodes again:

- While making a bed I flash back to when I was a boy. I'm a boy who wants to help his mother make it by cleaning the rooms of the boarders. *Notice that I let characters be easily transformed into other characters. I go from making a bed at home yesterday to making a bed as a boy, to creating a fictitious character who wants to help his mother.* The key word is *wants*. Neil Simon says that only recently he realized that nothing happens until his main character wants something and wants it badly. Thus I'll be looking for what each of these characters wants.

- In the second episode I find in my granddaughter a young girl who has special news for her grandmother. I suspect that she *wants* to tell her news, to share an accomplishment of some sort that will please her grandmother.

- In the third episode I discover a character who *wants* his world to be simpler in my own experience with my grandson's Christmas toy.

- In the fourth episode I find a character who relies on the rituals of Christmas. She *wants* Christmas to be the same every year, especially this year. This character took shape from my wondering about how our children now regard rituals.

If you try this Action at home before you introduce it to the children, take an hour or two and look for potential characters within yourself and in others. Take a situation or a trait and adapt it to a fictional character. Above all, think of what your character *wants*. When you feel comfortable, demonstrate how you do this in a mini-lesson.

ACTION 18.3:
Sketch in a character.

In this Action I'll look over my notes and choose one character to develop more completely. I'll choose the character who intrigues me, the one I may understand better than the others: the boy in the first episode who wants to help his mother. A good part of my sketching will involve probing into the history of this boy and his situation. There is a principle in writing fiction that it is most important to ponder: *When writers write fiction, they know far more about their main character than they are ever able to put into the story.* Thus, in this Action I am working to get acquainted with my main character. I'll take ten minutes to sketch in a profile of the boy and his mother:

- First, I'll give the boy a name. I sense that Jimmy is the right name. Sometimes I ponder a name for some time but right now Jimmy Wilkins seems right and he lives alone with his mother, Margaret Wilkins. His father died two years ago, and his mother is trying to make ends meet. If they make enough money they'll be able to move back to New England where they once lived before his father died of leukemia.

- In one sense Jimmy is an overly conscientious boy who imagines his mother marrying again someday so that he'll have a father at home. He wants the father, however, to be from New England so that he'll end up there. His grandparents also live in New England. Jimmy is ten years old, quite responsible, overly so I'd guess.

- His mother, Margaret, worries that Jimmy has taken on her seriousness and really needs to get outside and play with other children. Since his father died, he has become the "little man." She genuinely needs his help around the house while she works her regular job from 9:00 to 4:30 as a secretary for a shipping company.

- The situation is that there are two men who rent rooms in their large house. If she is to keep the house, she must have boarders. She needs to keep the house because she must be able to sell it in order to get back to New England. She worries about Jimmy, who has to be alone at the house after school, his need to get outside, make friends.

- Jimmy is just old enough to take on some of his mother's worries, especially about losing the house.

That was a quick ten-minute sketch of Jimmy and his mother. The characters now have just enough background to get me started. Jimmy *wants* to get back to New England with his mother and to keep the house so they can sell it. He has perhaps become an adult too soon. At least that's his mother's concern. She worries about keeping the house and takes in boarders, but she also worries that her son is too much alone and too serious to act like a real kid. My underlying question as I go to write is, "What do these characters want and why do they want it?" Their wants overlap, but mother and son are unique in how they play out their concerns.

Take some time now to sketch in your own character. Establish that there is something your character wants and dig as deeply as you can to unearth why your character wants it. In an immediate sense, the character may want something material: a book, a car, a bicycle, a trip to Disney World. For all of these I probe and ask, "What is there in this person's history, her makeup, her situation, that makes her have that want?"

ACTION 18.4:

Choose a situation that will reveal your character and write a short ten-minute piece of fiction.

You may wish to try this Action at home before you try it with the children. You can practice exploring the background of your characters to discover their wants and what might stand in the way of attaining them.

As I go to work, I have a rough picture in my mind of Jimmy and his mother. Now I need to think of a situation that will show or reveal what they are like, especially Jimmy. I think I'll choose a spot where their worlds intersect: The mother has just come home from work. She begins to prepare supper and inquires about Jimmy's day while she does so. Take a few moments now to sketch in a situation that will reveal your character. Try to see your character reacting to something, something that will suggest what she wants.

Follow these guidelines as you write for ten minutes. (These are a version of the same guidelines I mentioned back in Chapter 3):

- Write rapidly: allow thoughts in from the shadows.
- Change nothing: don't meddle.
- Lower your standards: first-draft work is rapid sketching. It works if you've done the background work in the two previous Actions.

Now, picture the scene in which your character will reveal herself. I'll write with you:

> Jimmy Wilkins looked out the window to see if his mother was in sight. He knew her habits well. She left work at 5:00 P.M. and she'd go straight out the door to her car in the parking lot, get in her car, and drive the fifteen minutes it took her to get home. Occasionally, she'd stop at Store 24 to pick up some milk, orange juice, or breakfast cereal, but that would take her only an extra ten minutes.
>
> This afternoon he'd done his usual cleaning of Mr. Pym's room, their elderly boarder. He'd vacuumed around the edges of the bed, a little under, and then put on clean sheets. Mr. Pym didn't say much. He'd had a mild stroke five months before. Oh, he could handle things all right and be alone, but Jimmy liked the feeling of helping him and doing small things. He wondered what it would be like for Mr. Pym after they sold their home and moved back to Cape Cod, where his grandparents lived.

Every bed made and every room cleaned brought them that much closer.

He heard the garage door open and the familiar click and slam as his mother shut the door to the car. Sometimes he'd listen for the speed of her footsteps. If they were slow, maybe he'd better be quiet and listen, or if they were fast, maybe she'd be in a good mood. He worried about his mother, especially in those first months after his father died. "Well, just the two of us now, Jimmy," she'd said. She put her head in her hands after that. "I'm sorry, Jimmy," she'd said. "You must feel terrible too." Jimmy had cried lots too, but he remembered one day saying to himself, "Got to grow up. Got to help Mom."

"Hi, Jimmy, what's new? How'd your day go?" she said cheerily. "Oh dear, I think I got something on my coat when I went by the woodpile."

My ten minutes is up. (If you wonder why you may not have written as much as I have, it is probably because I compose very rapidly on my computer.) I was surprised by some of the traits my writing revealed in Jimmy. He is so used to waiting for his mother to come home that he has learned all the signs of her coming: the time, the sounds, her moods. I think a boy who looked forward to his mother's coming home after he'd been alone for two hours would notice these kinds of details. In a ten-minute draft I can only achieve a general kind of plausibility; I am sure there are little inconsistencies that would make a reader say, "Hmmm, I'm not sure if a boy would say that under those circumstances."

As you reread your text, look for the little touches that reveal your character. I began with Jimmy waiting for his mother and simply wrote the answer to this simple question: "How would a boy who had been home alone for two hours wait for his mother, given the background already revealed about him?"

Now you have experienced what it means to begin to write fiction. Of course, it is unlikely that children will begin with the notion of character. A review of their use of character (see Figure 18.1) shows that their interests center on action. Children are fascinated by action. They are attracted to the "motion" aspects of fiction. Characters basically exist to serve a predetermined plot. Thus, when they write, they are expressing their impression of what fiction is, just as they made large motion marks with a pencil when they were three or four years old to signify writing. Indeed, a television program with a "good" plot is what will hold their interest. Their focus at this stage is on the action. They don't realize that it is how the characters are drawn that produces the true tension in the plot. Our task as teachers is to show children—in what they read and in mini-lessons—how to appreciate and write fiction.

ACTION 18.5:
Conduct a short mini-lesson with children to help them see what questions best develop a character.

To give children a feel for what questions help them gather information about characters, I conduct ten-minute mini-lessons. I choose a character, talk a little about the person, and then say, "I'm going to tell you a few things about a new character. Then you can ask questions to learn still more about that person. I'll make up the character in response to the kinds of questions you ask. I'll make believe I'm the character."

Don: My name is Jimmy and I'm ten years old and in the fifth grade. I just wish I had a dog. I've always wanted a dog. For two years now I've wanted a dog.

Child: What kind of a dog do you want?

Don: Any kind of dog. Just a dog.

Child: How come you want a dog so much?

Don: See, I want a dog to play with, go places, like the dog would always be there as your friend. He could sleep on my bed.

Child: Well, how come you don't have one?

Don: Well, my mom's allergic to them she says. The hair makes her sneeze. There must be some dogs that don't make people sneeze.

Child: What about getting another animal? Maybe she's just allergic to dogs.

In this mini-lesson the children are more concerned about dealing with Jimmy's problem, how to get a dog, than in developing background information on him. This is a natural thing to do. I can use my answers, however, to bring in background information. I'll stop now and use the mini-lesson for discussion:

Don: I want to stop now and see what we know about Jimmy. Tell me everything we've learned so far.

Child: He wants a dog.

Child: He's wanted one for two years.

Child: He's stuck because his mother has allergies and he can't get the dog.

Don: Tell me, if Jimmy was right here now what kind of person do you think he'd be?

Child: He'd be okay cuz he likes dogs.

Don: What could you ask to find out what kind of person he is?

Child: I could ask him what he likes in school.

Don: All right, you ask him. I'll be Jimmy again and you (the class) can ask some more questions.

Child: Okay, what do you like in school?

Don: Not much. I don't do too well. I work hard but I have so many papers I'm always behind. The teacher says I should try harder, but I really am trying hard. It takes me so long to answer the questions, I'm always behind.

Child: Have you talked this over with the teacher?

Don: Not really. I just don't think she'd understand.

The children are learning more about Jimmy now. Gradually, they begin to realize that when the character speaks about his values in relation to various events in his life, they learn a little more about him. At this point, or perhaps on another day, I'll turn to a piece of fiction by a professional author, read a short passage, and then ask the children what they have learned about the character thus far. I'll push them to the point of asking them how they'd like the character if they were to see him every day and press them for evidence to back up their conclusions. I'll demonstrate this mini-lesson by using the first page of E. B. White's *The Trumpet of the Swan.*

Walking back to camp through the swamp, Sam wondered whether to tell his father what he had seen.

"I know one thing," he said to himself. "I'm going back to that little pond again tomorrow. And I'd like to go alone. If I tell my father what I saw today, he will want to go with me. I'm not sure that's a very good idea."

Sam was eleven. His last name was Beaver. He was strong for his age and had black hair and dark eyes like an Indian. Sam walked like an Indian, too, putting one foot straight in front of the other and making very little noise. The swamp through which he was traveling was a wild place—there was no trail, and it was boggy underfoot, which made walking difficult. Every four or five minutes Sam took his compass out of his pocket and checked his course to make sure he was headed in a westerly direction. Canada is a big place. Much of it is wilderness. To get lost in the woods and swamps of western Canada would be a serious matter.

On the first page, E. B. White introduces Sam, describes the setting, and sets out the basic plot elements for the entire book. I'd begin my mini-lesson as simply as this: "I'm going to read the first page of *The Trumpet of the Swan*. I want you to be detectives and listen for clues that tell me everything you think Sam knows." We would compile a list of something like this:

- He has to be careful with his father. There's something he knows about him that means he has to be careful.
- He knows how to walk in the woods like an Indian and make very little noise.
- He knows how to use a compass.
- He knows how to be careful in the woods.

I find that if I focus on what the character *knows*, I can see more clearly how the author reveals clues that draw on the character's history. White immediately introduces tension between Sam and his father into the story. If we ask the basic question ("What does Sam want?"), these clues show us that Sam has a secret he wants to keep to himself, a secret special enough for him to bushwhack in the wilderness and follow a compass to an important location in the swamp.

ACTION 18.6:

Ask your children to take out the fiction they are reading and make a list of anything they know about their characters.

This is a good follow-up to the mini-lesson on *The Trumpet of the Swan*. Ask the children to try to figure out what their character knows and what their character wants. I recognize that both "knowing" and "wanting" are concepts that children only begin to assimilate over time. But they are at the heart of understanding characters. When I ask a child in conference, "Why did he do that?," he'll need to draw on what he's revealed about what the character knows and wants.

Reading and Writing Belong Together

ACTION 18.7:

Create a piece of fiction in which the children decide the elements that go into the story.

This mini-lesson is a joint venture in which you and the children create a story together. You ask the questions and the children come up with the information to keep the story moving. I often begin with the action or plot of the story, since children are more familiar with it. Then I take them back to the characters. Notice that I summarize to help the children keep in touch with the story and then go on to ask further questions. The following transcript is from a mini-lesson in a fourth-grade classroom (Graves 1989a, 29–31):

Don: I'd like you to come sit here on the floor or in chairs. Above all, it will be important for me to see you so that when you have a contribution to make I won't miss it. So, scrunch in close together. [*We are working in a corner of the room with probably no more than six feet from myself to the person in the back and no more than ten to twelve feet between children on the sides.*]

We are going to create a story together and as we do it, you are going to decide what happens, who the characters are. Things that happen decide the next things that happen. We'll do this so we can get a feel for all the things that go into a piece of fiction, and some of the questions authors ask themselves you can ask each other.

We're going to decide what goes into it, and I'll keep asking you questions to create the story. First, pick one problem to be solved. Try three and we'll talk about each. What could happen?

Child: Could have a mystery.

Don: Okay, a mystery. What's the mystery?

Child: Someone stole a book.

Don: Let's have a couple more.

Child: A murder mystery, people getting killed.

Don: Tell me more. Who killed the person?

Child: I don't know.

Don: We have two so far, a mystery with a stolen book and someone killed.

Child: There is going to be a kidnapping. Someone is missing, but we don't know if they are killed or not.

Don: So, we have three problems: a missing book, a murder, and someone who is missing. We'll vote on the three. Okay, looks like it is the missing person. [*Note that I continually restate details suggested by the children. Votes are taken on essential elements that go into a story: plot, characters, character names, descriptions of characters, etc.*]

The tone of the session is one of challenge. Note the following interchange:

Don: Tell me about the person who is missing.

Child: He is rich and famous.

Don: Why was he rich and famous?

Child: He wrote a book.

Don: Tell me about the book.

Child: It was a mystery book.

Don: What was special about the book?

Child: It was a big seller?

Don: What made it a big seller?

Child: It had certain things in the book . . . like jewels.

Don: Did that make it famous? We have a problem now. We have a person who is famous now, rich, has written a book, and we wonder why it became a best-seller.

Child: It was an imagination grabber. The book explains what it is. It made people want it most. Your main dream was in the book, and people identified with it.

In this beginning segment of the workshop with the children, the pattern of story construction with the leader becomes evident:

- plot: general
- characters
  - names
  - appearance
  - example of typical behavior
- setting
- specific plot action: beginning
- unfolding plot revealing characters

Notice that it is the role of the leader to call for the specific story components, then ask questions until children connect them to the main thrust of the story. Here is an example of a review of details following the introduction of a character and the addition of details about other characters:

Don: All right, let's look at what you have so far: a rich man, Mr. Mint, who is a writer, talkative, tending to brag about himself, who lives in Hollywood and is currently working on a screenplay. His daughter, Claire, is studying to be a nurse in a Boston hospital; she works very hard, is friendly, outgoing, but a little stuck on herself because of her wealth. She likes to manipulate people so they will come around to her way of thinking, and you are going to have her kidnapped in the Boston Common after her boyfriend tells her to sit on a bench while he gets her an ice cream cone. Now, tell me about the kidnappers.

Child: It is a man and a woman.

Don:	Tell me about the man.
Child:	He has a tattoo.
Don:	Why does he have a tattoo.
Child:	He got it when he was in the service?
Don:	You still didn't say why.
Child:	Well, all the guys on his ship wanted to get one so they had like a bond with everyone having this tattoo.
Don:	What did the tattoo look like?
Child:	It was a ship sailing on the ocean like.
Don:	There was some reason you chose a tattoo, called attention to it because it has to have something to do with this story.
Child:	The kidnapper and Mr. Mint have the same tattoo. See, Mr. Mint was in the service too about twenty years ago, and he was on the same ship with the kidnapper, and the kidnapper never forgave him for something he did to him, and he is going to get back at him by kidnapping his daughter. It's revenge.
Children:	Yeah, revenge.

Notice that the tone of this mini-lesson is one of direct challenge. I can question in this manner because my demands are directed at the entire class, not just one child. For example, in this mini-lesson one child suggested that one of the characters have a tattoo. My question, "Why does he have a tattoo?," is addressed to the entire class even though one child has made the suggestion. When the group tries to ignore the tattoo, I challenge them again: "There was some reason you chose a tattoo, called attention to it because it has to have something to do with this story."

Occasionally, children suggest bizarre elements. How well I remember a student in an eighth-grade classroom who suggested that the main character be four feet, five inches tall, and weigh 250 pounds. "Now that is interesting," I said. "You'll need a lot of detail to make that plausible. Tell me why this is important to the story and how he got that way. Must be quite a tale." I take the suggestion seriously, but I immediately challenge the student, because far more background is required for the implausible than for the conventional.

Although the main emphasis in this chapter is on characters in fiction, there is more to attend to than just characters. In one sense, right along with character I have also worked with plot. But there are other elements to teach: leads and conclusions, dialogue, showing what characters are like, setting, and so on. If you wish to continue to encourage children's fiction writing, consider reading *Experiment with Fiction* (Graves 1989a), in which these elements are developed more fully. You will be able to combine the children's reading right along with their writing. I also recommend Ralph Fletcher's *What a Writer Needs* (1992), which has an excellent chapter on "Creating a Character" and others that suggest still better ways to help children write in all genres.

Final Reflection

Children want to write in the genre they are reading. With fiction, they want to be known as writers who can excite others with the plots they spin in their stories. Unfortunately, children often turn to video stories, which prize high-action plots and in which characters play a minor role.

Fiction is a very demanding genre. Many find its demands are greater than those of other kinds of writing simply because the writer takes on the highly responsible job of creating believable characters. How hard it is to assume a godlike role and make characters believable. Many teachers don't want children to write fiction because they fill their plots with violence or create insipid characters whose actions have little sense or plausibility. Fiction, however, does offer children a unique opportunity to begin to analyze human behavior in order to create believable characters.

Professional writers of fiction say that "character is all." What occurs in the plot is a result of the nature of the characters themselves. In children's fiction, however, most of the characters exist for the plot. We need to help children become more proficient writers and readers by showing them through our mini-lessons just how to begin to enjoy their reading and how to write more plausible fiction.

The best way to help children read and write better fiction is to write fiction ourselves and show children how we create characters. If we don't we will continue to get stale, overly used TV plots with little regard for character. We must show children where we find characters, how we develop them, how we make them plausible: "What does my character want? Why did she do that? What does my character know?" We can use the good writing in the trade books they are reading to show children how professional authors set the scene, flesh out their characters, and handle dialogue.

19 SHOW CHILDREN HOW TO WRITE NONFICTION

Children want us to know what they think, and usually they let us know by speaking aloud. They are not alone. Adults prefer to talk on the telephone or address others in person. Writing is often the grudging medium for expressing opinions. Yet even before children come to school we notice that they use written language for signs and requests: "Kep ot" (Keep out!) or "CnIstaop" (Can I stay up?). They sense that the medium of writing has authority and they use it.

I notice that very young children try to persuade through "heaping" or accumulation. I refer to the "All About" books (Sowers 1985, 73) composed by young children, especially boys. These texts tend to be a listing of items: "There are hand-grenade shooters, bazookas, and flame throwers." In some instances each page contains a drawing of the particular weapon and a label in inventive spelling: bzuka (bazooka).

Personal narrative is another means of influencing others. The child writes "My Trip" and proceeds to compose a narrative she hopes will help others understand what a good time she had in her trip to the shore. In one sense all writing is persuasive. The writer works to hold the reader's attention long enough to present what she wishes to convey.

Unfortunately, little nonfiction, beyond personal narrative, is practiced in classrooms. Children are content to tell their own stories, but the notion that someone can write about an idea and thereby affect the lives and thinking of others is rarely discussed. Oral argument is important, but it is not enough. The letter, the essay, and the memo force us to be more precise with language. We want to persuade. We offer our point of view even as we acknowledge the point of view of others. A good storyteller must also be persuasive—she wants her audience to join her wholeheartedly in the story world she is creating. The essay, however, presents an opinion, one that requires some action of the reader. The writer knows there will be a reaction and intends to provoke one. Unfortunately, young children often address their essays to "to whom it may concern." Writing becomes an artificial exercise that teaches them little about the essay as a genre. A good share of this chapter will be devoted to what I call the "rhetorical construct," the situations in the course of a school day that present opportunities for these varieties of nonfiction.

ACTION 19.1:

Explore sources of nonfiction by reading the world.

Once again, I'll begin by recalling the events of yesterday from about 11:00 A.M. (when I finish my morning writing). I'll take ten minutes to write a first draft on my computer:

- 11:00 A.M.: I get a call to go skiing with friends from across town. This will be my first skiing of the season and I note a reluctance in myself to go. Takes so much preparation, skis (where are they), poles, boots. I really want to go with them. Further, the temperature is eight degrees above zero outside. I go because I know it will be good for me. I find that anything out of the usual pattern (first page in a chapter, first cross-country run, or first swim of the season) is hard to do. Is it age or what? *I see an essay here about the difficulty in making the first moves of the day, the season, the event. I finish with a question: "Is it age or what?" I wonder about that. I note that writing in all genres, any occasion for writing, begins with a question. I need to let children in on this. The time never seems right for something new, even though I've done it many times before.*

- By 12:30 A.M. I'm out skiing and loving it. Although we have had little snow, there is good cover at higher altitudes; only about another 800 feet up makes all the difference. *I am always amazed at the difference in snow from one level to another. This would be a good place to do research, a good hands-on study for myself. Of course, altitude affects temperature and one or two degrees make the difference between snow or rain.* "How come?" (the two most important words to a writer).

- On the way up in the ski touring center bus, I strike up a conversation with a group of young women from Smithfield, Rhode Island, who are cross-country skiing for the first time. I chat easily and openly, but I know that any male who does this usually causes problems with young women, who wonder what "this guy" is up to. Thus, I try to build in words about my wife and living locally, and I focus on their anticipation of skiing. The first conversation on their part is cautious, then one of openness and relief (I think). *I know that women have to be careful, and I don't want to worry them. I can see a nice joint article here starting with a letter from one of these women to a friend telling her what I did, and then the woman's point of view in return on whether she thinks I overstepped my bounds or was within them. My thesis is that it is too bad to have to remain silent for fear of worrying someone. On the other hand, I think there are signals a person can give that will help the other person to be comfortable with the situation.*

- I check with the bus driver to make sure I know when to get a ride back to my car. We both look at our watches. I want him to know that I mean business about time. *I sense that the bus driver isn't the least bit interested about my pushing him to say when he'll actually be present for the return trip. As an old Yankee bus driver, he'll arrive when he pleases. That bothers me. I see a short reflection here on my "time" system that bothers others.*

- I ski and chat with people along the way eventually catching up with my friends, who called me about skiing in the first place. I wonder if my first attempt to ski will be successful. I like to skate when I ski and I'm delighted to find that my cross-country running this fall makes a big difference. When I meet my friends, who are all better skiers than I am, there is a great delight in meeting on the trail. *What is there about meeting friends on the trail that is so delightful? I'd seen them the day before, but on the ski trail the setting has changed and maybe we are changed as people. There's an age piece here as well. At 63 will I still be able to ski like I did last year? I'm delighted to find things are better than last year. There's a short essay here: "We Never Stop Checking to See If We've Grown Up."*

- I'm also using a new ski suit, a one-piece suit that is a little more revealing of contours than I ought to dare. I wonder about the ego that purchased the suit. *Here's a good place for satire. A good laugh at myself. This might be a letter to a friend who skis or a short self-mocking essay.*

- I'm delighted at the grooming job the ski touring center has done on the snow. They've done miracles with only three to four inches. Further, they've been quite entrepreneurial at hiring a bus to take people to ski when there just isn't enough snow in the flat lands to encourage people to ski. *I'm so pleased with the manner in which our Ski Center does so much with so little snow. This is definitely a letter I want to write and will.*

Ten minutes are up. I've reflected briefly on what occurred over three hours and then looked back over the text to try to spot various writing opportunities. All my writing comes from an itch, an unanswered question just as it does in fiction, poetry, or any kind of prose. In this sense, all genres are the same: they deal with unanswered questions and with our sense of wonder. Sadly, we corrupt the purpose of writing by requiring our students to write about preordained learning that expects them to tell us what we already know. We want to demonstrate for children the origin of writing in the everyday life of the classroom.

Take a look at what happened yesterday from the time you left school and over the next several hours. As you jot down details, ask yourself, "How come or why do I feel that way?" I wrote some initial responses to this question as I reviewed the afternoon. Then I went back and looked over my writing to discover what topics might be appropriate for my nonfiction writing. This is what I found:

- Doing something new: I can see a reflective essay here. I write to find out why I delay in starting something new if

I've had a break from it. *According to the* American Heritage Dictionary *(1973) an essay is "a short literary composition on a single subject, usually presenting the personal views of the author." The essay, of all the genres, is the most highly personal.*

- Change in snow: This could be a research piece, a study of snow. *Whenever I sense that I need further reading or interviewing, I think of the short (or long) research report, which can be highly factual yet intermingle my sense of discovery.*

- Conversation with a woman: I'd try writing a letter to a woman friend or my wife about how a younger woman today reacts to my attempts to converse. This could also be an essay. *The origin of the essay is the letter. I find that writing a letter about a subject of high interest to me allows me to get a clearer picture of my own thinking.*

- Bus driver: I could see a character sketch of this "old Yankee," who apparently was doing a job he didn't care to do. *I enjoy describing people, sketching them out. This might be a human interest piece. Of course, he could be an excellent character for a short story.*

- Meeting friends: A delight to see friends in a setting we both enjoy but haven't visited for some time. A renewing of our friendship and our enjoyment. A short, reflective essay.

- Ski touring center grooming: This would be a letter to the staff thanking them for the job they've done in keeping us all skiing. *I enjoy writing letters when I initiate the subject. I find it much more difficult to answer letters. We need to help ourselves and our children initiate more letters. They are so much more powerful than phone calls.*

ACTION 19.2:
Write a short ten-minute piece of nonfiction.

It's time to choose one topic and write for ten minutes. I think I'll write a letter to a friend about initiating conversations with women. I'll choose a woman who will be frank with me about my views. I want you to make a selection from your exploratory list and follow the same guidelines you used when you wrote fiction in the last chapter:

- write rapidly.
- change nothing.
- lower your standards in order to get into the subject.

I'll write with you:

Dear Louise,

I know this letter comes out of the blue, but I've been doing some thinking following an incident I experienced yesterday. I wonder if you'd care to respond to what I write here, particularly giving your point of view from a woman's perspective. (I guess you could do no other, now that I think of it.)

I was riding on a bus up to a ski slope and I decided to strike up a conversation with the woman in the seat behind me. I enjoy speaking with people and obviously had no ulterior motive other than to have a friendly encounter. But, I realize in more recent times that women have to be on guard against men who start to operate. I'm obviously not a young man, with good white hair on the sides and no hair on the top. I've been told by some that "our kind" are the most difficult to deal with.

My whole point here is to ask your advice about how to put a woman at ease so it is clear there is no further attempt to be overly friendly. So, when I spoke with the woman about skiing and where she was from, I tried to intermingle conversation about my wife, Betty, and how much I've enjoyed skiing in the valley. She was with female companions, so I tried to open up the conversation so that she wasn't the sole focus. She helped me by speaking about her husband and children, how her husband was very helpful by shopping with the children while she skied.

I realize that I have a way of zeroing in on a person or situation and I suspect I can be overly focused when doing so. I want to be able to converse and meet people but not to the point that I frighten or put them off, particularly women. Of course, I was looking for signals that she might be ill at ease, which I suspect she might have been at first. I'm not the best in picking up signals, however, when I get overly enthusiastic or fascinated by what someone says.

So, I'd be most interested in what you make of what I'm saying. I've been warned by some of my women colleagues that they'll never respond to any conversation from a man for fear that the person may take advantage of them. Maybe all of this is just being overly concerned, but I'd appreciate it if you could give me a hand with your thinking. Thanks.

That's ten minutes of rapid composing at the computer. This is a typical first draft, with its winding search for a center. As I write, I realize I'm trying to be sensitive to three points of view: my own, that of the woman on the bus, and that of Louise. I focus most on my own point of view, and these questions run through my mind: "Why is this subject so important to me? Why am I writing this piece?" I know I want to converse with people, specifically women, but not in an inconsiderate way. Clearly, I'm trying to write my way into giving myself permission to do so.

Now that you've finished your ten-minute selection, reread it quickly and look for some of the following:

- What is your point of view? Where do you find the center of your feelings? Underline the sentence that shows it the most.

- Where are the facts to support that feeling? Facts are the details, the evidence to justify or represent a feeling. *In my letter I bring in the ways I try to help the woman be at ease. She does the same by mentioning her husband and children.*

- Draw a dotted line under the line or lines that surprise you. I was surprised by a line I remembered from somewhere: "Your kind, the men with white hair, can be the most difficult." I also was surprised that the woman sent signals about her husband and children. I didn't know that until I was writing. *The remarkable part about writing, if it is open to thoughts and observations without prior prejudice, is that facts creep in whose presence we knew nothing about before we sat down to write.*

ACTION 19.3:
Take one school day and observe the opportunities for using nonfiction.

This Action will help you to be aware of writing opportunities as they occur during the school day. If you can be sensitive to these moments, you will enter into the most powerful realm of teaching writing: showing children why people write and in what circumstances.

How well I remember the day in Mary Ellen Giacobbe's first-grade classroom when Gregory approached her to say in disgusted fashion, "Mrs. Giacobbe, someone from the other class is pushing papers under the door into our room. They can't do that. I want to go in and tell them to stop."

Mary Ellen responded, "No, they are busy in there right now, but you can write them a note. I suggest that you do that." Gregory, incensed by the episode, went straight to his table and wrote out a short cryptic note: "You are hereby ordered to stop pushing all papers under the door."

"How well do you respond to orders?" Mary Ellen asked Gregory. "Not very well."

"Then you might want to think of telling them why pushing papers under the door isn't a good idea. Maybe that would help them to see why they shouldn't." In this instance Mary Ellen does a marvelous job of steering Gregory from a first grader's usual response, the order, to the essay, a personal statement supported by facts.

I've seen other examples (Graves 1989b). A second grade class is incensed because the fifth graders have kicked their playground ball over the fence. The second graders address a letter (a precursor of the essay) to the fifth grade for a response. Four teens in Nancie Atwell's class had their ski tickets taken away because of a misunderstanding with the lift operator. They wrote a letter to the owner and got their tickets back. Children often come up with better ways to organize or run a class. I ask them to write, using careful, reasoned thinking that takes time, to express their views. This is what writing is for.

Consider the memo as an intermediary step between the letter and the essay. You might even consider displaying a memo board on which you post a daily memo that requests a response from the children:

From: Mr. Graves
To: The class

Subj: New children entering the classroom.

I need your help. We have two new children who will be arriving the day after tomorrow to our classroom. I need suggestions to help them feel more at home in our room. I'd appreciate your ideas on the subject. I'd like to know what you would do or what you'd suggest that the class do to help them become part of our class.

When the children respond, they use the same memo format: From, To, Subj. You can supply a memo box in which children place their responses. Further, open up the board as a place where children can address a memo to the class or to you.

ACTION 19.4:
Consider the meaning of knowing something well.

Nonfiction is an important genre for helping children and ourselves to know an area particularly well. In this sense, nonfiction is probably the most usable kind of writing for school and a lifetime of work. Sadly, children can complete their school careers and never experience the joy of really digging into information they wish to know well, of satisfying their curiosity about something that fascinates them. Until learners understand what it means to know something very well, they will settle too quickly for skimming the surface. And somehow we think that our splintered curricula can inspire a fascination about what it means to know.

Think this moment about an area of knowledge or a skill that you know particularly well and enjoy but didn't acquire in school. I've been writing a book for the past ten years on this subject. At first I was surprised by how few I had learned in school. Then I considered what these special skills had in common:

- A mentor was involved. I was able to spend large amounts of time observing how the mentor practiced the skill.
- The mentor showed me how he thought and actually used the skill in many contexts.
- I was able to spend large amounts of time pursuing and learning the skill.
- The mentor provided a picture and a vision of the completed work, so learning the skill made sense.
- The mentor invited me to do something he was already doing. A sense of invitation was important.

For this Action examine various skills or areas of knowledge you are acquainted with. I'll work on the Action with you to show what I mean. I'll list and comment on some things I enjoy doing and continue to read and study:

- Cross-country skiing, especially skating. *Thanks to Jane Hansen, my former colleague at UNH, I learned to skate on skis (see Graves, 1990). This took a fair investment of time, and I'm still working at learning how to ski that way.*
- Study of Birds. *I keep a careful journal on birds and the outdoors. I've been working at this for years, but I haven't really studied birds the way I'd like.*

- Bears. *Since we have bears in our area and in our yard from time to time I've taken up the study of bears both in my reading and in interviewing our local game warden. I've written a brief poem about one incident. I'd like to be more systematic about this.*

- Running. *Although I've jogged for nearly thirty years, just recently I've taken up the sport in order to be competitive. I am now in a running club which has a coach who reviews goals, helps us with speed workouts, and most importantly, I continually learn from other club members about their training and race experiences. Now I'm reading everything I can get my hands on about training schedules, diet, health, and physiology. Of all my interests, this one occupies center stage and therefore takes the most time for both the actual time spent running as well as the study of it.*

- Photography. *Last year I built a darkroom in order to return to this old interest of mine. Unfortunately, I haven't given it the time I'd like. I'd like to read more (I have the books and prints) and become immersed in it. I think the running has bumped this to one side. Years ago I spent a year as an apprentice to a photographer friend and was able to break into the art form. I miss the feeling of immersion in an expressive form.*

- Gardening. *This has taken off as an interest in the last few years and is something my wife and I have very much in common. She's the expert. I am the student. For me this is a seasonal interest (April–October) but during this period I devote large amounts of time to it.*

Each of these activities moves me to read and write nonfiction. Each of them, at one time or another, has brought me in contact with a mentor from whom I have learned. Unless I am involved in learning in some particular area, nonfiction holds little interest for me.

List specific areas of learning that interest you outside of your academic pursuits (see Figure 19.1). Some of the areas on your list may be highly active (running, interest in bears, and gardening) and inactive (birds and photography).

You may find that any one of these items will trigger the thought of an interest area of which you were unaware. It may be an awareness of what you were reading, someone who taught you a skill, or something you'd like to know more about. As I review my mentors,

▲▼ **Figure 19.1**

LEARNING AREA	MENTOR OR PERSON TEACHING YOU THE SKILL	NONFICTION READ IN CONNECTION WITH AREA
Cross-country ski skating	Jane Hansen	Didn't really read but kept a journal
Birds	Mother and high school biology teacher	Roger Tory Peterson bird book. *Bird Watcher's Digest.*
Bears	State game person and local wildlife person	*Black Bear*, local paper
Running	Bernie Livingston, Maggie Solomon, & other runners; Bob Johnson	*Runner's World, Running Times, The Lore of Running, Polar Heart Monitor Manual*
Photography	George Padginton	*Kodak Darkroom Guide* Ansel Adams, Yosuf Karsh
Gardening	Wife, Betty; Father, Hap Graves	Garden supply catalogs, state publications

some are quite obvious, as in the case of Jane Hansen with skiing or George Padginton with photography. On the other hand, my mentors in running (except for the coach, Bernie Livingston), learning about bears, gardening, or birding were probably unaware they were providing any mentoring or teaching at all.

I am also struck by how little writing I've done in these special interest areas. All are represented in my daily journal, but I have formally published on only bears and cross-country skiing. Perhaps the journal is enough, but the lack of formal writing, writing that is directed at others, has turned my head to think about publishing in these areas.

ACTION 19.5:

Help your children begin to understand what it means to know an area well.

Like ourselves, until children have a chance to begin to sense a territory of knowledge or a skill that interests them, nonfiction or writing nonfiction (outside of narrative accounts) will seem unimportant. I begin by helping children understand what it means to know something well. Take an area from your chart (Figure 19.1) that is close to you and has involved some mentoring and reading. If you can, choose an area that has some concrete aspects to it: cooking, sewing, ceramics, photography, plants, skiing, baseball, a place you have traveled, items of historical interest, or anything that can become a collection. Think back to Chapter 11 on portfolios. You may find an area to develop from the Action you tried there when you looked at collections. If you prefer, invite a guest speaker—an artist, a historian—to bring in a collection or some artifacts related to her topic of interest and ask her to speak briefly about her work. Here are some questions you and the children might find helpful:

- How did your interest begin?
- Were there people who helped you?
- Where do you find time to pursue your interest?
- How did you learn from your helpers?
- What have you read?
- What have you learned and what do you hope to learn next?

"What does it mean to know or to learn something quite well?" Curriculum coordinators, teachers, and children settle so quickly for so little. I have seen children become reinvigorated learners overnight when they were able to focus on one specific area and find out firsthand the joy of learning something well. Ironically, the children who need this experience most are children who are handicapped or have learning problems.

ACTION 19.6:

Help children work with nonfiction through the informal report.

Children need to know something about the content of their first report subjects before they even begin. I find that too many children are introduced to reports by trying to research something they know little about at the start. This approach usually guarantees that the child will see little sense in the function of the report other than to fulfill a school requirement. Further, their writing will be voiceless and the ordering of ideas will be unnecessarily difficult.

Think back to the three-column exercise you did in Chapter 2, when you learned the children's names and made a conscious effort to know something about each child. In those discoveries you probably saw something you could use to nudge children toward informal reports.

Children of all ages need to experience informal reporting before attempting longer, more extensive formal reports. For example, a first-grade child may have brought in a cricket or some nightcrawler worms she has found over the weekend. I'll receive and respond to what she has and, if it seems that she is quite interested in them, I might pursue it further:

Don: Angie, tell me how you found the cricket.

Angie: He was in the kitchen, actually. We heard him make a noise at bedtime and my mom helped me to catch him.

Don: What do you notice about the cricket right now? What do you see? What's he doing?

Angie: Well, he's got these things out front and those big legs and he's all black.

Don: What do you suppose they eat?

Angie: I don't know.

Don: That's something you can check out. I suggest that you head right down to the library and look over material about crickets. If you think you are interested and ready for this, we need someone to put together a one pager on crickets. This means you'd draw the cricket up here and then you'd write something down here about what you learn in the library. You might see if there is anything there about how they make that sound you heard. Do you think you are ready to try something like this? *[All the time we have been speaking about the cricket and reports, I'm trying to gauge Angie's readiness.]*

It is a good idea to have a selection of published materials on all kinds of subjects in science, social studies, or math so children can do one- or two-page informal reports. Older students can use the informal report as a way to get a quick overview of a subject for a more extensive piece. Include nonfiction sources on some of the following topics to interest children in the primary years:

Nature: frogs, crickets, worms, butterflies, chrysalis, plants, eagles, sharks, owls, weather, rocks, etc.

Pets: dogs, cats, gerbils, hamsters, turtles, parakeets, horses, etc.

Sports: specific players, hockey, baseball, football, basketball, soccer, gymnastics, stick ball, street hockey, etc.

Collections: Think back to Action 11.2 ("Consider different starting points for the children's portfolios").

Constructions: Some children like to put together directions to help others make things: puppet booth, model cars, instruments like the thermometer and barometer, small machines.

Of course, subjects for nonfiction in the primary years are limitless. I want children to include a number of elements in their one-page reports. Informal reports usually have a drawing of the main object or subject of the report. As much as possible, it is best that the child draw the object from direct observation. For example, I'd like Angie to draw the cricket by looking directly through the clear sides of her container. Admittedly, this is not easy for her to do because the cricket won't sit still, but she will notice details about the cricket that will give her a far greater appreciation of how the insect is put together.

Next, I want the child to include some facts that she feels are important for everyone to know. Sometimes this begins with a list, from which the writer needs particular items. The selection process is important. I want the child to be conscious of knowing more than she can include in a report and to make some value judgments about what readers need to "open" their interest in the subject. In some cases the child can refer the reader to other sources. One page of writing and art work is enough for young children, unless it is obvious that the child needs more space. Remember, the report is not exhaustive. Rather, it is meant to give the child practice in selecting information. "It's good if it's long," is a dictum waiting in the bushes to confuse the child into thinking length equals quality.

I've cited a number of nonfiction subjects for informal reports in the primary years. Many of these same areas appeal to the upper grades as well. (By "upper grades" I mean from grade four through middle school.) Virtually all the categories still apply. But if the informal report is final copy in the primary years, and is stored with the classroom's published collections, in the upper grades it is used to help students get into a subject, to view a larger study in shorter form.

Informal reports for older students follow the same guidelines as those for younger children. Students need to learn the process by reporting on something they know about in order to learn how to organize information and to discover their own voice. Older students often have a more difficult time finding a topic, since school experiences tend to remind them of what they don't know. Thus, it is even more important to do the three-column exercise in Chapter 2 for these students.

I'll write a report right along with the children. I begin by showing how I explore a subject, speaking aloud as I work:

Don: I've chosen to do a report on bears. First, let me say why I've chosen bears. Last June we had a black bear come into our yard twice. The first time he got the suet I'd put out for the birds; the second time he came back to see if he could get more suet or bird seed. They say bears never forget where they got their last meal. Let me tell you, this was a good-sized black bear, one of the largest I've ever seen. Well, I've seen a bear but since there have been lots of reports about them coming to homes where I live, I figure I ought to know more about them. So, I've got some questions I need to answer if I'm going to know more. *[Notice that I am trying to bring in at the outset the sense that an experience may be connected with what I'm trying to learn, and that I know a little about the subject but need to learn more.]*

Right away I know I have to answer this question: "What do they like to eat?" See, I'll put that question on one sheet of paper so when I get to reading or speaking with an expert I'll put information about food on just this sheet with the question on it.

I know that bears sleep in the winter and aren't so busy then but I don't really know when they sleep or wake up. I know that's called . . . Anyone know?

Child: Hibernation.

Don: Right. And I wonder if they hibernate earlier where we live because it's so cold. That brings me to another question, doesn't it. Any ideas?

Child: Where do they sleep? They say in caves.

Don: Good question, so when I do some reading I'll look to see where they sleep and I'm also wondering if they have a place to go, like a special place, to sleep at night, say in the summer time. There's another that hits me right now. How do they grow up, have their young? Okay, I'm going to stop there. I'm satisfied for the minute. No, wait, one more is real important. What experiences have people had with bears? I've had a little but I need to speak with some people who have had different experiences. Remember, I've put each of these questions on a separate piece of paper. *[If at all possible, have students speak to or interview someone who has experience in their area of interest. This is a great help to them in understanding the meaning of voice. At first, they adopt the voice of the person they interview; then they transform it into their own. See* Investigate Nonfiction *(Graves, 1989b) on how to help children learn how to interview.]*

This demonstration didn't allow the children to ask questions as much as it should. I could have asked them to state what they were curious about and then gone back to show how I'd focus on about four basic questions from a longer list to begin my reading. Above all, find some way to include the kinds of questions to ask in interviews.

ACTION 19.7:
Help children to use trade books as part of the process of writing the informal report.

In recent years we have seen a plethora of good nonfiction picture books. I think particularly of those books by Ruth Heller: *Plants That Never Bloom* (1984), *The Reason for a Flower* (1986), and *Animals Born Alive and Well* (1982), which are well illustrated and present the essential facts. Picture books are useful for students of any age, from the primary grades through graduate school, because the authors have to study the field under scrutiny, identify essential information, and then organize that information in meaningful ways.

The next mini-lesson comprises two parts: using a picture book and note-taking. I'll talk about the book's organization, then look for information and demonstrate notetaking.

Don: I have a book here entitled *Black Bear*, by Daniel Cox. Cox is a photographer and naturalist who has spent a great deal of time with bears. First, I want to look through his chapter headings to see how he's decided to tell about bears. I'll go over the headings and you tell me what he had in mind in organizing the information:

- Bears
- Spring
- Summer

I don't know if this is helpful or not. There's only three obvious headings. Still, what can you make of his approach?

Child: Well, I don't know about the first one but it looks like he'll follow the bear from spring to summer.

Don: Right, his organization is by time, first by spring, then summer. Makes me wonder why he didn't follow the bear through fall and winter to make it complete. Sometimes you discover things like this when you look at how it is put together.

Let me turn to the first part, "Bears," and see if there is any information to put on the sheets with our questions. I especially want to show you how to take notes, to put information down in a few words to go with your questions.

As I look through the picture book, I look under photos, drawings, and general illustrations. Usually the author takes key information, puts it into pictures, and then has a few words underneath to tell you what to look for. Look at this one:

A pair of young cubs explores the grasses for ants, grasshoppers, or anything else that may be edible.

What question does this go under?

Child: Food.

Don: Right. Look how I take notes from this. I'll just list the foods. What are they?

Child: Ants, grasshoppers. Or anything else.

Don: I'll probably just put down the ants and grasshoppers. Let's look at another picture and what it says underneath:

A sow curls tightly into a ball to help protect her cubs from the winter's cold. Entering the den in the fall, the sow built the grass nest they now rest on. The den is very clean and smells like hay. This particular den (left) is beneath a sparsely covered brush pile that offers almost no protection from the frigid winter temperatures.

Look at the questions I have and read this section. What is this about?

Child: Oh, this one is about where he goes in winter. Where he sleeps. I think it is that one.

Don: What's the den made out of?

Child: Grass. It isn't a cave.

Don: I always thought that the winter den of the bear was real solid, a cave or maybe a big hole the bear dug. Okay, I want to put down a few words under the question. Will someone come up here and underline what they think are the important words? *[Child will take a marker and mark on the acetate with the quote from the book.]* Someone has a question?

Child: What's a sow?

Don: Oh, that means the mother bear. See, bears come from the pig family. I didn't know that until last summer. They call a mother pig a sow too.

I'll take another book, *Whales: Friendly Dolphins and Mighty Giants of the Sea* by Jane Watson that will have more to look at for organization. One of my other interests is whales because my great, great-grandfather was a whaler and we have the letters he wrote home to his wife. Okay, let's look at it on the overhead. I'll just take the big headings:

- What Are Whales?
- The Baleen or Whalebone Whales
- Whales with Teeth
- Whales and Men

What do you see here? How is this author going to approach the subject?

Child: The author is going to tell us about all whales and then do different kinds?

Don: Yes, there are two kinds of whales, one is obvious, those that have teeth, and then the baleen whale, which don't have them. And finally the author will tell us how people and whales have gotten along together. Actually, not too well.

This session is actually two mini-lessons in one. I recommend that you break this into three parts:

1. Show children how to abstract information, choosing the key nouns and verbs. This kind of mini-lesson needs repeating many times.
2. Show children how to post the information under the right questions.
3. Show children where to find good data for their questions: in the table of contents, under pictures, and especially in picture books.

ACTION 19.8:

Help children to get their voice into the text.

Once children have finished posting their information beneath their questions, it is time for them to be interviewed about their topics. I find that interviews work best when children are in pairs or three-somes. One child talks and the other two children interview until all three have been interviewed. For example, once I had posted my information about the black bears, I'd have the children ask me questions about the bear. This allows me to get an "oral" feel for my content. I use my notes to share information, and the children get practice in asking questions to find out about the subject and the interviewee's relationship to it. This means that the children will try to find out about my interest in the topic, how I got started, what I learned along the way, and so on.

Once children are reasonably comfortable with the oral phase, I ask them to write a one-page piece without notes telling or teaching another person about their topic. Once again, this allows the child's own voice and sense of authority about the subject to get into the text. I don't want the child working from notes or examining encyclopedias. It is better to have him insert information he has forgotten rather than try to adopt the voices of others.

ACTION 19.9:

Line up several nonfiction books to read aloud to the children.

Children need to hear good nonfiction material read aloud to them. Find either picture books or nonfiction books that have a strong narrative bent in presenting the basic content. For example, Joanna Cole's *Magic School Bus* books combine the adventures of an elementary classroom with imaginative explorations of the human body, the water works, and the center of the earth.

Final Reflection

Nonfiction is a neglected genre in most classrooms, especially in the elementary years. Fiction seems to push nonfiction to one side, since children wish to write in the same genre in which they are reading. But children also have an urge to learn more about their interests and have strong opinions about issues that confront them every day in the classroom and at home. We need to help children be aware of how nonfiction fits into their lives as narratives, letters, essays, and informal reports by providing demonstrations of these forms.

Nonfiction is the genre that will dominate most children's school and vocational careers. It is an important medium of thought in which children learn to discover how they feel and what they think about certain subjects and issues. Usually, it requires further reading or interviewing in order to learn about the subject. Once again, we need to do reporting assignments right along with the children, showing them how to look at a subject, read picture books, raise questions, take notes, and write a discovery draft.

Informal reporting is the best way to start to learn the more formal aspects of nonfiction. The child learns the genre through topics in which he is already knowledgeable. This allows him to maintain his own voice through first drafts and beyond.

20 UNCOVER THE WORLD THROUGH POETRY

Poetry happens when people begin to look at the world differently. It is a way of uncovering the ordinary world: suddenly, in the hands of the poet, commonplace events take on new life and importance. A group of barefoot kindergarten children cross a stream during a spring field trip. One of the children reports, "We crossed the stream but the stones didn't mind us stepping on them."

Take a walk with a two-year-old child and let her lead the way. She sees a broken stick, picks it up and smells it. Her eye catches a wilted flower. She stoops to sniff, as she has seen her mother do. The "lowly" child, barely thirty inches high, explores the world with wonder. Through her eyes we see the world anew, the world of the poet. Someone once said, "Nothing is too small for a poem."

Margaret Shane Cusack, a fifth-grade teacher from Clarence, New York, writes along with her children:

sigh when you see it

red poppies in a row,
roses, robins, red-
winged blackbirds;
claret in a crystal glass, carpet in
a hotel lobby;

red cheeks in winter, red backs in summer sun.
Rednecks.
Queen of hearts,
Valentines,
crimson letters on a high school jersey, on the dance
floor red taffeta under black satin;
chili peppers,
red meat makes red blood;
red badges of courage,
red letter days, and oh, Old glory
red, white and blue,
sunsets,
red pens on black and
white words.
Redskins.
redwoods.
Red Riding Hood.
Cold War and the Reds. Pinko
red-faced, in the red,
rosy-fingered dawn,
raucous red rebellious
red outrageous
red.

sigh when you see it.

She thinks "red" and weaves a rich carpet of color in her poem.

Lewis Thomas, the award-winning writer and scientist, writes of poets:

> We must rely on our scientists to help us find the way through the near
> distance but for the longer stretch of the future we are dependent on
> the poets. We should learn to question them more closely, and listen
> more carefully. A poet is, after all, a sort of scientist, but engaged in a
> qualitative science in which nothing is measurable. He lives with data
> that cannot be numbered, and his experiments can be done only once.
> (1990, 178)

As Thomas points out, scientists, poets, and artists have much in common. It is teachers of science who remind us that children need to learn to see the world again in order to gather data more accurately. The scientist and the poet are fascinated by the details of the universe. Poetry is an essential part of the human survival kit.

Poetry Is for Everyone

For most of my school career, poetry was a genre on a lofty hill. It was written by people long since dead whose voices came back to haunt me. The teacher told us what various poems meant, and we were tested on that meaning.

We were drilled in reading poetry. Occasionally, I sensed that the teacher might have liked a poem, but in short order her delight gave way to the furrowed brow of interpretation. Rarely was poetry for those living in the present. From first grade through college I never met a teacher who dared to show us how to write poetry. I recall a Shakespeare class in which the professor asked us to write a scene such as the bard might have written in iambic pentameter. That was the first—and only—time in my school career I was asked to write poetry.

A few years ago, a Laotian teenager took a music class at his high school because he thought he would learn how to write music. The teacher was as confused by his request as I might have been in the same situation. The class was designed for choral singing. "In my country, we write songs to our sweethearts," he said. "I want to know how to write them in English." In most American schools, the course title "Music" does not usually mean that the student will compose in the art form, any more than a course billed "poetry" will mean the student will write poetry. Yet we have this marvelous opportunity to show our students how the process of self-expression can be theirs.

What Is Poetry?

I have already said that poetry is a way of uncovering the ordinary world. The world reveals itself to us and we combine sound and sense in the discipline of the line. Notice how Margaret Cusack creates a sense of red in the repeat of her r's,

> red poppies in a row
> roses, robins, red-
> winged blackbirds;

Although poetry is often associated with the notion of rhyme, it is the sound and simplicity of poetry that elicit our feelings. The poet selects the details—"red poppies in a row, roses, robins, red-winged blackbirds"—to create images. Poetry depends on the details to uncover the world in the compressed space of a few lines on a page. In *A Sky Full of Poems*, Eve Merriam shows us the inside of a poem:

Inside a Poem

It doesn't always have to rhyme,
but there's the repeat of a beat, somewhere
an inner chime that makes you want to
tap your feet or swerve in a curve;
a lilt, a leap, a lightning-split:—
thunderstruck the consonants jut,
while the vowels open wide as waves in the noon-
blue sea.

ACTION 20.1:
Help children read the world for sources of poems to write.

Once again, I'll think back over yesterday, this time looking for poems. The real issues in my life, the ones that are emotionally laden and ask the biggest questions, are usually what trigger poems for me. Of course, I often wonder if there is anything worth examining. On the surface, yesterday is only an ordinary day until I begin to push and prod. Ordinary things, with a little nudge, can be transformed into something extraordinary. I'll set my timer for fifteen minutes and write a first draft to see what's there. Comments in italic follow.

- Yesterday I was still filled with my Aunt's memorial service of the day before. I delivered a eulogy of about seven minutes at St. John's Episcopal Church in Northampton, Mass. It was an awesome task to choose those events or details of her life to bring my Aunt back that she might be remembered. I wonder if I selected well. I couldn't write it out in advance as I had to interview my cousins for their memories—to include them as much as possible and then produce something coherent. But the big questions are these: How to choose? What to choose?

  How would I choose and write a eulogy now about my own life? Certainly poetry, dealing with the vastness in short space, is a place to think.

- My wife is cooking soup downstairs. There's something about the smell of soup, with all the intermingling ingredients, that makes it more than food. I've never written about smells that I can recall. *But what of that notion: soup is more than soup. It speaks of home and stability and love. We will eat this soup together.*

- The phone keeps ringing while I work in my study. *Why don't I flip the button and shut the door so I won't hear it? Let my wife answer the phone downstairs. I think I'm nosey or I do want to be interrupted. I don't want to work today.*

- Today is a running day but the wind is blowing about twenty miles an hour on my anemometer and the temperature is ten degrees. I'm afraid I'll lose the conditioning I've built up all fall and into the race I had last Friday at the Dartmouth relays. *Why not take a day off? What am I afraid of? It's not big time fear but little nagging anxiety that at my age I won't continue to improve as a runner. I ran a 6:09 mile at the relays and placed third for my over 60 age group and now I want to be better. What's better? So who cares?*

- I run and once I am out there the cold doesn't bother me, but the footing does. We've had a lot of snow lately and the running is more like running in soft beach sand which is tiring over the eight miles I plan to run. The footing. *I spot a metaphor there for so many things. If I can just get good pavement under my feet, a good computer under my fingers that will work, good wheels under me when I drive, a lovely wife whom I can love . . . all is footing, a place to put my feet, my life, my love.*

That's fifteen minutes of rambling on the computer keys. I'm delighted with what words can turn up. I'm surprised by what I find in what seemed to be an ordinary day. The two words, "How come?," continue to unfold the details that make living worthwhile.

Take fifteen minutes now and put your words down as you remember the events of yesterday. As you compose, write down some questions and put the answers, the beginnings of answers, right on the page in note form, as I have done.

Any one of the events I recalled from yesterday could be made into a poem. (Sometimes I wonder why I don't do this exercise for myself more often.) I'll choose two very different ones to see how they might play out in a poem, the one about my aunt, which I think may be more difficult yet is one I want to write, and the one about my wife making soup, which I sense may be easier.

ACTION 20.2:

Choose an episode from your exercise and experiment with a list poem.

I've decided to use the episode about my aunt to try a list poem. This means that I'll free associate for three minutes and list everything that comes to mind. William Carlos Williams says, "No ideas but in things." I will try to list the things in my aunt's life, and, as in any brainstorming session, I'll write rapidly, changing nothing:

diary
envelopes
letters
school bells
grandfather clock
old schoolhouse
chalk tray
antique secretary
hardwood floor
porch
bible
weather
pain entries
photographs
school photo, grade four
table, father Harry made
clippings
school smell
chalk line maker, five lines
drop leaf secretary
playing cards
file tin with whiskey bottles
upper room, devotional
Calvin Coolidge's wife
tea room on porch
food in diary

In my mind's eye, I was sitting in my aunt's living room, wondering about the things in her life that would tell her story. My aunt lived in a red brick schoolhouse built in 1845, the one-room school her mother, my grandmother, first taught in at the turn of the century. Many school artifacts are still there in the living room of what was the school. I also realize I could do a list poem just from her diary entries. The events she chose to record in her diary showed what was important to her. Imagine an archaeologist on a dig, carefully turning over the earth to discover the story of a civilization. When we write poetry, we choose the things that will tell a story or answer the questions hidden behind them.

ACTION 20.3:

Choose another episode from yesterday and write a five-minute poem after a three-minute list poem.

The Actions we are experimenting with here are very much like the rapid sketching an artist does. We are sketching in with words in order to feel an impression of what occurred. At the heart of the sketching are nouns, the things, for they will make poetry specific. I'll take the soup episode now, do a three-minute list, and then use the list to write a five-minute poem:

onions
bacon
soup bowl
corn
creamy corn
table
family
children
crackers
Betty
halter top dress
spinach soup
friday night
liberty
Coast Guard
first love
ring
marriage
biscuits
butter

place mat
computer
printer
hug
upstairs
downstairs
her work
my work
house
kitchen
study
odor

The list reflects a bit of the history of a soup I remember my wife, Betty, making when we were first married forty years ago. I was in the military and home on liberty. I could even take off now on another brainstorming session and list soups we've eaten together. Somehow different soups recall different memories. I notice another shift in the list: I am upstairs in my study doing my work and she is downstairs in the kitchen doing hers. The smell of her soup is like a visitation to me while I work. I'll take some of these notions now and try to work them into a five-minute poem, using these details to help me compose:

Upstairs, Downstairs

I punch at words on a Compaq 425,
a gritty bunch of details,
my jaw set in the rightness
of my composing, my focus
a grey screen with the syncopated
vowels and consonants hopping
their way to return to another line,
and another

the smell of onions,
creeps across the room,
around my back and under my nose,
then bacon, potatoes, now
blending to memories
of spinach soup and first love,
my wife in blue halter
telling me she's pregnant,
our first child,

we crumble crackers
and stare, lifting the soup
to our open mouths,
tears

The approach to writing the poem is the same as that of writing the list: let everything in during the first draft. I began with my own mechanical action of pounding away on my computer, let myself be interrupted by the aroma of Betty's soup, then take off again with a soup memory. My time ran when I reached "tears," but you can bet your life I'll be back at work on this one. The poem is built on things: Compaq 425, jaw, focus, screen, vowels, consonants, onions, crackers. I try not to let on that I'm into my rather mechanical task in the study. I stay away from adjectives, although a few creep in (rightness, gritty) and let the nouns do the work along with one verb (punch).

ACTION 20.4:
Help children get started with poetry.

The list poem is a good way to introduce children to the writing of poetry. Use a chalkboard or an overhead projector to start a list. Choose a theme, something timely in the life of the classroom, and then have children contribute to the list.

> *Don:* Today, I want to show you a new kind of poem. It's called a list poem. I'll choose a theme, something that interests me, and then go straight down the board with words that come to mind.
>
> Do you remember the bear I told you about? The one who visited us looking for our bird feeders? Well, I'll make a list out of anything that comes to mind when the bear came or about the bear himself. Watch:
> black
> furry
> bear
> sniffing
> moves head
> side to side
> hungry
> big
> paws
> claws

    bird feeder
    quiet
    suet
    shoulders
    quiet
    friendly?
    glides
    stick snap
    dangerous

Okay, I'll stop there. What do you see in those words? What was I thinking about when I was trying to recall that time with the bear?

Child: Mostly what he looked like.

Child: You said what he did, like moved his head from side to side.

Child: You had a rhyme, paws and claws.

The list poem works well with just about any age. Once I've demonstrated what a list poem is, the children choose a theme or focus for a list. Children then contribute to the list and I write it down. This works well with an entire class.

Line Starters

I don't use story starters for children's writing, but I do find that line starters help children to get the feel of poetry. Although the line helps with ideas, the fact that it is a line tends to set children up for beginning to feel the shape of poetry. Line starters work best with children nine and older, but you may have younger children who you think will be helped by them. I've found these lines to be helpful:

    "I am the person who . . ."

    "Remember me . . ."

In this poem the child becomes a particular person and role plays that person through the poem:

    Remember me?
    Elvis Presley, the king
    of Rock 'n Roll, from Memphis,
    Tennessee, me and my guitar
    changed the country,
    got everybody swingin'
    to that beat, "Ain't nothin'
    but a hound dog."

Children could choose historical figures, sports figures, etc.

"Let me tell you about my dog . . ."

Of course, this could be a cat, gerbil, snake, gecko, etc.

ACTION 20.5:
Respond to children's poetry.

I respond to children's poetry in much the same way that I respond to any piece of writing: I want the child to tell me what the poem is about. At first, children are often caught up in the "form" of poetry. This is especially true of children who insist on rhyming. Unfortunately, the form of the poem, the straining for rhyme, can push meaning to the sidelines.

A writing conference with a child writing poetry might go like this:

Don: Tell me what your poem is about, Martha.

Martha: It's about my rabbit, Sniffles.

Don: What's he like? Is he a he?

Martha: Nope, she's a she. My Mom lets me bring her into the house sometimes.

Don: Is that in the poem?

Martha: Yeah.

Don: Read that part to me.

My basic objective in the poetry conference is to find out the main idea of the poem and the details that support that idea. You will find more about responding to children's poetry in *Explore Poetry* (Graves, 1992).

Children instinctively know that feelings belong in poetry. What is hard about using feelings is that a statement of feeling in the poem doesn't necessarily inspire the same feeling in the reader. Consider this poem by a twelve-year-old (Graves 1992):

The Dregs

Sometimes I feel so down,
the aches inside hurt,
and I keep going

until the tears
roll over me like
some wave and nobody
knows how much pain
there is and I just
don't feel like doing
anything at all.

We know the poet is hurting, yet we are unable to participate in that pain because we don't know the details. I will certainly accept this poem as a genuine attempt to share hurt, to open the door on a painful incident. On the other hand, the child may wish to provide details that will allow the reader to empathize. And if the child does not wish to share the poem with the group, we must fully respect her privacy. I've reworked the poem simply to show what I mean by using details:

The Dregs

The voice harps
from the first floor,
"Cleaned your room yet,
done the laundry?"
"Seems like you're
never here . . ."
and like a saw blade
that cuts in
chewing away on my backbone
until I feel
so weak I run
to my room
soaking up pillows
and thinking about friends
I'll leave and their voices
that comfort and listen
will fade and only the voice
with a knife in it
will be left in the air.

I take the general notion of aches and hurts and give them the details the readers need to feel the same pain as the author. Things enter the poem: floor, room, laundry, saw blade, backbone. I use verbs to give more of a feeling to the detail: harps, cleaned, cuts, chewing, soaking, and so on.

ACTION 20.6:

Read other poets aloud to the children.

Children need to hear the voices of many poets when they are writing poetry, to discover how they shape words and sounds to meaning.

This Action carries you into reading poetry to the children. It is important to read poems aloud a number of times by yourself before reading to the children. I have chosen four very different poems to give some sense of the flavor and the range within the genre. It is important that you hear a different voice in yourself since the words will dictate a different tone.

This first poem, "The Pickety Fence," by David McCord, produces the actual sounds of a stick running along the boards in a picket fence. Read this poem aloud several times. As you read, listen for the punch of the p's in pickety, and the c's in clickety.

The Pickety Fence

The pickety fence
The pickety fence
Give it a lick it's
The pickety fence
Give it a lick it's
A clickety fence
Give it a lick it's
A lickety fence
Give it a lick
Give it a lick
Give it a lick
With a rickety stick
Pickety
Pickety
Pickety
Pick.

This poem is intended to be read rather quickly at about the pace you'd walk if you were running a stick along a fence.

I usually read the next poem, "Icicles," by Mark Irwin, very slowly, letting the words form in my mouth like water dripping from an icicle. Try to be aware of the pause at the end of the lines (with the exception of "Look, he says laughing, a pinocchio nose," which I try to make sound like a child laughing). The art of reading poetry is in letting the voice caress each word. These types of poems usually take more practice than "The Pickety Fence," since there is much more variation in the lines. You may find it helpful to record your voice to practice different ways of reading the poem.

Icicles

Slender beads of light
hang from the ceiling.

My son shows me
their array of sizes:

one oddly shaped,
the queer curve,

a clear walrus tooth,
illumined, tinseled.

We watch crystal cones
against blue sky;

suddenly some break loose;
an echo of piano notes.

The sun argues
ice to liquid.

Tiny buds of water,
pendent on dropper tips,

push to pear shapes:
prisms that shiver silver

in a slight wind
before falling.

Look, he says laughing,
a pinocchio nose,

and grabs one
in his tiny hand,

touching the clear carrot
cold to his lips.

The next poem, "Where Would You Be?," by Karla Kuskin, is rich with rhythm and rhyme, and I want to hear those sounds as I read. But don't be lulled by the rhyme and miss the meaning. For example, in the first two lines, be sure to use the intonation of a question. The next line is also a question, and your voice should rise as you read it. This lovely poem is filled with the wide-eyed wonder of a stormy night. Convey that wonder in your voice as you read the poem aloud several times before sharing it with the children.

Where Would You Be?

Where would you be on a night like this
With the wind so dark and howling?
Close to the light
Wrapped warm and tight
Or there where the cats are prowling?

Where would you wish you on such a night
When the twisting trees are tossed?
Safe in a chair
In the lamp-lit air
Or out where the moon is lost?

Where would you be when the white waves roar
On the tumbling storm-torn sea?
Tucked inside
Where it's calm and dry
Or searching for stars in the furious sky
Whipped by the whine of the gale's wild cry
Out in the night with me?

Emilio De Grazia's poem, "Pasttime," a sports poem expressing the wonder of a nine-year-old at a baseball game, is a lovely statement about the young girl and the game itself. Try to read this poem in several ways. Experiment. Try on different voices, then share it with the children in the one you like best:

Pasttime

A girl, nine years of wonder
Still on her face,
Stands directly on the bag at third
Running amazed fingers along the wrinkles
Of my old leather mitt.
It is the bottom of the ninth,
And everywhere in the world
The bases are loaded.

Share only the poems you like with the children. Remember, there are few neutral feelings about poetry. You may be saying to yourself, "How could he choose that poem? It merely confirms the fact that there are some things about poetry I can't stand." Well, that's a normal reaction. To some of you, these poems may sound like hard rock or far eastern music. Find poems you do like and practice them, allowing your voice to convey a rich variety of interpretations.

Final Reflection

We are surrounded by poetry in the ordinary moments of our days. We can take the ordinary and, through poetry, turn the smallest, least significant moment into something important. In this respect, poetry is for everyone.

Poetry, like all art forms, conveys a range of emotion, from burning anger to quiet joy. It is one of many entry points to understanding the world. I want the children in my classroom to hear and experience all kinds of poetry. I want as many children as possible to discover what language can do.

Children need to see the everyday world that poetry comes from, and how poets write poems. I find that free verse helps children to focus on the meaning of their poems, rather than sound alone. Naturally, sound and sense are at the heart of poetry, and children need to hear and experiment. If you enjoy and experiment with poetry yourself, bring it into the classroom so it can become part of the children's lives.

V

CONTINUE TO LEARN
WITH OTHERS

21 WORK WITH PARENTS AND ADMINISTRATORS

Parents and administrators need information about children's progress. At the same time, parents and administrators possess information that will help you teach. In this chapter you will involve yourself in Actions in which you exchange data about the progress of particular children and learn how to help both parents and administrators tell you what they know about those children.

Work with Parents

How well I remember my first parent meeting in my first year of teaching. The principal informed me that the parents of John, one of my students, were concerned that their son was not performing up to their expectations. They wished to meet with me at my earliest convenience. My first reaction was one of fear, "Did they think my teaching substandard? Would they be hostile?" My attention was focused more on myself than on their son or what they, as parents, might contribute to our meeting. Above all, I wanted to impress them and convince them that I was a competent teacher.

The meeting went poorly, though I thought well of it at the time. The child's parents were concerned that his papers were incomplete and shoddy in appearance. They wanted to know what they could do to help him. I said I would do everything I could to make sure John completed his work; each day they would check John's papers when he got home.

I was relieved that the meeting turned out to be pleasant. They wanted me to think they were good parents; I wanted them to think I was a good teacher. Unfortunately, at the conclusion of the meeting neither of us was any more informed about how to help John as a writer than we were at the beginning. There was little exchange of information between us.

Meetings with parents take preparation. You need to take time to gather data on the child beforehand—on what the child can do, and what his direction as a learner and a writer might be—and report as many details about his progress as you can. I want to be equally prepared to learn more about the child from his parents. For better or worse, parents see their child in ways that we need to understand in order to teach. They also come to conferences with notions about writing from their own experience as learners. We often forget that parents' learning experiences at school can play an important part in our meetings with them.

I remember well my interviews with adults when I was gathering data for the Ford Foundation study (Graves 1978) on the status of writing in the United States. Person after person shared horrific stories about learning to write: "The teacher made me stand up and read my errors aloud to the entire class." "I had to write a three hundred word composition on how I would improve my attitude toward school." "I was so embarrassed at the look of red marks on my paper I tried to hide it so no one would see it." Many adults freely admitted that they would never pick up a pencil to write unless they were made to do so.

Later in these same interviews I made a final request: "I want you to stand in the doorway of a classroom today. Choose any grade level and tell me what you want to see happening in the room." The adults responded quite universally by saying, in effect, "I want those kids to sit up straight, be quiet, and if they make mistakes the teacher should nail 'em." The model they imagined was the only one they had experienced: writing as a medium of punishment.

Before I begin a conference with parents, there are a number of factors I want to keep in mind:

- *Writing concept:* What is the parents' concept of writing and what writing is for? What is my concept?

- *Parent and teacher concerns:* What possible concerns does the parent have about the child's learning before, during, and after the conference? *Parents' concerns may shift from one focus to another as you proceed through the conference.* Does my concept of what the child needs change during the conference?

- *Child's progress:* I show parents their child's growth as a writer in the folder or portfolio collection. *It is absolutely essential that the child's written collection be present for the conference. I know of no conference more difficult than the conference about* one paper *when neither teacher nor parent has a historical context for discussion.*

- *Child's potential and needed areas of learning:* Above all I want to show what the child can do and what he needs to learn in the future.

- *Parent knowledge:* I want to learn as much as I can about the abilities the child evidences at home but may not show in school. I might catch a glimpse of these in the section on "Stories the Child May Be Able to Tell" in the interview (see Figure 6.1).

Keep in mind the fact that both you and the parents are concerned about the child's learning. Though you may have different perspectives on the matter, it is very important to be as specific about what you know as possible in terms of the papers the child has written and of what you have observed about what the child knows.

My wife and I have attended many parent-teacher conferences for our five children over twenty-four years in the public schools (they are grown up now and on their own). I find it good discipline to switch roles and recall what I looked for in a conference from a parent's perspective:

- *Does the teacher respect my child?* Though we have different responsibilities, there has to be caring before anything significant can happen. Usually enjoyment is part of respect. Does the teacher enjoy my child and approach my child's foibles with a good sense of humor?

- *Does the teacher know my child?* Though my child may behave differently in school than at home, do the teacher's observations seem plausible? Plausibility is very much dependent on the *specificity* of comments about learning.

- *Does the teacher know the field?* I want to feel assured that the teacher has professional knowledge about the area under discussion. I find that if the teacher knows the field, she doesn't have to call on jargon. I like to hear about specific examples of teaching situations and whether learning did or did not seem to take place.

- *Is the conference jargon-free?* One of my pet peeves is the litany of jargon that tends to emerge in conferences: self-assured, self-concept, self-esteem, below grade level, above grade level, works below ability, could do better if he tried harder, etc. Jargon takes the place of specificity. It expresses shortcut conclusions usually unsubstantiated by facts.

- *Is the teacher interested in my perspective on my child?* In short, is the conference a sit and listen session on the part of the parent? Is the teacher confident enough in his own knowledge of my child to ask me, "What do you make of this?"

- *Is the teacher in a hurry?* Do I have the feeling that we have a very limited time to explore a topic very important to both of us? If new issues come up, can we explore them or, at the very least, set up a new appointment?

- *Do we leave with a mutual plan?* Is there something for me, the teacher, and the child to do? How have we decided to engage the child in learning? Ultimately, we want him to take over learning for himself. How is our plan directed toward that end?

I'm not suggesting that every parent comes to a conference with the same expectations or concerns. Still, I do believe that the first question,

"Does the teacher respect my child?," is paramount and universal. I also believe that parents want details of their child's progress and potential in straightforward terms, not professional jargon.

ACTION 21.1:
Choose a child and review her progress in preparation for a meeting with her parents.

This Action carries me back to Chapter 6, where we examined student potential. I suggest that you use the same procedure shown in Figure 6.1, "Worksheet for Writer Potential Based on Paper and Interview": examine a child's paper and then interview him in order to find out what he knows beyond what you have observed in the text. You will want to know far more about your student than you can use in the conference. Figure 6.1 is reproduced here as Figure 21.1 since I will use it as resource for my conference demonstration.

My interview with Jason touches on his understanding of conventions, his background knowledge, his own sense of what he will learn next, and how he will use the conference in working on his next piece. It also reveals Jason's skill as a problem solver.

The following information will be particularly useful to me in my meeting with Jason's parents:

WHAT JASON KNOWS

- *Content:* Jason is well-versed in outdoor lore and is a good observer. He knows how to build fires and set up a tent, and he is observant about the woodpecker. *Notice the section, "Stories or information I suspect student knows but has not yet written." This will also be a useful area to discuss with his parents, who probably know his background in these same areas.*

- *Use of detail:* Details—size of woodchips, smoke pattern, how to build a fire—even if he has not yet written about them, show the depth of a person's knowledge.

- *Conventions observed:* good narrative sequence, indenting of paragraphs, serial comma, use of titles, good sentence sense. *To learn: spelling, a sense of when certain conventions are actually used. At this stage his usage is more instinctive than knowledgeable.*

▲▼ **Figure 21.1**
Worksheet for Writer Potential Based on Paper and Interview

WHAT DOES THE STUDENT KNOW?

Context—text	Content—interview
Generally *what goes into a hike, How to build a fire, outdoor cooking*	Generally *About friend, Joey. Hiking—not an isolated event*
Use of specifics *smoke followed me, holes in tree, sawdust, wig-chips*	Use of specifics *Forgot raincoat—the details of the whole process of building a fire.*
What has child observed? *what a woodpecker has done, Noticed size of chips, How smoke travels from a fire*	What has child observed? *Carefully observed and learned from Joey*
Process—text *Can handle a narrative appears as though he thinks he has finished*	**Process—interview** *Jason writes to relive his experience*
Stories or information I *suspect* student knows but has not yet written *How to plan what to take on the hike. How do you build a fire in the woods? How do you know so much about birds? Does smoke really follow you? Tell me about the others who were with you.*	**Stories or information child *can* tell but has not yet written** *Details on fire Birds from Joey*
Use of conventions—text *Indent, left to right, spaces between words, potential serial comma, good sentence sense, use of titles*	**Conventions known but not used** *Periods go when you have something new. a general sense*
Language—Text Verbs *hiked, wanted, stay, blow, followed, cooking, tasted figured, knocked*	**Language—Oral** Verbs elicited *good process verbs when talking about building the fire. Good detail of sequence here.*
Use of time/space markers *last saturday overnight looks back on trip*	Use of time/space markers *good sense of what happens when he builds a fire.*
Individual language use *"figured it was done by a big woodpecker the way he knocked it out"*	Individual language use *Didn't notice any*

▲▼ Figure 21.1 (continued)

---

1. Find the best part here and tell me about it.

The part where I try to get away from the smoke.

---

2. Anything you learned in writing this one?
(Notes from following section appear in narrative in text.)

---

3. How is this piece different from other pieces you have written?
(Have the child take out four to five pieces he has written and place them in front of him as you ask the question.)

---

4. Look for something the child has done correctly. E.G. "I see you got this period in just the right place. How did you know how to do that?"

---

5. As best you can, give an oral summary to the child of what he knows from the data you have gathered thus far. Then ask, Now that you know all this, what else would you like to learn order to be a better writer?

- *Process sense:* Jason tires of a piece rather quickly and needs to have others listen to it. He is not at the point of revising effectively: he is his own audience at this point and he writes to relive the experience. That is all.

MY ROLE IN JASON'S NEXT STEPS

- *Conventions:* Help him know why he uses conventions correctly. Offer him more mini-lessons. Keep a better list of the conventions he already knows.

- *Audience:* Although it is important for him to write for himself, I want him to be exposed to audience situations where he will need to be sensitive to what his readers enjoy and need.

HOW HIS PARENTS CAN HELP

- Tell me about Jason's interest in the outdoors. Why do you think he knows so much?

- I'm curious about what Jason knows how to do—anything at all. What does he like to do that has little apparent connection with school?

- What do you remember about being taught writing when you were in school? Does that make you wonder about what I am doing here with Jason?

- In what areas are you wondering whether or not Jason is making progress?

The Parent Interview

Now I will try to use my conference preparation in my meeting with Jason's mother. Remember, I will only be able to use a small part of it. My main responsibility is to both teach and learn, and effective teaching requires us to be selective rather than exhaustive with information.

Don: Good afternoon, Mrs. Thurston. I appreciate your coming in. As I mentioned on the telephone, I wanted to share Jason's progress with you and learn more about him from you.

Mrs. T: I can't imagine what I can contribute, but I am curious about how he is doing. When you first called, I thought he'd done something wrong or his studies were going downhill. I have to tell you I was relieved that you just wanted to discuss his progress. Well, how is he doing?

Don: Let me take out his folder so we can look through his papers. [*One of the easiest ways to be specific is to let the child's work speak for itself. Mrs. Thurston's question invites a global statement. Of course, until we look at Jason's writing, my detailed statements will be meaningless.*] Here's his paper, "My Hike."

Mrs. T: Heavens, look at the misspellings.

Don: Yes, there are some misspellings here: *friends, Saturday, canteen.* I find it interesting that when he started out, he misspelled many more words than later on. For example, he got some tough ones

350

Keep Parents and Administrators Informed

down here like *knocked, laughed,* and *wouldn't* with the contraction in. He came pretty close to getting *figured.* It's possible that Jason was thinking so much of getting started, the spelling suffered. I'll be interested to know if Jason can explain it. You'll be pleased to know that he said he wanted to work on his spelling. *(Parents comment on spelling errors more than on any other convention. Above all, be prepared to speak of the child's progress or your approach to teaching spelling.) I also notice, with a bit of humor, that I didn't see this spelling pattern until I had to explain it to his mother.*

Don: Jason is quite knowledgeable about the outdoors. He attributes it to his friend, Joey. What do you make of his know-how here?

Mrs. T: The minute he comes home he's out the door again heading for the woods. At least he isn't inside watching TV all the time. He's bugging me to send him to the same camp with Joey next summer. The two of them! Always together. Of course, my husband hunts so maybe he gets it from him, this outdoor stuff. I'm an inside person.

Don: Can you tell me some things that Jason enjoys doing that maybe aren't so connected to school?

Mrs. T: Sports. He must have about six hundred baseball cards. He's constantly running through them. He and Joey. I think they trade them. They talk numbers, averages, hits, homeruns. Now if he could apply some of that to his math he'd get somewhere.

Don: You've given me a thought. I hadn't considered using baseball statistics in math. Let's take a closer look at his writing.

I'm pleased to see that he uses writing for his own ends. That is, he wrote about the hike because he wanted to relive the experience. This shows me that he knows what writing can do. I'm pleased with that because that's one of the basic signs that assures me he'll use writing later on in his life.

His ideas follow in sequence here: he knows how to tell this story so that one idea logically follows the next.

As far as conventions go, you'll see a big change from how he wrote last fall. Take a look at this September piece. Sentences . . . well, there are many that got marked off. Now he's using commas. He doesn't know yet why, but he seems to do a good job of getting them in the right place now, along with his periods.

Mrs. T: I never could get that stuff right. I'm glad you are teaching him that. I don't know much about this fancy stuff, but I'm glad you're teaching it to him. What's a convention anyway? (*Without realizing it, I used some jargon. I was lucky that Mrs. T interrupted me. Most parents do not.*)

Don: I'm glad you interrupted me. I should have explained that. In fact, if I use any words that don't make sense, do just like you did with your last question.

Conventions are ways of acting on the page so the next person can understand what you are saying. Jason goes from left to right with his words. That's a convention. He goes from top to bottom, not bottom to top. Or, he puts spaces between words. Those are the easy ones. But if you capitalize at the beginning of the sentence and put a period at the end, those are conventions too, and the same goes for spelling. Does that make sense?

Mrs. T: Yes, it does. Thanks. So what can I do that will help him at home?

Don: I think one of the greatest things we do as parents is to be interested in what our children are doing. Help Jason talk more about his outdoor experiences, his baseball cards. Get him to teach you about what he knows. I know you aren't an outdoor person, as you said, but to listen carefully to his mind at work helps him to know what he knows. That's what I'm trying to do here. He'll probably ask you about our conference today. Tell him what you learned today about his progress.

We haven't discussed his reading yet, but you won't be surprised to hear that books about the outdoors interest him. Gary Paulsen's *Hatchet* and John Gardiner's *Stone Fox* have really gotten him going in reading. He didn't really care to read that much, but now I'd say he's comfortable with a book. Actually, he likes nonfiction books even more than fiction—books about sports and owls (since we had a visit from the curator at the nature center).

Mrs. T: That's all he's talked about, those owls. He wants us to go up there on a Saturday to the center. I suppose that would help.

Don: There's another book I'd recommend that we don't have here. It's Farley Mowat's *Owls in the Family*. That's an easy-to-read Mowat book for younger children. It may be available at the local library. We don't have it here but that book could be an opener to some of Mowat's books written for adults. There's a lot about the outdoors in them, especially *The Dog Who Wouldn't Be*. That book's a riot. With Jason's sense of humor, I think he'd take off with it. I'll write them down here if you'd like to see about getting them at the store or the library. Are there some things we haven't reviewed or you'd like to ask questions about?

Mrs. T: Hmmm, let's see. As I said before, I was worried when I came here. I'm glad he's doing okay. He doesn't say much about school when he comes home, though the woman who talked about owls got to him. He won't stop talking about owls. I should have picked up on that one. I hope his spelling gets better. He's just like his father, who can't spell worth a darn. *[Parents often worry about problems in their own learning that may turn up in their children.]*

Don: I don't mean to interrupt, but Jason is a good speller, an ambitious one, I'd say. He tackles tough words. He makes some mistakes but he's coming along.

Mrs. T: Well, I'm glad he's writing so much. That sure is different than when I went to school. I hate to write and I'm glad he's getting along.

Don: Thank you for coming in Mrs. Thurston. Please call or drop a note if I can be of help in the future. I'll be curious to see how Jason continues to change as a writer/reader.

Note that I pulled together much more information before the conference with Mrs. Thurston than I used. If children had been keeping track of their use of conventions (see Chapters 10 and 12), I could have shown Mrs. Thurston how Jason's use of conventions had changed.

I am pleased that we could both enjoy Jason's knowledge of the outdoors. I hope that his mother will listen to her son and help him teach her about all the things he knows. As I write these words, I realize that we need to do far more to show parents what we mean when we say this. I suspect that his mother may find it very difficult to do.

Questions Teachers Frequently Ask About Parent-Teacher Conferences

1. How do you handle parents who want to know how their child compares with other children in the class or in the country?

I wish I could forget to include this question. It is one of the most perplexing ones confronting teachers today, particularly in high-flying, competitive suburban communities. I will try to provide enough information on several sides of the question so you can make up your own mind about how to respond to parents.

The paradox at the heart of this question is what parents have a right to know versus what, in your estimation, will help the child learn tomorrow. Parents do have a right to know about the progress of their children and how they have changed as learners in your classroom. If there are standardized test data, they have a right to know how their children have scored and their percentile score relative to others in the country. I have a problem, however, when parents wish to know how their children compare with others in the classroom. They may not be asking for names, but they wish to know the child's relative ability placement. I am reluctant to share this information simply because it will not be helpful to other parents in the room: "Mr. Graves says that my child is among the top five in the classroom."

When a parent asks me how their child compares with others, I have to ask a question in return: "There's a reason you need this information, Mrs. Thurston. Can you tell me what you have in mind?" If you feel you are faced with a difficult question that is hard to answer, try to remember that you don't have to give a quick reply. I usually need to know the reason behind the person's question. Otherwise, I won't respond with helpful information.

"Do you believe in teaching grammar, Mr. Graves?"

"When you say grammar, what do you have in mind, Mrs. Thurston?" I might have asked her a question about Jason's spelling when she noticed the misspelled words at the beginning of his piece: "You are worried about Jason's spelling?"

"Yes, I wonder if he'll be as poor a speller as his father." This information helps me respond more specifically to Mrs. Thurston's question.

Remember that the main purpose of a parent-teacher conference is to exchange information about the child and direct our attention to the child's learning. I may frame the question about relative ability by asking, "You think the information will help us know what to do in our plan for your child's learning?" Unless the child is severely retarded or exceptionally intelligent, I do not find such discussions productive. But even in these cases, how I teach or help the child will not change. We need to come to a mutual understanding of where the child is, assess the learning situation, and proceed with the next step.

2. What do you do when there is a major difference between your philosophy of teaching and how parents wish their child to be taught?
Above all, clarify what the parent thinks is the difference. I find that our differences are often not nearly as great as they appear if we can clarify each other's position: "Would you please tell me what you think my approach is, Mr. Jones?" Indeed, there may be mutual disagreement but at least we should both be dealing with the heart of the matter. "Your concern, Mr. Jones, is that we are not correcting each of the errors on your son's papers? Is that right? How do you feel that correcting all the errors will help your son to be a better writer?" Once again, I direct my question to our next step, the improvement of the child's work. The parent often believes that if we miss any error, the errors will proliferate. In short, correcting is teaching.

I want the parent to know that I am aware of the errors and that there is a specific teaching plan for dealing with problems like this. I do point out to the child the errors he should have been able to handle. I focus on the one or two elements the child should be able to get for himself.

3. What do you do to reach parents who simply won't show up for a conference? The ones I need to see the most are the toughest to reach.
I think our first conclusion about parents who seldom come near the school is that they simply don't care. Of course, for many children the

word is singular: parent. So many children have only one parent, who is trying to cope with job, family, and school simultaneously. We need to provide a range of access for parents who do care yet cannot possibly get to the school in the afternoon. Evening hours, telephone messages, exchanged notes are not ideal, but they will open doors.

Mrs. Thurston thought that a call from a teacher for a conference could only mean bad news. (Sometimes a note that prefaces some of the positive elements in the child's profile helps a parent to realize that you have a genuine interest in the overall picture.)

Parents who have had poor school experiences of their own find it particularly difficult to even walk through the door of the school. "I had the same heavy feeling walkin' through that door for my kid that I had when I was his age. This place [the school] is bad news." Many of the children who struggle today have parents with troubled learning histories of their own. We need their support. I have a hunch that if it were possible for parents who had a difficult time in school to talk about how hard it was for them, they might experience some relief and then be able to work with the school on their child's learning.

Reflection on Parent Conferences

Conferences take preparation. We prepare by carefully reviewing children's present and potential performance along very specific lines: their use of information, process, conventions, and language. We need a folder or a portfolio to follow progress over time. If children's papers go home each day or even each week, we will not have the full perspective we needed to show parents how their children are changing. Thus, at the conference I have the child's work and even spread it out on the table so we can look at it. Occasionally I ask the parent, "What do you make of this? You know your child, what do you see here that surprises you?"

Teachers and parents need to learn from each other. I can't afford to leave a conference without knowing more about the child at home, since children possess many skills and abilities that schools don't necessarily reveal.

We need to work hard to avoid jargon in our conferences. Jargon excludes people and makes them feel as though they have little to share. Deep down, parents want to know that we respect their children and see new and interesting things they have not seen. Then parents and teachers together can construct a profile of the child to help her assume more responsibility for her own learning.

Work with Administrators

I find it important to take the initiative in meeting with school administrators to explain my approach to teaching writing and show how my students are developing. It is virtually impossible to explain how I teach writing unless I have examples of children's work to show them. This means that in September I set up an appointment with the principal to discuss children's progress and then work hard over the first six or seven weeks of school to accumulate materials for the meeting.

Principals need to stay informed about how the children in their school are progressing. When I was a principal, I carefully looked at test scores to see how we needed to adjust our curriculum and teaching. At that time I didn't realize how unreliable test data were in giving us a true learning profile. As an administrator, I was also unprepared to teach writing. There were few college courses in the teaching of writing, especially for administrators. I needed to see what progress looked like in the actual stuff of learning—children's papers. Once I saw that progress I got curious: "How did you get these results? What did you do?" Every administrator needs to tell someone else about how the students in their school are progressing, but good, solid learning stories from actual classrooms are hard to find.

ACTION 21.2:

Schedule a meeting with an administrator in which you share data about the learning progress and potential of specific children in your class.

I suggest that you allow yourself four weeks to prepare for the conference unless you are in the middle of the year and already have good, solid data. Choose three children, one in the low, one in the middle, and one in the high ability range. Prepare each case as you did for the parent conference. Be sure to include the Writer Potential sheet in Chapter 6. If your children have kept any of the records suggested in

Chapter 10, and you have put together lists of the conventions the children are learning, be sure to bring those records as well. Be prepared to show your data in these areas (see the Writer Potential sheet, Figure 21.1):

- child's knowledge base, particularly as shown in the details
- child's use of the process
- child's knowledge base beyond the text
- language: note Writer Potential sheet (Figure 21.1)
- child's use of conventions—*If you are using the sheet in Figures 10.4 and 10.5, then you are ahead of the game. If you have not put these into practice yet, you could make them up for your three cases.*
- spelling: be prepared to show development in this important and controversial area

Consider doing a dry run with another teacher before your meeting with the administrator. Above all, show specific changes with your record sheets and student portfolios. Of course, some areas may not have changed the way you'd hoped. That's perfectly normal. But be prepared to state what you'll do through mini-lessons and conferences to help the student improve as a writer.

Administrators, like parents, will be able to see things in the data that you may not have seen. Sometimes I ask the administrator, "What do you make of this?" (Some administrators may be a little uneasy with this question. You'll have to judge its appropriateness.)

Questions Teachers Ask About Administrators

1. How do you work with an administrator who thinks the only important things in writing are grammar, punctuation, and spelling?
I acknowledge that they are important. If children do not observe these conventions, the reader isn't going to be able to understand the text. But I have a hunch that what the administrator is worried about are the political issues related to weakness in these areas. Somewhere in the midst of our preoccupation with test scores and parent comments, the issue of what writing is for is forgotten. Writing is not for punishment, it is not solely for answering questions at the end of a

chapter, nor is it for passing tests. Writing is an essential medium for communicating ideas and information.

If the administrator is concerned about conventions, I need to show how our children are progressing in this regard. Of course, some conditions make it difficult for our children to show what they can do. Folders and portfolios of children's writing allow us to demonstrate what they can do better than an annual standardized assessment. As professionals, we need to raise questions in faculty meetings about what research shows us about children's use of conventions and what writers do in order to write well.

2. My administrator gives me an annual evaluation in April after just one visit. This year he came during writing time, saw me conferring with some children and said, "I'll come back when you are teaching." How can I avoid this problem?

Once again, it is our responsibility to show and explain what we are doing before an annual evaluation. Make an appointment with your administrator in the fall to discuss your plans and your children's progress.

3. You say it is important to have enough time to teach writing. Well, in my building writing is way down the list of curriculum priorities. Other curriculum areas consume any time I might have to teach writing. How do I find time?

Include writing in all the subjects you teach. Although you may relish a set time block, writing is a tool to include in reading, science, social studies, or math (see Chapter 3 in *Investigate Nonfiction* [Graves, 1989b). Indeed, the greatest problem with most writing programs is that the children only write during "writing time."

Final Reflection

We need to take the initiative to help administrators know how our children are progressing as learners. We also need to invite them into the classroom to see what we do that helps children learn. I also recommend that we share what we are doing to improve ourselves as writers and teachers of writing. The next chapter, "Live the Professional Life," expands on ways to continue to grow as a teacher.

22 LIVE THE PROFESSIONAL LIFE

The art of a teaching is the art of continuing to learn. Teachers are the most important learners in the classroom. It is the quality of our learning, it is our continual engagement in new approaches to help the children, that are the source of our greatest influence, far transcending any elegant methodologies we may have acquired. We invite children to join us as we explore better ways of writing, to try new investigations in science, to look for other ways to solve a mathematical problem.

This book is intended to engage you in exploring the teaching of writing in a wide range of situations. We all learn by doing, reflecting on what we have done, and improving our first attempts. If you try a new form of record keeping and find that certain children simply cannot focus well enough to follow it or that others see no sense in it, you pull these children together to discuss the matter, trying to understand the problem from their point of view and teaching what is needed to help them keep records.

There are more Actions in this book than can possibly be accomplished in any one course or even several courses. If you have never taught writing, there are many entry points that will help you begin. If you are an experienced teacher of writing, you can choose those Actions that will help you refine what you are already doing. Most of the Actions need to be repeated in order to make the practice your own. Indeed, to become a top teacher of writing is to enter into a lifetime of learning. I don't simply take a course in writing and say the job is done. I deliberately engage in those acts that will help me continue to learn and grow over the long haul. This chapter focuses on how to continue to learn throughout your career.

Connect with Other Teachers

Our profession is isolated. In recent years, the proliferation of new curriculum has resulted in less contact time with children and reduced access to our colleagues. If we do see them in the lunchroom or during brief breaks in the teachers' room, we seldom speak about professional matters. Rather, we use the time to chat about our families, exchange personal gossip, or grumble about the latest demands from administrators. This is understandable. Teaching is so demanding, we need a time-out with easy conversation.

Yet each day we work around people who possess valuable lore about teaching, whose experience and wisdom can contribute to our ongoing education. Their classrooms are some of the best contexts for a dialogue about teaching. Think back to Chapter 1, where we examined the teachers in our own past. Notice again how different some of them were from each other, although they all contributed to our education.

I find that I learn as much from teachers whose teaching style is different from mine as from those who teach like me. Maybe more. I visited a first grade classroom near Chicago recently, where the children were seated in a rather traditional fashion. When the teacher spoke, they responded on cue with well-polished remarks. "Nice show," I thought to myself. When the children spoke or read their work, they stood next to their seats, as if at attention and read in a crisp, almost militant manner. "Humph," I thought, "glad I'm not the principal of this school, or have a grandchild in this room." I looked forward to reading their work expecting to find neat, safe, homogeneous texts.

I was surprised to find some of the best first-grade writing I had seen in years. The children's choices of topics and language were highly individual. They wrote voluminously, legibly, and with an extraordinary range of conventions. I have a hunch that if I had met this strong-minded teacher in the teacher's room, I might have dismissed her as "old school," not like me. I wish my travels had permitted me to spend more time in her classroom to learn more about her teaching. Obviously, her teaching was thorough and demanding yet liberating to her children. The proof was in their texts.

Unfortunately, our isolation in the profession makes us look even more strongly for the perfect match, the teacher who has the same philosophy we do. Make no mistake, we do need one or two teachers with whom we have a close match, but notice that I had to go into that first grade teacher's classroom to be struck by what I needed to learn.

ACTION 22.1:

Schedule a meeting with two teachers, one who teaches as you do and one who teaches differently.

The purpose of this Action is to open the door to a future of intentional learning from your colleagues. You will make after-school

Teachers Confer with Other Teachers

appointments with two teachers, one with whom you feel a closer philosophical agreement on the teaching of writing, the other with a different approach. When you speak with them, say that you are trying to learn more from your colleagues and that you'd like to interview them, exchange information, and ultimately visit in their classroom. If possible, you'd like them to visit yours as well.

The Interview

It is best to interview your colleague in her classroom in order to have materials close at hand so that she can document her views and practices. Emphasize the fact that the interview is a two-way street; you ask her questions, and she is free to ask you questions as well. Here are some suggestions about how to start.

- Bring two writing folders or portfolios: Share the children's progress just as you did with the administrator and/or the parent. Let her tell you what she sees in the contents. Discuss your teaching in relation to the children's progress. You will want discussions to be specific; children's work keeps it that way.

- Consider these questions:
  - Have you taught children like these? What did you do?
  - How do you approach the teaching of writing?
  - How has teaching changed for you over the last five years?
  - What are you trying right now in teaching that's new for you?

If you feel that the comfort level is a good one, propose a mutual exchange in which you have a chance to see how her children handle the room and understand their work. Your emphasis, as always, will be on learning from the children. Since you have already interviewed some of your own students, you will understand the meaning of the statements your colleague's children make even better. Above all, share their answers with your colleague. Ask your colleague if there are particular children she'd like you to interview, then use some of these questions and statements:

- Would you take me around the room and show me how the room works?
- What's it like during writing?

- Tell me about this piece you are working on right now.
- Show me a place where you got stuck and how you solved the problem.
- Why do people write?

Once again, it will helpful if your colleague will ask the same questions of children in your room. Next, discuss the implications of what you've learned and what you'd like to change.

ACTION 22.2:

Continue to grow as a writer.

There are few teachers who write during a summer program or occasionally in class who don't say, "I've got to find a way to do this more often." We are often surprised by our ability after being told in our early school years that we had little to say and our work was filled with errors. Yet, for some reason, we end up looking back at the summer or the course in which we were helped to write with fond memories; we have not written since. Our audience disappeared when the course was over and everyday teaching crept in to consume all our time and attention. We do need an audience and we do need to establish regular habits. I strongly suggest that you use your writing in your classroom to teach through mini-lessons and class sharing.

Continue to show children how to "read the world" and you will discover that writing becomes part of your everyday teaching. Now when you discover topics, you will have a ready-made audience: the children. Composing a ten-minute piece on the overhead, the chalkboard, or experience chart paper once every eight or nine teaching days will leaven your writing on the other days. It is enough to say to the class, "I'll be working for the next ten minutes on that piece I was telling you about the other day. I'm not to be disturbed."

"You can't be serious," you say, "I don't have enough time for conferences now. I could see three children in those ten minutes." Yes, that may be so; we'll always be behind. But in our research, we've found that when the teacher writes instead of moving around the room conducting conferences, the children write even more intensely.

Occasionally, share what you are writing at your desk with the children. Keep them in touch with your writing. In one study, a researcher asked children several questions about her writing: What is she writing? Where is she in the piece? Why does she write? Should teachers write and why? Their answers showed us that when teachers write and share their writing, children internalize important concepts about what writing can do and absorb particular skills in the composing process. "Today I'm going to work on my lead; I'll talk with you later on about how this comes out."

Share with Colleagues

Try to enlist the help of another teacher. See if you can make a pact to compose with your students, but in this instance you will also share your writing with each other. If you can find more than one teacher to join you so much the better. The larger the group, however, the more difficult it is to arrange times and places to meet.

Work to improve your writing just as I did in Chapter 13 on teaching the children to read their own work. Make no mistake, every time I try to show children how to write with my own writing, I help myself as well. There are particular ways I've found to help others to help me. I'll list them here (Graves 1990, 124–26) to give you some options for keeping your writing moving ahead:

- Listen to this and don't say anything when I'm done. I just want an audience. I need a face, a human being who is here. No more.
  Sometimes I don't want any help at all, just a friendly ear, so that I can hear my own voice as I read.

- Listen to this. I'd like you to say what this is about, what you remember. No more than that.
  This is probably the most important and common directive to a reader. Notice that I don't ask, "What do you think of this?" or, "Is this any good?" The quality of the piece is revealed more by what the person can actually say she understands or what she will do and how she'd do it. As I listen to the person's response, I judge whether this is what I want her to understand.

- Listen to this. Tell me what this is about. Then tell me what is clearest to you and what isn't so clear.
  This directive requires more of the reader. If I think I have a reader who can handle this, I'll ask it. Above all, notice that I am setting the

reader up to get what I want. That's my job, to sense what will help me and try to show someone else how to provide that information.

- Would you please read this and tell me what this is about?
In this instance I want the reader to decide what the main thrust of the piece is. Sometimes I think I already know, but I'm so close to the piece I can't tell. There are some instances in which I'll tell the reader what I think it is about and then ask him to read and tell me what he thinks, but I prefer the former approach.

- Would you please read this, decide what the piece is about, and then find the place, the story, or the image that most reveals it?
Sometimes my best material doesn't appear until much later in the piece. It's often hard for me to know what strikes a reader most forcefully, or which material is best and belongs up front.

- Would you please read this and mark the places that just don't make sense? Even if you just wonder what they mean, please underline them.
Asking a reader to underline the "fuzzy" places is a good preliminary for help in editing. This should precede any attention to spelling, punctuation, or grammatical problems. Until I deal with the issues in logic I am wasting a friend's time asking for judgments about surface features.

- Would you please read this and check any "errors" that will turn a reader off?
This particular request comes at the end of the process, when I am sending a piece off or going to press. I make this request after I have gone as far as I can on my own and after I have dealt with other issues.

Consider Publication

Many of our New Hampshire teachers have published in national journals. We've convinced them that they ought to step forward and share what they know. They already had data that should be shared with other professionals. "You mean this wouldn't be old hat to other teachers?" they asked.

"No," we answered, "because you have data specific to your children that showed how they learned and continued to grow, your data will never be 'old hat.'" If you look back over the Actions you have tried with this book, you will see many places in which you listened to children, recorded data, kept records of their progress, and then taught accordingly. In many instances the information from those Actions is publishable if you begin to think in terms of articles.

A Few Hints for Publishing

Editors are always looking for teachers who can write using good, solid data from their classrooms. Consider some of these approaches as you look back over the Actions in this book. I'll choose one and show how I'd convert the information into an article.

In Chapter Six, I examined Jason's piece, "My Hike," and then interviewed him to find out still more about his writing. I'll try to show you how I take those data and turn the material into an article for other teachers.

What Do I Have?

My first question focuses on looking at the information to see if there are questions that would interest teachers embedded in the data. I ask myself, "What did I find useful to me as a teacher? How did the data on Jason help me? What did I learn?" I'll brainstorm about the last one:

- Jason learns a lot from his friend, Joey.
- He enjoys the outdoors.
- Jason feels the experience when he writes.
- Jason isn't aware of all that he knows. He liked knowing what he wasn't aware of.
- Being funny, humor, is important to Jason.
- Jason, like other children, gets bored with his writing and wants to start something new.

Ask the "So What?" Question

My "so what" is related to what I found useful. Above all, I learned so much more about Jason in our conferences that on subsequent occasions, I felt as though I knew him. Best of all, he knew that I knew him. We could also speak more frankly about his work.

Sometimes I get at the "so what?" question by asking another one: "Suppose I didn't have these data on Jason. What would be missing for me as a teacher and for Jason as a student?" That question usually helps me find a way to see what I've discovered.

I think the best thing about interviewing Jason was that I gained a sense of his learning. If I hadn't looked at his paper or interviewed him, I would be unaware of what he'd achieved. When children are learning and we can see it specifically in their work, we feel better about ourselves as teachers.

The odds are that if my data helped me to teach, what I learned can help others. This means that I will write as one learner to another, one learning teacher to another. My writing will be more like a conversation over coffee in the teachers' room.

Consider the Structure or Your Approach to the Article

The structure reflects a teaching paradigm: "Let me show you something I've learned. Interested? Okay, let me continue to show you how I learned that. Finally, what is the significance of this experience for me?"

The Structure in Action

I'll write a brief lead to show you how I'd handle the first part of the article, move from there to show the beginning of the teaching section, and then draft a short beginning to the significance portion. My comments on my work in progress appear in italic:

> I often have doubts about what my children are learning. When I have doubts about them I doubt myself as a teacher. I don't need days like that. I'll go home with a queasy feeling in my stomach. When I feel that way I'm dragging. *(Notice that I begin with myself. The use of first person allows me to converse and bring in the universal experience: There are days when we wonder if our children are learning anything. The underlying question here is, "So what did you do?" That leads me to the next paragraph.)*
>
> The other day I decided to see for myself what the children know and are learning. I figured a good hard look at Jason, a child I've wondered about for some time, might give me the spark I needed to teach, and a spark in turn for him to learn. I found a procedure, a simple one that worked. It took me about twenty minutes at home and thirty minutes in school during two recesses to get what I needed. *(I let the reader know right*

away that I've found a way to deal with that initial problem. Further, if you've had this experience, you'll find a solution right along with me. The reader also asks, "Well, what's the price in time?" I'll be as frank as I can about this.)

I asked Jason, the child I studied, to choose a paper he liked. Then I took it home and really looked at all the different things he knew. I told Jason I'd get back to him for an interview. I have to admit that he looked a little puzzled at the prospect. I think he might have been a little worried as well, but I assured him it would be a good experience for both of us, since I was confident that he knew many things of which I was unaware. Here's what I did. *(I give a quick picture of just what I do and then follow with the very details I show in Chapter 6 in the split column diagram. I want as much upfront information, my best information, in as early as possible. Writers don't withhold information until the end; they put the best material right up front for the reader. Editors know that readers decide within two minutes and the first ten lines whether they will continue reading.)*

After my experience in studying Jason's piece and speaking with him, I've begun to see potential in other children. I'm more sensitive now to the stories not yet told that are suggested in a single line like, "The vet said that we had to put the big white collar on the dog so he couldn't get at the scab." I realized that there was a whole story about going to the vet that the child could probably tell. I have a hunch that Jason hasn't kept quiet about his positive experience. Other children are beginning to ask me to take their papers home. *(This is the significance paragraph. I show the reader what this information means to me today. It's a continuation of the "so what" question.)*

This is a brief look at how I go about writing one kind of article. If you have done many of the Actions in this book or if your children have kept records, you have much that you can use for articles. Perhaps you have information from sharing sessions and you've found a way to do them better than you've done them before. The critical variable here is learning. Even if you have just begun to teach, if you can show a good, solid learning experience, you have a publishable article. Remember, new teachers need your article. There is always a need for your experience as long as you write with details and base it on good, solid information about you and your students.

A new journal, *Teacher Research Journal* (Johnson Press, 49 Sheridan Avenue, Albany, New York 12210), is interested in data you may have gathered in your classroom that could be useful to other professionals.

ACTION 22.3:

Contact a national, professional group dedicated to the improvement of literacy.

You should become part of national organizations that seek to improve the literacy of your students. These groups offer continuing education and updates through national and regional workshops, national conventions, and monthly publications. As you become better acquainted with the growth of your children and related issues, you will want to broaden your awareness of what is new in the field.

I'd suggest two organizations in particular: the International Reading Association and the National Council of Teachers of English. Write to them and request membership applications and materials, which describe their various benefits, so you can decide which ones you wish to join:

National Council of Teachers of English
1111 W. Kenyon Road
Urbana, IL 61801-9981

International Reading Association
800 Barksdale Road, P. O. Box 8139
Newark, DE 19714-8139

Whole Language Umbrella
Box 2029
Bloomington, IN 47402

Although these are national organizations, they also have regional and state meetings that will allow you to come in contact with other professionals from the workday classroom.

The whole language group is active at the local level through TAWL (Teachers Applying Whole Language), which meets regularly, invites speakers, and conducts workshops. This is a rapidly growing organization, particularly because teachers' extensive involvement in running and organizing contacts for other teachers.

ACTION 22.4:
Investigate books written by teachers at your grade level.

We are fortunate in recent years to have authors who write books about the teaching of writing from the inside. That is, we finally have classroom teachers who write about their own teaching experiences.

Although I spend a great deal of time in classrooms, I have not lived the day-to-day experience of teaching writing for a while.

As part of this Action I suggest that you investigate the book or books written about your grade level to see how other teachers make the many decisions that go with the teaching of writing.

Primary Years

Carol Avery's book, . . . *And with a Light Touch* (1993), gives extensive details about first-grade teaching in a classroom with a wide range of children of different backgrounds. The book focuses on teaching both reading and writing from day to day over an entire year. It is the most practical book to date, since it shows through transcripts of conferences and examples of children's work how a teacher learns and struggles. You will see both the successes and failures of someone who constantly pushes to the edge of learning for herself and her students.

Ellen Blackburn Karelitz was the teacher with whom Jane Hansen and I did our first research on the reading/writing process thirteen years ago. The term, "the author's chair," was born in Ellen's room and is now part of the pedagogical vocabulary of teachers everywhere. Ellen, of course, has continued to expand her notions of teaching writing since those early days and has written a very helpful, practical book called *The Author's Chair and Beyond* (1993).

Intermediate Years

Jack Wilde's gift is the range of genres he teaches in *A Door Opens: Writing in Fifth Grade* (1993). This is one of the best books available demonstrating how writing should be used across the curriculum. Note these chapter titles: "Uncovering Poetry," "Shorter Bus Routes: Developing a Persuasive Writing Assignment," "Engaging and Informing: Reconsidering the Written Report," and "Writing Our Way into the Middle Ages."

Middle School Years

We have two classics for middle school teachers: Nancie Atwell's *In the Middle* (1987) and Linda Rief's *Seeking Diversity* (1992). How fortunate we are that two such extraordinary teachers demonstrate what students can do in the middle school years. Both books detail specific strategies for teaching adolescents, for helping them to discover the power of writing in their lives.

In the Middle was the first of the books written for teachers by a teacher, and it actually paved the way for a very important new kind of professionalism. The large sales of all these books shows the eagerness with which other teachers have welcomed the opportunity to learn from another teacher. Professors will no longer have a corner on the market.

High School Years

Tom Romano is a writer's writer. He was a high school English teacher in Trenton, Ohio, with many years teaching experience when he wrote *Clearing the Way: Working With Teenage Writers* (1987). It is difficult to teach writing responsively in the high school years because of the large numbers of students, yet here is a teacher who conducts conferences and responds to multiple drafts with students of all abilities. This high school teacher has very high expectations for his students, and he shows how students' writing changes from conference to conference.

I strongly suggest that you also read one of these books from a grade level other than your own. Find out how writing is taught with older or younger children. You will find that the teaching of writing is quite similar at all ages. At the same time, you will discover approaches to writing that you can easily borrow for your students. Somehow, the age difference helps you to see the underpinnings of the process at your own grade level and discusses approaches that may be useful for your more advanced children.

Another resource teachers have found invaluable is Regie Routman's *Invitations* (1994). Although Routman's work is not grade-specific like the texts I've just discussed, this is a practical book filled with specific suggestions to help teachers deal with the details of teaching reading and writing. Her writing shows teachers and children at work in the classrooms she visits every day. She understands the life of the teacher and contextualizes her instruction in an understanding, informative manner.

ACTION 22.5:
Investigate courses in the teaching of writing or in writing itself.

Sometimes universities provide courses in writing or the teaching of writing. A writing course can help you to both maintain your current writing and stay up-to-date with teaching practices. I find that contact with the other teachers in the course is a stimulating source of professional discussion.

Be cautious in your selection of courses. You will want courses that actually help you to write. Too many courses that are billed as "writing" courses spend more time *talking* about writing than doing it. Before you enroll, talk with the professor to find how much writing is involved, the manner of response, and (if your courage is up) whether the professor writes with the class.

Final Reflection

You began this book with Actions that helped you to look at your own history as a learner. You knew what helped you to learn and you were aware of what kept you from learning. From those experiences you began to fashion a philosophy about what you thought would help you to teach children to write. You've learned what an exciting, but at times discouraging, enterprise teaching can be, especially the teaching of writing. Both writing and teaching are crafts, and as such their pursuit is filled with failures and mistakes. Children rebel or don't work up to their abilities. We struggle to be the teacher we'd envisioned when we first entered the profession. People are unpredictable, especially when they try to learn. Of course, we are trying to learn along with the students who are struggling to write.

You began to listen to children, to find out what they know, and to use that information to help them learn. You explored children's potential through your listening and mini-lessons, and your own demonstrations of writing. Children are caught up in your own discoveries and want to discover for themselves. You knew that in *showing* them, learning was taking place. Most of all, when you wrote, they saw what writing was for: to learn and to communicate with oneself and others.

You have discovered and tried many new practices in this book. Now that you are about to put it down, think carefully about how you will continue to educate yourself so that it becomes a lifelong proposition. Teaching can be an isolating profession. In this last chapter you have decided to break out of the isolation through planned meetings with colleagues, continued writing, and expanded contacts with professional groups and teachers who have published articles about their experiences.

Perhaps, just perhaps, you have realized that in your classroom and in your writing, you have something unique to say. I'd say the odds are two to one that you would write and publish if you could only believe in your own learning. Why not?

CLASSIFICATION OF ACTIONS

A. *Learn from the Children*

2.1 Practice listening to children.

2.4 Find a child for whom words are probably not the easiest means of communicating what she knows.

2.5 Learn about the child beyond the walls of the school.

4.7 Conduct a series of writing conferences in which the children teach you about what they know.

6.3 Look through the current writing the children are doing. Think through some appropriate nudges that will help them become better writers. Leave nudge paper to allow them to experiment.

10.3 Spot the lifetime writer.

14.1 Interview a child in order to help her have a sense of her own recent writing history.

14.2 Interview children to see if they have a sense of their options.

14.3 Confer with several children to find out about their readiness for revision.

B. Learning from Children but Actually Recording Data

2.2   Follow one child and record data about what that child does during a forty-five minute block of time.

2.3   Ask a child to tell you how his classroom works.

2.6   Get to know your children through a three-column exercise.

5.1   Interview three children while they are engaged in the writing process.

6.1   Study one child's potential by examining one piece of writing the child selects for review.

6.2   Within two days, re-interview the same child and ask her what she remembers about what she knows, as well as what new things she can add to her list.

6.5   Interview five children to find out what they are working on to become better writers.

8.1   Hold a small group or class meeting to find out children's sense of limits and their understanding of the various guidelines you have established for the class.

8.3   Teach a small group of children (two or three) to take on a classroom responsibility. Keep records of their progress for a week. Conduct two short sessions to trouble-shoot as well as celebrate their progress.

9.4   Keep track of small group, then large group sharing.

10.1 Review how writing is evaluated in your school.

15.1 Observe three children during composing.

15.3 Gather basic data on handwriting speed.

16.1 Observe a child who is using inventive spelling.

21.1 Choose a child and review her progress in preparation for a meeting with her parents.

C. Classroom Data but not from Children

7.1   Examine the amount of time your students have for writing. Rethink the way time is used in your classroom in order to have at least four days a week when they can write.

8.2   Check the predictability of your time for writing and work to structure your use of the time.

10.1 Review how writing is evaluated in your school.

22.1 Schedule a meeting with two teachers, one who teaches as you do and one who teaches differently.

22.2 Continue to grow as a writer.

22.3 Contact a national, professional group dedicated to the improvement of literacy.

22.4 Investigate books written by teachers at your grade level.

22.5 Investigate courses in the teaching of writing or in writing itself.

D. Teaching Practices—Doing Things with Children

4.1 If you are teaching kindergarten or first grade, choose a small group of children who exemplify the criteria mentioned on page 48 and introduce them to writing through your own oral discussion and demonstration.

4.2 Choose a small group of children who don't seem to be as interested in the narrative side and try exploring lists. (If appropriate, have them help you invent the spelling of the words.)

4.3 Experiment with making and reading signs and messages with a small group of children.

4.4 Practice writing short messages to children and note how they make meaning out of them.

4.5 Demonstrate where topics come from in the everyday experience, selecting incidents from your own life that will interest your students.

4.6 Show children the options for writing topics from an everyday reading of the world.

4.7 Conduct a series of writing conferences in which the children teach you about what they know.

4.8 Conduct a writing share session with a small group or with the entire class.

6.3 Look through the current writing the children are doing. Think through some appropriate nudges that will help them become better writers. Leave nudge paper to allow them to experiment.

6.4 Practice directives.

8.3 Teach a small group of children (two or three) to take on a classroom responsibility. Keep records of their progress for a week. Conduct two short sessions to trouble-shoot as well as celebrate their progress.

9.1 Try sharing with a small group in which group members remember, make connections, and ask questions.

9.2   Broaden the content of the share session.

9.3   Help children to practice evaluating their own work and the work of professional writers.

10.4 Introduce one aspect of a new system of record keeping that students will maintain themselves.

10.7 Take four folders home each night for a week. Write short, two- to three-sentence letters to students about what you see in their folders and records.

11.3 Make the transition from folders to portfolios.

12.1 Conduct a small mini-lesson to show five children the conventions they already know or apply.

12.2 Use mini-lessons and keep track of them in a notebook.

12.3 Set the tone for conventions.

12.4 Help children speculate about conventions.

12.5 Share conventions.

12.6 Introduce the Convention Game to the children.

12.8 Use trade books to demonstrate conventions.

12.9 Work on scheduling mini-lessons.

12.10 Help children conduct mini-lessons.

13.1 Conduct a short mini-lesson as a review of reading the world.

13.2 Conduct a mini-lesson in which you show children how you decide the one thing your piece is about.

13.3 Conduct a mini-lesson on how to show the subject of a piece in the text.

13.4 Look for a line that tells what the piece is about.

13.5 Examine the nouns in your "showing" section.

13.6 Conduct a mini-lesson on rereading a piece to see what verbs the writer has used.

13.7 Find one or two lines you just like and try to say why you like them.

13.8 Reread the sentence that tells what the piece is about, and then find the one or two sentences that have the least to do with the main purpose.

15.2 Work with a child who needs help with handwriting.

16.2 Help one child or several to sound out slowly. Place their finger on a letter they have written down and listen to the remainder of the word.

16.3   Help the poor speller.

18.2   Read the world for characters.

18.3   Sketch in a character.

18.5   Conduct a short mini-lesson with children to help them see what questions best develop a character.

18.6   Ask your children to take out the fiction they are reading and make a list of anything they know about their characters.

18.7   Create a piece of fiction in which the children decide the elements that go into the story.

19.1   Explore sources of nonfiction by reading the world.

19.2   Write a short ten-minute piece of nonfiction.

19.5   Help your children begin to understand what it means to know an area well.

19.6   Help children work with nonfiction through the informal report.

19.7   Help children to use trade books as part of the process of writing the informal report.

20.1   Help children read the world for sources of poems to write.

20.2   Choose an episode from your exercise and experiment with a list poem.

20.3   Choose another episode from yesterday and write a five-minute poem after a three-minute list poem.

20.4   Help children get started with poetry.

20.5   Respond to children's poetry.

20.6   Read other poets aloud to the children.

E. A Teacher's Own Writing

1.1   Recall the teachers in your past who particularly affected your learning.

1.2   Post names of any teachers associated with the teaching of writing.

1.3   Identify important attributes of teachers in your past to plan the kind of teacher you wish to be in the years ahead.

3.1   Begin to learn to read the world.

3.2   Go back twenty-four hours and begin to record the details of your day. When you have finished, jot down some quick questions about yourself and the world.

3.3   Take one of the elements from the list you made when you "read the world" and write a ten-minute piece from it.

3.4   Continue to write short pieces until you feel relaxed about what is on the page.

4.5   Demonstrate where topics come the from in the everyday experience, selecting incidents from your own life that will interest your students.

4.6   Show children the options for writing topics from an everyday reading of the world.

10.2 Review your own personal practices in writing.

11.1 Begin to keep your own portfolio.

13.1 Conduct a short mini-lesson as a review of reading the world.

13.2 Conduct a mini-lesson in which you show children how you decide the one thing your piece is about.

13.3 Conduct a mini-lesson on how to show the subject of a piece in the text.

13.4 Look for a line that tells what the piece is about.

13.5 Examine the nouns in your "showing" section.

13.6 Conduct a mini-lesson on rereading a piece to see what verbs the writer has used.

13.7 Find one or two lines you just like and try to say why you like them.

13.8 Reread the sentence that tells what the piece is about and then find the one or two sentences that have the least to do with the main purpose.

18.2 Read the world for characters.

18.3 Sketch in a character.

18.4 Choose a situation that will reveal your character and write a short, ten-minute piece of fiction.

19.1 Explore sources of nonfiction by reading the world.

19.2 Write a short ten-minute piece of nonfiction.

20.1 Help children read the world for sources of poems to write.

20.2 Choose an episode from your exercise and experiment with a list poem.

22.2 Continue to grow as a writer.

F. Actions not Requiring Children

Chapter One   Three reviewing teacher history.

Chapter Three   Four that are involved with the teacher's own writing.

10.6 Consider different ways of using children's records.

10.8 Consider the strategic use of your time in designing your evaluation program.

10.9 Consider the children who have problems with evaluation and record keeping.

11.2 Consider different starting points for children's portfolios.

16.4 Construct a spelling program.

19.3 Take one school day and observe the opportunities for using nonfiction.

22.1 Schedule a meeting with two teachers, one who teaches as you do, and one who teaches differently.

22.2 Continue to grow as a writer.

22.3 Contact a national, professional group dedicated to the improvement of literacy.

22.4 Investigate books written by teachers at your grade level.

22.5 Investigate courses in the teaching of writing or in writing itself.

REFERENCES

Atwell, Nancie. 1987. *In the Middle*. Portsmouth, NH: Boynton/Cook.

Avery, Carol. 1993 . . . . *And with a Light Touch*. Portsmouth, NH: Heinemann.

Burden, Jean. 1974. "Poetry is a Celebration of the Concrete." *Yankee*. January, p. 173.

Chomsky, Carol. 1971. Invented spelling in the open classroom. *Word*, 27, 499–518.

Clay, Marie. 1993. *Reading Recovery: A Guide for Teachers in Training*. Portsmouth, NH: Heinemann.

Cohen, Leo A. 1969. *Evaluating Stuctural Analysis Methods in Spelling Books*. Unpublished doctoral dissertation, Boston University.

Cole, Joanna. 1986. *The Magic School Bus at the Waterworks*. New York: Scholastic Books.

———. 1987. *The Magic School Bus Inside the Earth*. New York: Scholastic Books.

Cox, Daniel J. 1989. *Black Bear*. San Francisco: Chronicle Books.

De Grazia, Emilio. 1987. From *This Sporting Life*. Minneapolis: Milkweed Editions.

Fletcher, Ralph. 1992. *What a Writer Needs*. Portsmouth, NH: Heinemann.

Fly, Edward. 1992. *Spelling Book*. Laguna Beach, CA: Laguna Beach Educational Books.

Fry, E., D. Fountoukidis, and J. Polk. 1985. *The NEW Reading Teacher's Book of Lists*. Englewood Cliffs, NJ: Prentice Hall.

Gardiner, John. 1980. *Stone Fox*. New York: HarperCollins.

Goldstein, Bobbye, ed. 1992. *Inner Chimes*. Honesdale, PA: Boyds Mills Press.

Graves, Donald H. 1977. "Spelling Texts and Structural Analysis Methods: *Language Arts* 54 (1) (January).

——— 1978. *Balance the Basics: Let Them Write*. New York: Ford Foundation.

——— 1983. *Writing Teachers and Children at Work*. Portsmouth, NH: Heinemann.

——— 1989a. *Experiment with Fiction*. Portsmouth, NH: Heinemann.

——— 1989b. *Investigate Nonfiction*. Portsmouth, NH: Heinemann.

——— 1990. *Discover Your Own Literacy*. Portsmouth, NH: Heinemann.

——— 1991. *Build a Literate Classroom*. Portsmouth, NH: Heinemann.

——— 1992. *Explore Poetry*. Portsmouth, NH: Heinemann.

——— 1993. "Children Can Write Authentically If We Help Them." *Primary Voices* 1 (1) (August):2–6.

Graves, Donald H., and Bonnie Sunstein. 1992. *Portfolio Portraits*. Portsmouth, NH: Heinemann.

Hansen, Jane. 1987. *When Writers Read*. Portsmouth, NH: Heinemann.

Hansen, Jane, Thomas Newkirk, and Donald Graves. 1985. *Breaking Ground*. Portsmouth, NH: Heinemann.

Harste, Jerome C., Virginia A. Woodward, and Carolyn Burke. 1984. *Language Stories and Literacy Lessons*. Portsmouth, NH: Heinemann.

Heller, Ruth. 1982. *Animals Born Alive and Well*. New York: Grosset and Dunlap.

——— 1984. *Plants that Never Bloom*. New York: Grosset and Dunlap.

——— 1986. *The Reason for a Flower*. New York: Grosset and Dunlap.

Irwin, Mark. 1987. *The Halo of Desire*. Baltimore: Galileo Press.

Jerome, John. 1992. *The Writing Trade*. New York: Viking.

Karelitz, Ellen Blackburn. 1993. *The Author's Chair and Beyond*. Portsmouth, NH: Heinemann.

Kuskin, Karla. 1980. *Dogs and Dragons, Trees and Dreams*. New York: HarperCollins.

Lederer, Richard. 1991. *The Miracle of Language*. New York: Pocket Books.

Mandelbaum, Paul. 1993. *First Words*. Chapel Hill: Algonquin.

Martin, Ann M. 1989. *Kristy and the Walking Disaster* (Baby-Sitters Club #20). New York: Scholastic.

McCord, David. 1952. *One at a Time*. Boston: Little, Brown.

Merriam, Eve. 1986. *A Sky Full of Poems.* New York: Dell.

Mowat, Farley. 1957. *The Dog Who Wouldn't Be*. Boston: Little, Brown.

——— 1961. *Owls in the Family.* Boston: Little, Brown.

Murray, Donald M. 1968. *A Writer Teaches Writing.* Boston: Houghton Mifflin.

——— 1990a. *Read to Write*. Fort Worth, TX: Holt, Rinehart, & Winston.

——— 1990b. *Shoptalk*. Portsmouth, NH: Boynton/Cook-Heinemann.

Newkirk, Thomas. 1989. *More Than Stories*. Portsmouth, NH: Heinemann.

One Classroom: A Child's View, dev. by Jane Hansen and Donald Graves. Videocassette. Portsmouth, NH: Heinemann.

Paulsen, Gary. 1988. *Hatchet*. New York: Puffin.

Rief, Linda. 1992. *Seeking Diversity*. Portsmouth, NH: Heinemann.

Romano, Tom. 1987. *Clearing the Way: Working with Teenage Writers*. Portsmouth, NH: Heinemann.

Routman, Regie. 1994. *Invitations*. Portsmouth, NH: Heinemann.

Rule, Rebecca. 1991. "Three Kids vs. the School Budget." *Christian Science Monitor* February 13.

Shaughnessy, Mina P. 1977. *Errors and Expectations*. New York: Oxford University Press.

Simon, Neil. 1992. "The Art of the Theatre X." *Paris Review* No. 125, Winter.

Smith, Frank. 1982. *Writing and the Writer*. New York: Holt, Rinehart, & Winston.

Sowers, Susan. 1985. "The Story and the All-About Book." In *Breaking Ground: Teachers Related Reading and Writing in the Elementary School,* ed. Jane Hansen, Thomas Newkirk, and Donald Graves. Portsmouth, NH: Heinemann.

Temple, Charles, Ruth Nathan, Nancy Burris, and Frances Temple. 1988. *The Beginnings of Writing*. Needham Heights, MA: Allyn and Bacon.

Thomas, Lewis. 1990. "A Trip Abroad." *A Long Line of Cells: Collected Essays.* New York: Viking.

Vygotsky, L.S. 1962. *Thought and Language*. Cambridge, MA: M.I.T. Press.

Watson, Jane Werner. 1975. *Whales: Friendly Dolphins and Mighty Giants of the Sea.* Racine, WI: Western Publishing.

White, E. B. 1970. *The Trumpet of the Swan.* New York: Harper and Row.

Wilcox, Carol. 1993. *Portfolios: Finding a Focus.* (Writing Lab Monograph) Durham, NH: No.1.

Wilde, Jack. 1993. *A Door Opens: Writing in Fifth Grade.* Portsmouth, NH: Heinemann.

Wilde, Sandra. 1991. *You Kan Red This!* Portsmouth, NH: Heinemann.

Williams, William C. 1961. *Farmers' Daughters: Collected Short Stories.* New York: New Directions.

CREDITS

INDEX